BLACK
IN
BLUE

BLACK
IN
BLUE

AFRICAN-AMERICAN
POLICE OFFICERS
AND RACISM

Kenneth Bolton Jr.
and
Joe R. Feagin

ROUTLEDGE
New York and London

Published in 2004 by
Routledge
29 West 35th Street
New York, New York 10001
www.routledge-ny.com

Published in Great Britain by
Routledge
11 New Fetter Lane
London EC4P 4EE
www.routledge.co.uk

10   9   8   7   6   5   4   3   2   1

Library of Congress Cataloging-in-Publication Data

Bolton, Kenneth, 1959–
    Black in blue : African-American police officers and racism / Kenneth Bolton Jr. and Joe R. Feagin.
        p. cm.
Includes bibliographical references and index.
    ISBN 0-415-94518-6 (acid-free)
    1. African-American police. 2. Discrimination in employment—United States. 3. Occupations and race. I. Feagin, Joe R. II. Title.
    HV8138.B556 2004
    363.2'089'96073—dc22   2003017150

CONTENTS

PREFACE

In 2003, a Louisiana appellate court upheld a jury's award of $1 mil-
lion for two African-American officers who faced racial harassment
and other discrimination in a major city police department. The two
officers had joined the force in the early 1970s. They reported enduring
frequent racist comments in their department and over the police radio
from white officers. They presented evidence that they had been denied
promotions because they were black and that, at some point during
their career, white officers openly displayed Klan logos and a hang-
man's noose. When they confronted officers who were using the *nigger*
epithet, the term was changed to *they*, but the racist conversations continued. According to their accounts, early on white supervisors refused
to shake their hands, and when one of them was finally promoted in the
1990s, a superior officer told him that he was going to be the "head
nigger in charge." When they complained about their mistreatment,
they were sometimes assigned punitive foot patrols in bad weather.
Reporting harassment and discrimination to superiors was generally to
no avail. Interestingly, the appellate court noted that the jury had to
decide on the credibility of the officers' reports, because of denials of
racism by white department officials. The higher court also found the
black officers' reports very credible.[1]

   In this book we too take seriously the accounts of fifty African-
Americans officers in sixteen different law enforcement agencies in the
Sunbelt. These officers are a contradiction personified. As relatively

new entrants in historically white and male social-control institutions, they must police, "protect and serve," and at the same time negotiate difficult organizational pathways designed to exclude or marginalize them. As they reach for important life goals that all people seek, they must constantly prove themselves worthy to the many whites who view black Americans as unworthy. As they try to make policing fairer for residents of black communities, their fellow white officers often view them as "radicals," while some members of black communities perceive them to be traitors.

Moreover, as black officers have become more numerous and vocal in many police agencies across the United States, strangely enough both white researchers and public commentators have generally ignored them and their impact. As have other successful African Americans, they have become in this regard an invisible "racial other." In reviewing the scholarly and popular literatures, we have noticed that a person is often either a black person or a police officer, but not both. In many discussions of policing, all the law enforcement officers are, implicitly or explicitly, taken to be white.

Few public accounts of black life and communities, especially in the mainstream media and official government reports, tell the contemporary story of black America like it really is. There are indeed in black communities the much-noted street criminals, the hard drug addicts, and the chronic welfare recipients, yet the substantial majority of black Americans do not fit into these categories. As we will see in our interviews, the majority of black Americans grow up with positive family instructions and values about work, education, achievement, family, and community that are similar in many ways to those that white politicians and other whites often pontificate about in public. Indeed, these important family lessons and parental values enable the majority of black Americans not only to survive but also to succeed under difficult, often racialized, conditions in U.S. society.

One of the officers we interviewed makes this clear in reflecting on the discriminatory acts by whites he has encountered:

> Well, they bother me, but it's nothing that I can't get a hold of. I realize that there's still prejudice in the world. And I guess it angers me that people . . . just don't realize that people are the same. They're the same; they have the same problems. And times have changed where if the world was to blow up today, everybody here, everybody would be gone. . . . Everybody is going to be affected. I guess it's just the belief of what your

parents teach you to believe—that is what you grow up with, and you turn into.

In this still-racist United States, black Americans get an education, secure a job, and raise a family while facing a *lifetime* of individual and institutionalized discrimination that is created and maintained by large numbers of white Americans, in towns and cities across the United States.

In our interviews numerous accounts show the great efforts that these officers' parents, as well as other important black adults, have made so that their children can survive, thrive, and have a good life. Listen, for example, to this life story of a black police officer who was accused, unfairly, by fellow white officers of being biased in favor of a local black community during a very divisive local dispute:

> I'm just telling you my struggles as a black patrolman coming out of the projects until now. And you're told to—growing up as a black young man, my father worked two jobs to raise us. There was six of us. He worked as a maintenance person for the county school board and he worked as a supervisor at night at [the hospital] as a custodian. And you've been told by him and by the school to don't be a thug, better yourself, educate yourself, be a better person. And you do that. And then when something happens . . . you get looked at like the common thug that we're told of to grow up not to be like. So it's like, I've bettered myself, I don't steal, I don't even drink, I don't smoke cigarettes, never used drugs, never burglarized, never did any of that, and I did what I was taught to do at school by my parents and then to be scrutinized just as if I was a common thug. It's like, it makes some blacks in [this] position say, "Where's the credit?" And then people wonder why so many people go wrong. Sometimes it's like, you're damned if you do, you're damned if you don't.

Most of the officers we interviewed do not mind the sacrifices they have made and the hard hours that they work to serve and protect local communities, but they do get upset and frustrated about the persisting racial hostility and discrimination that cause them great stress and pain—to the point of periodically asking, "Where's the credit?"

Over the course of their life, black parents and children must face not only long hours of hard work but also long days, months, and years of persisting antiblack discrimination at the hands of an array of white colleagues, clients, supervisors, teachers, and strangers. Not only must black Americans expend the normal amount of human energy used to get an education, pursue jobs and careers, and build a family and raise children but they must also expend the large amounts of human energy, over a lifetime, required to contend with and counter a constant barrage of white-generated hostility and discrimination. Although the majority of white Americans seem to be in denial about the extent of this everyday hostility and discrimination, such denial of reality is hard for African Americans and other sentient observers of the U.S. scene to understand.

At the beginning of this research project, we were somewhat surprised by the almost total lack of information about African-American law enforcement officers in the Sunbelt states. We knew that entry into law enforcement agencies was denied virtually all southern African Americans until the 1960s, but we assumed that research into their experiences had been conducted since that time and that there was an existing body of literature for researchers to draw upon. Yet this literature does not exist. Instead, we discovered that what few studies had been done were about African-American officers in a few large northern cities such as New York and Detroit. Even these studies were mainly conducted before the mid-1980s, and none seemed to be theoretically honed and developed.

In addition, all the recent research we have found on the relations between racial groups and police agencies, North or South, treat African Americans more or less as *objects* of police activities. There are no substantial analyses of the experiences of black law enforcement officers, or of their actions in trying to reduce racism in their police agencies. When asked why this was the case, some of our knowledgeable research colleagues said that a primary reason is that police officers do not want to be studied and that it would be especially difficult to persuade black officers to talk with researchers. Indeed, many of our colleagues tried to dissuade us from doing the field interview project that we envisioned. Yet we persisted and contacted a national African-American police officer association, whose officials gave us a few names of possible contacts for interviews.

After we spent some weeks trying unsuccessfully to meet these contacts, we were beginning to think that our colleagues had been correct. We traveled long distances for appointments that were never kept and played phone tag. Finally, one officer extended an invitation to be interviewed in her home. The next week another officer from another agency requested an interview while on a workday break. Gradually, in the months following these initial conversations, we developed a list of fifty-nine officers who wished to be interviewed. As we did more interviews, it became apparent that these law enforcement officers not only had something very significant to say but also had begun to trust us. Eventually, in a real sense, they became joint proprietors of this research project.

Because of this trust, we became the recipients of a wealth of information about the history of black officers in the Sunbelt, their day-to-day life on and off duty, their experiences with and understandings of everyday racism, and their goals and visions for their future and the country's future. One of the significant findings of our interviews with these mostly veteran officers is that, although they and their views have been omitted from most social science literature and mass media portrayals, they provide important and detailed accounts of being active agents of change in their agencies and communities. These African-American officers see themselves as strongly rooted in their communities of origin and at the same time struggling within one critical organizational setting as part of a larger collective struggle for justice in the United States.

Contrary to much white opinion, the substantial majority of black Americans, including the officers we interviewed, have a strong collective and community orientation. They have learned important collective values and views about work, commitment, fairness, and justice at home, at church, and in the community, from previous generations of African Americans. Thus, they often go into jobs and careers like policing not just to succeed as individuals but also to make a difference for their communities. Still, they face major obstacles in trying to implement this community orientation. Dealing with recurring racism entails much patience and endurance, as this veteran officer makes clear:

> There are some things you have to endure. I endured things like certain stuff: I'd sit on the front row, and [white officers] would say things like "Yeah, we caught some of those niggers breaking in a car last week." And that was very distasteful, of course. [I] just came out of the military . . . and my first thought was to get up and, you know, tear the place apart. And that wouldn't have done any good. So you have to sit there and endure those things, and I was able to endure because my rationale was, not everyone was like that. . . . I was able to fulfill my mission, my mission was at least make a difference. . . . So you have to take those

kind of things. And you get vindicated in the end because down the line, if you stay here long enough that impact [you have]. For example, down the line after all that, I wind up being chief of community affairs which, of course, improves the relationship within the public community, so I got a chance to put something back in.

Most of the black officers we interviewed indicated, explicitly or implicitly, that they see themselves to some degree as the moral conscience of their policing institutions. Indeed, those who are veterans often take credit for some reduction of overt racial hostility and discrimination within their law enforcement agency or improvement of police–community relations in their area.

In their interviews these officers often explain how they have worked to change important aspects of local policing and to introduce new understandings and know-how to dealing with local conflicts. In one sage commentary, another very experienced officer describes how African-American officers are frequently caught in challenging community situations:

> Being a black police officer puts you in a trying situation. The average black family's only association with law enforcement is very negative. And you're going out, you're in a profession where you are basically there to bring two groups together. And that is not the police department, but the . . . two different communities. That's who you're bringing together. Because people interact every day, blacks and whites work there, they have auto accidents with each other. . . . They steal from each other; they curse at each other. Anything that happens in an all-white neighborhood or an all-black neighborhood will happen between the races. That's just inevitable.

After these pointed and nuanced comments on intergroup *and* intragroup relations and conflicts that he has observed, this respondent continues with an example of what a black officer can often accomplish:

> I've seen a lot of black officers who have made friends out of blacks and whites, just by resolving a dispute. And I've found that on numerous occasions where I've had a situation where, someone in a store, a white store manager might have caught a black female shoplifting. It's all right to go and put her in jail, satisfy the manager. He'll pat me on my back; I'm doing a good job. But it was more important to me to find out why

the person did that. And once I found out that she has five children in the home, and her husband was out drinking, and she didn't have nothing to eat, and I expressed that to the store manager, then the store manager looked a whole lot differently upon that. Or when I took the woman home, and I had a chance to go by her home and see the condition that she was in and she was telling me the truth . . . I would go back to the store and reach in my pocket and pay for whatever she took. And take it back there. And then I had store managers who made me put my money away and gave it to them, and say, well, . . . I'll give her a job, make her clean up or make a cashier out of her. . . . When you don't know about people, it makes things bad. But the black police officers' impact is bringing everybody together.

Black officers, as do black employees in many other organizations, contribute new knowledge and wisdom that can help such organizations operate in a more professional and humane way.

W. E. B. Du Bois, one of the most perceptive analysts of racism in U.S. history, argued that by excluding some people in society from mainstream opportunities and institutions, you leave out "vast stores of wisdom." Only by adding in the "whole experience" of those excluded, he noted, can the United States hope to meet the many difficult challenges of the future. The ending of racial exclusion and the inclusion of African Americans and other people of color in all institutions not only meet the highest liberty-and-justice ideals of U.S. society but also make much wisdom and knowledge available for current and future human and community development.[2]

Generally speaking, these African-American officers are realistic about their limitations and poignantly discuss their many racial trials and humiliations. They are very insightful, and often probing, in analyzing the complex dimensions and contradictions of their life. They show us clearly the importance that they place on their and others' humanity. Indeed, their conversations were frequently painful, intense, and emotional, and they constantly underlined the strength of their character. Through conversations with women and men who have often been ignored by white scholars, politicians, and media commentators, we have gained a better understanding of the great complexity and variation in human understandings about racial matters and recognized the critical importance of black agency in changing the character of racism in U.S. society.

These black officers have also underscored for us how important it is to challenge continually the often simplistic or stereotyped assumptions that a majority of white Americans seem to have in regard to the operation and arrangements of this highly racialized society. We have learned from these experienced, perceptive, and often heroic women and men that all those Americans concerned about a more just future for the United States must not be disheartened but must indeed strive to be collectively better than we have ever been:

> You always have to have hope. . . . You know, I wanted to quit. I'm not going to sit here and lie about it. I was going to find me something else to do that didn't cause me as much stress, but as I kind of say in all times, "The good Lord normally has something in mind if you're doing the right thing." I ended up here doing something that I really love because I can see some positive things that it does in the community.

ACKNOWLEDGMENTS

We would like to thank all those officers who promoted this project by contacting other officers, providing contacts, and sitting down with us to relate their experiences and life story. We, and indeed their communities and the larger society, owe these brave women and men a debt of gratitude that can never be repaid. We hope that this book provides an accurate and fair account of their experiences and helps to make them and their struggles more visible. They and their colleagues across the country deserve much credit for making policing institutions better than they were just a few decades in the past.

We would also like to thank Southeastern Louisiana University for financial support for purchasing equipment and software to facilitate the transcription of the taped interviews. We are indebted as well to Ilene Kalish and her staff at Routledge for their strong support for this project. We would also like to thank a number of our colleagues who took time out from busy lives to give some input on various versions of the draft manuscript, including Danielle Dirks, Marlese Durr, Brian Hewlett, William Smith, David Thornton, and Bernice McNair Barnett.

Ken Bolton would like to thank his parents, Kenneth and Margaret Bolton, for their unequivocal lifelong love and support. He is indebted to his wife, Làzara, and his son, Gianni, who have pushed and guided him to strive to be the best he can be. Joe Feagin would like to thank his parents, Frank and Hanna Feagin, for giving their love and support and for teaching him to be inquisitive about life's unexpected turns and twists.

Black in Blue

My [white] riding partner and I learned something. He said to me one time, we were riding along one day and just out of the clear, blue sky just talking about a whole lot of things and he says, "You know what I've learned since you and I've been riding together?" And I said, "What's that?" And he said, "You know, I found out that you have a family and you feel about them just about the same way I do about mine." He says, "I've also found out you have about the same moral values that I have, but I was raised to think that you were different." He said, "I've felt like black people were stupid and dumb and, you know, didn't know anything about anything." And he says, "You know, you and I talk about all kinds of things and a lot of times you know a lot more about it than I do." And I said, "Well you see that's the problem in this world. A lot of times kids grow up listening to what people tell them and they never question it and, unless they have an opportunity to actually get to know somebody one on one, they never know the difference. They just go through life taking their attitudes out on other people and, and most of the time if you ask them why, a plain old answer: that's the way it's always been. That's the way my mother and father or whoever taught me." You see? (Black police officer)

INTRODUCTION: THE HISTORICAL BACKGROUND

Black police officers in historically white police agencies are a relatively new reality in U.S. society. Historically, whites not only have been almost all of the police officers in the society but also have maintained full control of policing agencies. For several centuries, white Americans have used their monopoly of police power to coerce and control the communities of African Americans and other Americans of color. Indeed, numerous scholars have traced the origins of policing in the United States to the white goal of controlling enslaved African Americans and, after the Civil War, controlling the newly freed black population.

Researchers examining the history of U.S. policing have shown how powerful groups of whites developed police forces as a means of ensuring their power over the less powerful. For two centuries now, white authorities and citizens have viewed a police force as the first line of defense against, as some have said, the black "hordes" and therefore authorized the use of coercion and violence to keep black Americans subordinated in segregated communities. Thus, after the Civil War, the white elites in the South authorized the use of naked violence and police power to subordinate the newly freed black citizens. By the end of Reconstruction, unofficial (for example, Ku Klux Klan) and official white violence virtually reenslaved most black southerners. Moreover, between the late nineteenth century and the 1960s, many white police officials and officers continued to aid white mobs who attacked or killed (often, lynched) black citizens. White Americans have long exercised a monopoly over physical force as authorized by the law.[1] From the seventeenth century to the present, the justice system has frequently failed to provide legal protection and social justice for African Americans and other darker-skinned Americans.

Today, black communities and other communities of color are still disproportionately the focal point of much policing effort in the United States. The mass media and the courts, among other institutions, have fostered images of many communities of color as much more criminal than white communities, and such images have legitimized selective and forceful policing in these communities. Thus, one content analysis of "reality-based" police shows on television found that white characters in them were more likely to be portrayed as police officers, and black and Latino characters were more likely to be portrayed as criminals. In the television footage, the usually white officers were generally more aggressive than criminal suspects, and black and Latino suspects were more likely than white suspects to suffer physical aggression from officers. This study concludes that the entertainment media often portray people of color as the "bad guys" in society and white police officers as the "good guys," the restorers of justice.[2] Another study found that many white officials promote an exaggerated image of the "good cop" in the policing and justice system, a view that leads to according police officers a great deal of deference and that indicates a misplaced confidence that police officers routinely use their discretion appropriately. Because white police officers are usually seen as good when they disproportionately sanction black men for crime, the nonblack public is supported in the view that a majority of black men are stereotypically bad and criminal.[3]

Accenting the active role of police authorities, William Chambliss, among other scholars, has argued that a coalition of political, law enforcement, and media interests have often worked to create public panics over street crime in order to support a growth in funding for policing and to build up the "prison-industrial complex."[4] Numerous scholars have shown how police authorities periodically promote the idea of a crime "crisis" and relate that exaggerated crisis to black Americans or other people of color in order to extend their legal or bureaucratic powers and to justify increases in their legislative funding. In this process, they create or reinforce numerous stereotypes of Americans of color in the minds of many whites, images that in turn often justify the unjust treatment of Americans of color within the justice system.[5]

Following these earlier researchers, we argue here that an array of major structural and ideological forces have operated to relegate black people to secondary citizenship status in the United States, and that one significant set of such forces is rooted in the origin, development, and institutionalization of policing. In previous centuries, and still today, a lack of economic and political power among racially oppressed African Americans has been translated into a lack of adequate legal and juridical protection, a lack that has meant that African Americans must constantly endure targeted political and bureaucratic controls and, thus, much official police violence. The ideological justification for this targeted social control is powerful, particularly in times of social or political crisis when law enforcement agencies, the media, and various political institutions create panics over street crime that promote the public image of people of color as "deviants" who must be controlled at almost any cost.

In this book we examine the views and experiences of a significant sample of black law enforcement officers in a number of different state, local, and federal government agencies. These women and men have an experienced, distinctive, and nuanced comprehension of how racial characteristics affect policing within their law enforcement agency, in other law enforcement agencies with which they are familiar, and in the civilian society. Our analysis examines how African-American officers view themselves as African Americans and as police officers, as well as how they view the sometimes discriminatory relations with their coworkers, their department, and the communities in which they live and work.

POLICING BLACK COMMUNITIES
The White Policing Syndrome: Negative Views of Black Communities

The perceptions and actions of white officers in relation to black citizens in their communities demonstrate some of the daily realities of these broad social control factors. Homer Hawkins and Richard Thomas have discussed the reality of the "white policing syndrome," which began at least a century ago and has been carried over to modern policing in most urban communities. This syndrome involves the routinely negative white police perceptions of, and treatment of, black citizens in local communities.[6] Offering support for this view, numerous other scholars have shown how white officers demonstrate these views and orientations in the daily performance of their job. This is a complex matter, however, as we will see in the sometimes conflicting studies on these issues.

In general, white police officers reflect the dominant attitudes of the majority population toward Americans of color. For example, the common stereotype of a black man (less often, woman) as likely to be criminal particularly affects nonblack police officers whose job it is to deal with crime in the local community. Several researchers have concluded from field research and reviews of the literature that white officers' attitudes about and behavior directed at black Americans differ greatly from those directed to whites. A major social function of policing is to maintain existing group-based hierarchies, and white officers tend to hold stereotypes and prejudices that are linked to or shaped by their policing role. One illustration of this point is commonplace racial profiling; many white officers today believe that the racial marker "black" is a sufficient reason to suspect, detain, or search blacks, and particularly black men.[7]

It is not just those white officers who openly express racist stereotypes who discriminate against black citizens and other citizens of color. Those who suppress their racist feelings in public often act to discriminate as well. In one 1960s study, Black and Reiss concluded that the racial attitudes of white officers were for the most part unrelated to their treatment of black citizens. However, Friedrich reanalyzed their data and found that the more white officers disliked blacks, the more likely they were than others to arrest black suspects, but not to treat black complainants differentially.[8] More recently, one 1990s study found that white officers were more likely to view the actions of black people as guilty-looking than those of whites. Other surveys of police officers have found significant proportions (for example, 25 percent in Los Angeles) who believe that racial prejudice affects officers' perceptions of people of color.[9]

Given that white police officers are likely to be similar to the general white population in their racial views, it is likely that the majority hold negative stereotypes of African Americans and a significant percentage also hold negative views of other people of color. Thus, one 2001 national survey found that more than half of whites still openly agree with one or more of four negative stereotypes of African Americans, and several recent studies of white students have found that the majority accept some stereotypes of African Americans as true.[10] In addition, because many whites give socially desirable responses to the opinion surveys, the percentages may well underestimate the degree to which whites hold negative stereotypes of African Americans and other Americans of color. Research shows that when whites, including white students, are given more time to discuss their views, they often articulate more stereotypes and racial animosity than they do in response to brief survey questions.[11] This is particularly true when whites are "backstage," in more private settings with family or friends, where they often make blatantly racist comments they would not normally make in public.[12]

Specific racial attitudes are not the only factors shaping white police officers' treatment of citizens of color. Most whites, including most police officers, have grown up and live in a highly segregated community where they have very few, or no, enduring equal-status contacts with African Americans. Michael Banton has suggested that generally police officers are more likely to adopt a service perspective in neighborhoods similar to their own. The less social distance between an officer and the citizens of a neighborhood, the more likely the officer will adopt a helping and friendly orientation in encounters with citizens. Recent research confirms Banton's suggestion.[13] Major influences on police officers' behavior are their knowledge of a particular community and their interpretation of that community's expectations of how the police should act. Substantial racial segregation of rural and urban communities promotes those conditions in which white officers lack ability to understand the behavior of citizens of color.

Another important factor affecting the attitudes and actions of white police officers is the distinctive police culture that develops in most historically white departments. Because of their difficult working conditions and odd hours, as well as other factors we examine in later chapters, police officers often socialize mainly with each other and develop tight in-groups and a strong police culture. Historical studies indicate that the earliest generations of police officers were aggressive and often brutal in attempts to establish authority in urban communities. Given the recurring tension with or antagonism toward certain communities they police, over time the majority of white officers have become more or less isolated from the people in these communities and thus most concerned with internal group solidarity and with protection of one other. New officers are thus greatly pressured by other officers to conform to the preexisting occupational roles, including common-place stereotyping of and hostility toward people of color. The sense of isolation, as well as the reported difficulty in communicating with their superiors, regularly create situations in which many officers are inclined to devalue official rules and to use shortcuts in their policing procedures.[14] White officers' behavior can be racist to the extent that institutional controls are weak and that insular police cultures express active attitudinal and behavioral racism, such as condoning excessive violence against citizens of color. Knowledge of the police culture often assists one in understanding discriminatory police behavior directed toward citizens of color.

Contemporary Evidence of Discrimination in Policing

Oddly enough, some criminologists continue to debate whether there is racial discrimination in the U.S. policing and justice system. We find much of this debate to be strange because evidence of racial discrimination in other major institutions that have been studied is generally quite substantial, as is the evidence previously noted that a majority of white Americans still hold some racist stereotypes today. It would be extraordinary indeed if the criminal justice system were so different from other major institutions as to have no serious problems with racial discrimination. One reason for this debate is that much attention is focused on whether the statistical data indicating that a disproportionate number of black men are arrested, convicted, and sent to prison are evidence of racial bias in policing and other aspects of the criminal justice system. Considering these statistics, some researchers have argued that they simply represent a greater level of engagement in crime by black Americans. Yet numerous others have found that there is a dual standard in the criminal justice system in U.S. towns and cities.[15] For example, one Yale study discovered racial discrimination in bail setting by judges in New England.[16]

There is also much evidence of routine racial discrimination in everyday policing. Black communities are more frequently patrolled than other areas, a practice that increases the likelihood of black citizens' being stopped and arrested. In several surveys, African-American respondents often reported racialized mistreatment by white officers. Both black women and black men are more likely than whites to be stopped and searched by the police for no good cause. One national survey found that 37 percent of black respondents felt that police officers had stopped them unfairly only because they were black, including about half the black men in the survey. Another city survey found that black respondents were much more likely than whites to be unfairly stopped and searched by police.[17] In addition, a study of police stops on a Maryland interstate highway discovered that black drivers constituted about three-quarters of all those stopped and searched by the police, more than four times their proportion among those drivers in violation of traffic laws.[18]

Another study examined more than one hundred published accounts of police brutality and found that 97 percent of the victims were people of color, and 93 percent of the offending officers were white. More citizens of color were assaulted for not complying than for posing a serious threat to the officer or another citizen. This study clearly suggests that whites make up a very small percentage of the victims of police brutality.[19] In addition, black citizens are more likely to be killed by the police than are whites. Some explanations for this differential in police killings accent the point that the proportion of blacks killed is similar to the proportion of blacks arrested for violent crimes, and thus that such police killings only occur when there is a serious threat to police officers.[20] Yet other researchers who have studied particular cities have found racial differentials in the pattern of police killings in some cities, yet not in others.[21] This significant variation suggests that the level of police violence may well be linked to the variable character of police cultures across cities, rather than to the street situations that white officers find themselves in.

Images of White Police Officers in Communities of Color

In his classic study of U.S. racism in the 1930s and 1940s, Gunnar Myrdal observed, "The Negro's most important public contact is with the policeman. He is the personification of white authority in the Negro community."[22] This is still often the case in counties, towns, and cities across the United States. The above discussion of police practices, and malpractice, indicates the prominent and often oppressive role that white police officers play in black communities. Not surprisingly, police officers are often negatively viewed in these communities.

Since the racial riots and revolts of the 1960s, which were often triggered by police brutality incidents, numerous researchers have examined the views of black citizens about police and policing in local communities. Examining conditions in cities across the country that led to the 1960s riots, the 1968 National Advisory Commission on Civil Disorders concluded that many black Americans believed that police brutality and harassment occur repeatedly in their communities.[23] More recently, studies have reached similar conclusions. African Americans still report problems with police malpractice in their communities, and for that reason there is substantial concern about police brutality and other malpractice in most black communities. This means there are substantial suspicion and caution in regard to dealing with white police officers. A late-1980s Miami study found that black residents were much more negative toward the police than were Cuban Americans, who were more recent residents there.[24] Other studies since the 1980s have found that black Americans often have a positive view of the police in general yet are usually more critical of both police services and responses in time of need, and of police malpractice, than whites.[25] A number of studies have found that black views of the police are shaped by concrete experiences in local neighborhoods. It is the cumulative nature of negative contacts with police officers in neighborhoods that accounts for the low level of support for the police in many black communities.[26] In an earlier assessment of this research, which is still accurate today, Jerome Skolnick commented, "There is no reason to suppose that anti-black hostility is a new development brought on by recent conflicts between the police and the black community. What appears to have changed is not police attitudes, but the fact that black people are fighting back."[27]

BLACK POLICE OFFICERS: A BRIEF HISTORY

When modern policing began in the United States in the first decades of the nineteenth century, there were no black police officers. It has taken many decades for black Americans to move from enslavement and legal segregation to a situation of some access to historically white institutions, such as law enforcement agencies. Looking at the history of black police officers, W. Marvin Dulaney has underscored the changes over three historical periods. From the period of Reconstruction after the Civil War to the 1940s, there were few black officers anywhere, and these few "crime fighters" typically served as the tough arm of whites who sought to maintain control over impoverished black communities.[28] Samuel Walker has pointed out that "during the Segregation Era (1890s–1960s), Southern cities did not hire any African-American officers, and police departments in Northern states engaged in systematic employment discrimination."[29] It has only been in recent decades that we have seen significant changes in the representation of African Americans in U.S. policing. Thus, during the 1950s and 1960s, the number of black officers began to increase slowly. As grassroots movements grew, black citizens demanded more political and police power, which translated in part into greater numbers of black law enforcement officers. Since several large, primarily northern cities had used small numbers of black officers to police black communities for some time, police administrations everywhere had evidence that black Americans could be effective officers. The integration of black officers into historically white agencies was viewed as one solution for racial tensions, so that these officers were often seen as "reformers." Many people felt that black officers would be more sensitive to black communities and less likely to harass them and would therefore reduce community tensions.

Since the late 1960s, black leaders have worked to recruit better-educated officers, and these officers have generally worked to redefine their role in historically white institutions, such as by pressing for an end to discrimination and by creating black police associations. Gradually, black police leaders sought to end blatant discriminatory practices in historically white departments and to develop a view of black officers as "professionals," as public servants whose job was to reduce racial tensions while protecting citizens from criminals.[30] Beginning in the late 1960s, another solution promoted to overcome tensions between black communities and police departments involved community-oriented policing strategies. These strategies stressed greater cooperation and communication between communities of color and police departments and a deemphasis on traditional patrol-and-control strategies. The link between community-oriented policing and hiring of officers representative of those communities continues to be strong. As Skolnick and Fyfe have suggested, "Policing should reflect and be informed by the values and views of all people served, and all the people should at least occasionally see others who look like them in police uniform."[31]

Contending with Barriers to Hiring and Promotions: Federal Intervention

The convergence of numerous factors—including increased black political power, the need for jobs in black communities, and the desire of many white officials to pacify black communities in the 1960s—culminated in a new phase of the history of African-American police officers. Yet, a problem remained as how to overcome white opposition to hiring and promotion of African-American officers. In 1972, the Equal Employment Opportunity Act extended the 1964 Civil Rights Act to state and local governments and empowered the Equal Employment Opportunity Commission (EEOC) to fight discrimination in employment in organizations such as police departments. This facilitated actions by black citizens and officers seeking to reshape practices within traditionally white departments by providing some legal backing. Indeed, numerous police departments have been sued, often because of their employment practices.[32]

Samuel Walker has devised an Equal Employment Opportunity Index (EEOI) to measure compliance efforts of police departments in employment of officers of color. If the percentage of officers of color in a department equals the percentage of people of color in the community, the EEOI number is 1.0. An examination of departments in the fifty largest cities from 1972 to 1982 found little movement toward this EEOI goal. A later study of the years 1983 to 1992 found modest progress in meeting the 1.0 guideline. Just 38 percent of the large departments had achieved the level of at least 0.75 for black officers.[33] Various other studies suggest that factors contributing to the successful desegregation of some historically white departments include an increase of black political power, an increase in employment litigation, and an administrative leadership committed to employment of more officers of color.

A variety of factors continue to limit black representation in many historically white police departments. These factors range from discriminatory barriers in hiring, to discrimination within law enforcement agencies, to a potential black officer's concern with being labeled a traitor in the community, to aspirations for better occupations than police work.

Some research suggests that an important factor is black citizens' choosing not to pursue a police career. However, this is a constrained choice because of the fact—as shown in several studies, including our own here—that job opportunities are affected by the discriminatory practices of many historically white police organizations.[34] Much research shows the considerable resistance to hiring black officers by historically white police agencies. Today, various discriminatory procedures within law enforcement departments adversely affect the hiring and promoting of black officers. This discrimination has been documented in autobiographies of, and interviews with, pioneering black police officers.[35]

Racial discrimination also takes place in the promotion process through subjective evaluations, despite guidelines that are supposed to promote objective procedures. A few research studies and some court cases have identified three areas in which this can occur: performance evaluations by supervisors, personal interviews with higher-ranking officers, and job assignments that are "dead-end."[36] Some other research suggests the importance of promotion and assignment to officer motivation. Black officers like to feel that they have the ability to do a good job and be rewarded for it by being allowed to develop more satisfying police interests. When this does not happen, they may become increasingly disillusioned with their department and are likely to feel a greater sense of unity with other black officers. When white officers are given preference, black officers feel that their goals can only be achieved through black police organizations.[37] Moreover, a study by Buzawa found that in police departments with successful affirmative action policies and some black executives, black officers expressed greater job satisfaction; white officers expressed greater dissatisfaction for the same reasons.[38]

Numerous observers have suggested that tension between police departments and black communities, as well as the problems black officers encounter, can be overcome by the appointment of black law enforcement executives. One 1970s study found that black officers believed that top-ranking black officers could have a positive effect by establishing rapport with citizens and ensuring that their officers treat citizens in a fair manner.[39] More recently, writing in the 1990s, Dulaney has noted that black executives are often innovators in the police profession. They often deliberately solicit support from the communities of color that they serve.[40] Nevertheless, the presence of black executives is not a cure-all for discrimination faced by black officers. Leinen's 1984 study discovered that promoting black officers to supervisory positions does not necessarily result in improved conditions for other black officers because of the inability of these executives to develop the requisite social networks to exercise authority effectively within the organization.[41] More recently, black executives themselves have reported the problem of being promoted to supervisory positions without legitimate authority.[42] Black executives are often caught between the pressures for change and the pressures of existing rules and regulations. For example, some black officers in Los Angeles complained that the new black police chief, Willie Williams, was being "too" fair. They argued that black officers had suffered such extensive discrimination for so many years that they now deserved more attention and more than technical equality of treatment.[43]

The Value of Black Officers: Local Black Communities

Since the 1960s, numerous advocates of reducing community–police tensions have argued that the presence of black officers will significantly alter some policing patterns in local communities. Jerome Skolnick and James Fyfe have suggested that black officers can reduce community tensions in two major ways: community members see black officers and feel that the police department is representative, and the presence of black officers affects the actions of their white partners and makes them more sensitive. Other commentators have expected black officers to be better in dealing with citizens of color in day-to-day policing.[44]

As for policing styles, most research studies have concluded that, generally speaking, white and black officers do not do their policing in significantly different ways. For example, a few researchers have examined police shootings. Two studies found that black officers had higher shooting rates, although the differences are likely explained by assignment location and the residence of black officers, which can mean higher off-duty shooting rates. A third study did not find a relationship between the racial characteristics of officers and the frequency of shootings.[45] Other research has found that black and white officers have similar arrest patterns, patterns of citizen complaints against them, and levels of police deviance.[46] Nonetheless, a few researchers have found some significant differences in certain attitudes that can influence day-to-day policing. Thus, one sociopsychological study of police officers found that the black officers studied were less social-dominance-oriented in their attitudes than their white counterparts.[47]

Studies of the nature of the relationship between black officers and black communities have so far reported somewhat contradictory findings. Some researchers have found that black officers believe they have a positive impact on black citizens' evaluations of police because of their greater knowledge of the community and its norms. Studies have also shown that black officers generally want to make their community a better place to live. However, other studies have found significant proportions of black officers reporting that they felt more respected by white citizens than by black citizens and that most lived outside the community where they worked.[48] Other studies of police–community relations have concluded that black community attitudes toward the police are often shaped more by socioeconomic conditions or by the general negative image of the police role than by the actions of individual officers.[49]

In addition, a few studies that have focused on particular communities show variations by place and time. For example, in Detroit during the 1960s there were considerable tensions between a then mostly white police department and local black communities. However, as the city has changed, so has this relationship. A 1996 opinion survey there found that black citizens generally held more favorable attitudes toward the police than did white citizens.[50] This differential probably reflects not only the majority black population there but also the greatly increased representation of black officers on the police force and the presence of a black police chief and mayor. In contrast, nationally the view of the policing system differs greatly between white and black Americans. A number of recent national opinion surveys have shown that black views of the criminal justice system and of the police are generally more negative than are those of whites. Thus, in contrast to the much more positive views of white respondents in regard to the justice system, two-thirds of black respondents polled in a Gallup survey believed the criminal justice system was biased against black people. Some 63 percent also said that they would not assign greater value to the testimony of a police witness than to the testimony of other witnesses.[51] It is interesting to contrast these national survey results with the Detroit opinion survey. This contrast does indeed suggest that a racially representative police force can have a positive impact on black communities.

Research on Women Officers

Women officers, white and black, entered policing in great numbers about the same time as black men and under similar social and political circumstances.

Research on women officers has found some significant data. The in-depth interview methods employed by some researchers have resulted in rich descriptions of the experiences and interpretations of women officers. These researchers have found that women officers face considerable resistance and discrimination from male officers and consequently suffer high levels of stress. Male officers often treat women as a general class and not in terms of their individual characteristics. Women officers and prison guards face institutional barriers, harassment, and discrimination, which are often based on the traditional idea of policing's being a masculine profession.[52] In response to this treatment and the resulting stress, the female officers who remain on the job must develop a range of survival mechanisms. Despite the confrontational environment encountered by women, numerous studies have found that there are no significant differences in the job performance of male and female officers, though community perceptions often are that female officers are more empathetic and communicate better in police–citizen confrontations.[53]

However, most of this research fails to examine in a significant way the differences in the experiences of women officers of different racial and ethnic groups. This omission is important, considering that white Americans, including police officers, traditionally perceive white women and black women very differently. Black women often have been portrayed in the media and in political commentary as social "deviants" and, therefore, are more likely to be perceived by white police officers and officials as more likely to commit certain criminal acts. They are much more likely than white women to be confronted and questioned by police officers.[54] One of the few studies that specifically examine the situations of black women officers found that institutional racism and sexism both operated as monumental barriers for them. For example, they faced discrimination in assignments and promotions.[55] In addition, a more recent study has found that for black female officers racism and sexism are interlocking systems of oppression. Black women officers have experiences with discrimination that are sometimes different from those of white women officers, as well as from those of black men officers.[56]

OUR CONCEPTUAL FRAMEWORK: THE SYSTEMIC CHARACTER OF EVERYDAY RACISM

Most empirical studies of the police, community policing, and racial matters are not theoretically driven. That is, there is typically a lack of clarity regarding definitions of important concepts such as discrimination, stereotyping, "race," and racism. In addition, the connections between key concepts are often underexplored. Without a clear theory of racism, the interpretation of research results can be problematic. Let us be clear then about our theoretical understandings and perspective.

Systemic Racism

We accent here a conceptual framework that views racism as a matter of extensive everyday experience, and thus as well institutionalized and systemic across all institutions in the United States. In the late nineteenth century, Frederick Douglass, one of the first analysts to accent the institutionalization of racism, made an observation about the racism faced by black Americans: "In nearly every department of American life they are confronted by this insidious influence. It fills the air. It meets them at the workshop and factory, when they apply for work. It meets them at the church, at the hotel, at the ballot-box, and worst of all, it meets them in the jury-box. . . . He [the black American] has ceased to be a *slave of an individual,* but has in some sense become *the slave of society.*"[57] Systemic racism, in some sense, makes African Americans subordinate slaves of white society generally. The first extended analysis of racism as a system was developed by the sociologist Oliver Cox, who argued in the 1940s that in the case of African Americans, the white elite had early decided "to proletarianize a whole people—that is to say, the whole people is looked upon as a class— whereas white proletarianization involves only a section of the white people."[58] By the 1960s Kwame Ture and Charles Hamilton, among other important researchers, defined *institutional racism* as the patterns of racial discrimination that are built into and supported by the major social institutions of the society, such as the economic, political, educational, and health care institutions.[59]

Drawing on this tradition, we define *systemic racism* as a centuries-old system of racial oppression created and maintained by white Americans, one that encompasses widespread discriminatory practices targeting African Americans and other Americans of color; the racialized emotions, ideologies, and attitudes that generate and undergird these discriminatory practices; the social in-groups, networks, and institutions that embed and buttress the pervasive racial discrimination; and the unjustly gained economic and political privileges, resources, and power of whites that have resulted from this institutionalized discrimination over nearly four centuries. Thus, racism is not just a matter of a few bigots; it is well institutionalized, systemic, and enduring. Racism is not just about the construction of racial images and attitudes in white minds; it is also about the creation and maintenance of substantial white privileges and power.

At its heart, systemic racism embeds very unequal relationships of privilege and power between racially defined groups. In this society, most people do not experience "race" in the abstract, but in recurring relationships, in experiences with other Americans directly or as they are represented in the media. Whether one is a perpetrator of racial discrimination, a target of racial discrimination, a bystander to discrimination, or an activist working against discrimination, each individual is caught in a complex web of alienating racial relations in the society. In everyday operation, a complex array of discriminatory and other racialized relationships distort what could be fully egalitarian societal relationships into relationships that are in fact harmful, separating, and alienating. This means that racism is fully *experiential* as well as systemic. Constantly at work, systemic racism categorizes and divides human beings from each other and thus severely restricts the development of a common human consciousness and egalitarian society. Everyday life under this system of racism involves an ongoing struggle between racially defined human communities—one community whose members are generally seeking to preserve unjustly derived privileges and power, and other communities whose members are seeking to overthrow racial oppression and garner a fair share of societal resources and opportunities. The alienation that is racial oppression extends to many areas. In the case of African Americans, that which should most be their own—control over their own life and work—is that which is often taken from them by the persisting system of racism.[60]

The Centrality and Character of Experiential Racism

Since the legal segregation era that ended in the late 1960s, numerous white scholars, public commentators, and jurists have moved from the complete rejection of accounts from black Americans of discriminatory experiences characteristic of the pre-1960s period to a closer attending to black accounts of everyday discrimination. If one examines landmark statements and court decisions on racial matters from the late eighteenth century to the early decades of the twentieth century, one finds that very few white social scientists, jurists, or other white commentators took seriously the reports and perspectives of black Americans on the racial oppression that they faced.

Thus, in the *Dred Scott v. Sandford* (1857) U.S. Supreme Court decision on the petition of an enslaved black American named Dred Scott, a substantial majority of the Court ruled that Scott's view that he had constitutional rights was of no consequence. Chief Justice Roger Taney ruled that black Americans "had for more than a century before [the U.S. Constitution] been regarded as beings of an inferior order, and altogether unfit to associate with the white race, either in social or political relations; and so far inferior, that they had no rights which the white man was bound to respect."[61] Similarly, half a century later in a famous 1896 decision (*Plessy v. Ferguson)* supporting racial segregation laws, the U.S. Supreme Court concluded that black people's view "that the enforced separation of the two races stamps the colored race with a badge of inferiority" is not worthy of consideration because that sense of inferiority is *only* a notion in black minds.[62] All but one justice on that Court, and most social scientists in the period, saw no reason to attend to black accounts of everyday experience with discrimination and other aspects of antiblack racism.

It was only a half-century later, beginning in the 1940s, that more white social scientists and other social analysts started to pay much more attention to the experiences reported by black Americans in regard to the discrimination they faced. One example of this shift was Gunnar Myrdal's *An American Dilemma,* a lengthy volume that drew in substantial part on interviews with black leaders and citizens in regard to experiences with everyday discrimination at the hands of whites.[63] By the 1950s, we also saw a movement by some jurists away from the *Plessy* decision that segregation was necessary and legal to a complete rejection of that position, most notably in the 1954 *Brown* decision of the U.S. Supreme Court, which cited social science data to buttress its conclusions.[64] Today, numerous white social scientists and jurists understand that they must pay *substantial attention* to the concrete experiences of African Americans if they are to understand how discrimination works in U.S. society.

In this book we examine the everyday lives of black officers in terms of the concept of *experiential racism,* which has been developed in recent years by a number of scholars, including the authors. Using this approach, we and other researchers have shown previously how racial discrimination is experienced as a routine, recurring, and everyday reality for black Americans and other Americans of color across and within an array of societal institutions. This experiential racism involves discrimination that is motivated by racial stereotyping and racial images that have become so integrated into the woodwork of the society that they are barely noticeable to most white Americans. Sets of these embedded understandings and the practices triggered by them constitute substantial institutionalized racism in each of society's major sectors. Discrimination is more than an activity of individuals, for individual acts of discrimination fit into, and are shaped by, the larger and encompassing racialized ingroups, networks, organizations, and institutions.[65] Human actors operate within structural boundaries and make decisions within structural contexts, supports, and constraints. We should also keep in mind that awareness of these organizational and other structural contexts, and of reasons for discrimination, is not always a conscious process. Indeed, many people discriminate more or less unconsciously.

Today, experiential racism continues to have an impact on the lives of all Americans of color, and especially on the lives of African Americans, the longest term (with Native Americans) racially oppressed group within this white-dominated society. This discrimination ranges from intentional and easily documented acts, to less obvious and subtler forms of discrimination, to covert discrimination that takes place behind the scenes. Discriminatory acts by whites range from avoidance maneuvers, to exclusion and rejection, to verbal or physical attacks, to insults and insensitivity. Racial discrimination also varies in character and impact, depending on the site and location. For example, black Americans often encounter different forms of discrimination in the workplace than they do in impersonal public locations such as malls and on the streets.

Recurring Experience with Racial Discrimination: Some Illustrative Examples

Numerous recent studies reveal the fact that discriminatory practices targeting African Americans are still commonplace across the country. We will note numerous studies in later chapters, but let us cite a few examples here. One recent study of health and the effects of racial discrimination gave two thousand African Americans a list of seven social settings, such as the workplace. A substantial majority of the respondents reported that they had faced discrimination by whites in at least one of these settings.[66] A late 1990s Gallup opinion survey asked African Americans whether they had experienced discrimination in workplaces, in dining out, in shopping, with police, or in mass transit during the last month. Just less than half said that they had faced discrimination in one or more of these settings.[67]

Discrimination is commonplace in the U.S. workplaces that have been studied. For example, surveying black workers in Los Angeles, one major study found that six in ten among a sample of more than a thousand respondents had faced discrimination in the workplace within the past year. Similarly, a survey of thousands of military personnel discovered that large proportions of the African-American respondents had recently faced racist jokes, discussions, comments, published materials, stares, and barriers in their job in the military.[68]

Public places and shopping areas are also still racialized. A 2001 national survey found that most of the black respondents had faced discrimination in public places and shopping areas, such as being the recipients of racial slurs and of defensive or openly disrespectful behavior from whites. Another 2001 survey, of black tourists, found that most had experienced discrimination while shopping, dining, or staying at a hotel.[69] Even these substantial data likely underestimate the frequency of discrimination, for brief surveys have not generally examined the great range of discriminatory actions encountered daily by African Americans.

Field researchers have also found discrimination against black customers shopping for new cars. They have reported on the substantial degree of discriminatory treatment faced by black Americans from white professionals such as medical practitioners. And numerous field-audit studies using black and white housing testers have discovered very high levels of discrimination. Audit studies in numerous cities across the United States have found that black tester-renters confront exclusionary discrimination about 60 to 80 percent of the time in looking for housing.[70] In turn, enforced residential segregation limits the opportunities that many African Americans have to get better schooling and jobs.

The Cumulative Character of Experiential Racism

We have found no research on the frequency of the discriminatory incidents faced by individual African Americans during the course of a lifetime. In previous research, the second author has asked a few respondents about how often they face discrimination over the course of a typical year. The answer tends to be, *a hundred or more times a year*. Thus, one retired New York printer, after some reflection, estimated that he faced at least 250 significant incidents of discrimination annually, and he noted that he was only counting incidents that he had consciously noticed. Thus, over the course of a lifetime, a typical black woman or man probably encounters thousands of incidents of blatant, covert, and subtle discrimination at the hands of whites. Encounters with racial discrimination constitute a painful, constant, and accumulating experience.[71]

Not surprisingly, thus, our respondents do not view experiential racism with detachment but in terms of their own, and their relatives' and friends' experiences with discrimination by whites—both in the past and in the present. When our respondents talk about racial mistreatment, they describe experiences as being painful when they occur as well as having a cumulative impact on their life and those of other African Americans in their social networks and communities. Individual African Americans frequently discuss such experiences with each other, and over time a strong collective memory of racial discrimination and how to combat it is created.[72]

Generally speaking, recurring experiences with discrimination at the hands of whites shape one's life perspective. Necessarily, this life perspective and orientation must include a repertoire of responses to hostile acts by whites. African Americans learn to contend with racial mistreatment in a variety of more or less successful ways. Research on middle-class African Americans shows that they respond to discrimination according to their perception of the site in which the act occurs and the form of the act.[73] They and other black Americans actively respond to racism with an array of important strategies for countering and coping, including deference to whites, evaluation of a situation before concluding that racism has occurred, and active resistance—including verbal reprimands, sarcasm, physical counterattacks, and lawsuits. Most African Americans struggle to maintain some kind of balance and to contain their frustrations while searching for the best response. The costs of racial discrimination to the victims are extensive, ranging from the immediate to the long term. They include embarrassment, frustration, bitterness, anger, rage, and an array of stress-related physical illnesses such as hypertension and stress diabetes. They also include energy loss and, often, a significant impact on the families of those who are victims of discrimination. Racial discrimination is a recurring, damaging, energy-consuming, and life-consuming experience.[74]

DIMENSIONS OF EXPERIENTIAL RACISM: SOME BASIC CONCEPTS

Let us now examine several sensitizing concepts that we use throughout this book to examine the racialized events and incidents faced by African-American police officers in their workaday world. These concepts signal what we see as relevant in the interviews. We draw here on sensitizing concepts grouped into four areas. These are drawn from the experiential-racism theoretical framework: the cumulative knowledge of racism, problematization and denigration, marginalization and exclusion, and active resistance to racism (see figure 1).

Gaining Knowledge of Racism: Cumulative and Collective

Central to this book is the concept of the cumulative knowledge of racism. Over time black Americans acquire, develop, and understand through their everyday experiences just what "race" and racism are in actual operation. They learn how to evaluate, interpret, and respond to specific discriminatory acts. A key idea here is that those who endure racism more or less daily gain a sophisticated knowledge of its reality and reproduction over time. One pioneering scholar, Philomena Essed, has suggested that to know how everyday racism operates one must pay attention "to the knowledge, beliefs, opinions, and attitudes of blacks with respect to the meaning of racism."[75] Whereas *experience* always

Figure 1:
Sensitizing Concepts

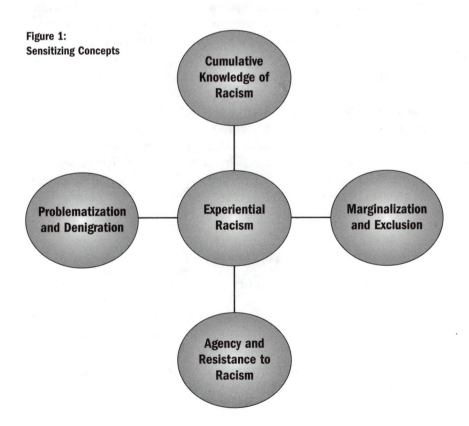

involves specific events that happen to an individual, the particular events are interpreted on the basis of knowledge gained from previous events as well as from the collective knowledge of the relevant black families and communities. People act on the basis of meanings they attach to social events and interactions. As we will see in chapter 2, the black police officers we interviewed use their gradually acquired knowledge of everyday racism to understand, interpret, and counter discriminatory experiences with white officers and civilians. It is significant that a majority of whites seem blind to, or at least unconcerned with, the reality and harsh consequences of their discriminatory actions, in part perhaps because they have never had to face racial discrimination themselves.

Since African Americans, such as the police officers we interviewed, operate from experience with and distinctive knowledge of everyday racism, they usually have much greater insight into discrimination and its aspects than whites. Marginalized and exploited racial groups generally have a better understanding of how discrimination operates that is a result of their collective experience with oppression and the cumulative stock of knowledge they share across families and friendship groups, and over generations. Experiences with racism, therefore, constitute a cumulative process of knowledge acquisition in which the new experiences of black people "are interpreted and evaluated against the background of earlier personal experiences, vicarious experiences, and general knowledge of racism in society."[76] Individuals are socialized by their elders and others with a fundamental stock of knowledge needed to cope in everyday situations: the ways to move about and survive in hostile social worlds. For black people in a racist society, this means that they generally have a special stock of knowledge as to racist attitudes, behavior, and acts that white people are not privy to. The knowledge of racism transcends immediate and individual occurrences: "past memories flow into present memories as past communities are the basis for present communities."[77]

Contexts of Contemporary Racism: White Networks and Networking

For nearly three and a half centuries slavery and segregation were legal, first in the North American colonies and later in the United States. A high level of social segregation of racial groups was created and mandated by white Americans from the first decades of colonization, and this social segregation was buttressed and reinforced by housing segregation. Housing segregation became ever more important as villages and towns grew into cities and large areas of cities became homogeneous along racial lines. Residential segregation and homogeneity were created not, or primarily maintained, by African Americans but rather by white Americans concerned that the two racial populations not mix, socialize, and intermarry. Now, for nearly four hundred years, this country has been mostly segregated, and, though now only informally maintained, substantial social and residential segregation persists into the twenty-first century. Such racial segregation has many serious consequences, not the least of which are the generation and fostering of important segregated social networks, along which white Americans pass critical information about an array of employment and other issues and within which they trade resources, make decisions, and provide social support. As they try to integrate historically white institutions, black Americans have frequently found established and entrenched white (usually "old-boy") networks to be a very serious impediment to improving their circumstances in society.

In our analysis, we focus centrally on the U.S. workplace, specifically in historically white law enforcement agencies. In social science research on organizational workplaces, researchers have made an important distinction between the formal organization and the informal social networks that develop and become important within a typical employing organization. One can see the contours of the formal organization by looking at organizational charts and official regulations, yet these are often *not* accurate in terms of depicting how workplaces actually operate and how decisions are made. In practice, informal networks of existing employees, especially influential employees, shape much of the way that most workplaces operate on a daily basis.[78] In assessing what happens to workers of color in employment settings, it is generally important to pay attention to the reality, operation, and impact of informal social groups, for they usually become critical contexts within which discriminatory actions are formulated and reinforced. In historically white employment settings, many whites discriminate as prejudiced individuals, but much of their power to harm their targets originates in membership in the white-dominated networks, what one sociologist has called "enforcement coalitions."[79] The norms and views of historically white enforcement coalitions within most employing organizations typically include racial stereotypes that caricature and problematize Americans of color. Not surprisingly, such views shape the character of the workplaces within which workers of color are being integrated. Research on predominantly white workplaces and business settings has often discovered a continuing racial hierarchy grounded in an informal culture and substantially reinforced by the informal enforcement networks.[80]

The workplaces of historically white police agencies, our focus, show patterns very much in line with the findings of this organizational research. The literature on contemporary policing reports data indicating that police officers have often created within their departments strong informal groups with a distinctive police subculture. This phenomenon is so strong that it is sometimes described by the metaphor of officers' living behind a "blue curtain." Because of emotionally and physically stressful jobs and odd hours, as well as the fact that they do dangerous "dirty work" for the community, many police officers, today as in the past, socialize substantially with other officers off duty and thus often become more insulated from the civilian population than those who work in many other fields. Not surprisingly, in most contemporary police departments those in control of the informal police groups and subculture are white. Although the situation in some departments has changed somewhat as women, African Americans, and other nontraditional employees are hired, the police culture in most departments often has an orientation that accents "us" versus "them," isolation from civilians when off duty, a tough and aggressive crime-fighter orientation, and a strong loyalty to fellow officers. Moreover, in the view of many officers, one cannot catch criminals without violating official rules. Officers are the "good guys" in the war against society's "bad guys."[81] Since those identified by the larger society as the most serious bad guys are often Americans of color, such as those who are street criminals, it is not surprising that the police culture often negatively stereotypes Americans of color, especially black Americans.

In addition, most white officers, like other whites, have grown up in overwhelmingly white, relatively segregated residential areas in the United States. Numerous research studies have shown that major cities, North and South, have a substantial degree of residential segregation that is changing, but slowly.[82] This extensive segregation means social isolation from other racial groups and, significantly, a paucity of equal-status experiences with black individuals and families. In one Chicago study, *New York Times* journalists interviewed working-class Chicagoans in two adjacent suburbs, one mostly white and the other mostly black. The journalists found that white interviewees were very isolated and went through life "without ever getting to know a black person." Each group was fearful of the other. Yet, the black respondents were "fearful because much of their contact with white people was negative," whereas "whites were fearful because they had little or no contact" with black Chicagoans similar to them.[83]

Given the racial ecology of everyday living, a majority of blacks spend much more time interacting with whites than the majority of whites spend interacting with blacks. Not surprisingly, this white isolation feeds negative stereotyping among white Americans, including many white law enforcement officers. Typically, they have learned and share the negative views of African Americans and other Americans of color that are circulated and reinforced within their family of origin and friendship networks and among their neighbors. Given the often negative view of Americans of color circulating among many white officers, black American officers face an especially difficult task in trying to become fully integrated into historically white police agencies. More or less daily, they face a majority of white officers who hold to at least some negative stereotypes of African Americans and other Americans of color. For that reason, black law enforcement officers regularly report that many white police officials and officers see them more or less as intruders into white networks and comfort zones.

The Minds of White Folk: Problematization and Denigration of African Americans

As we have just suggested, it is within white-dominated social networks that most whites develop their views of black Americans and other Americans of color. These networks begin at an early age—in families, on playgrounds, and in elementary schools—and continue to be important as whites become older and enter other educational institutions, the military, and workplaces. Whites, as other people do, learn much about the world from these informal groups and networks. Some information is accurate, but much that is related to racial out-groups involves racial stereotyping and rationalizations designed to buttress preexisting racial privileges. Given the lack of sustained equal-status contacts that most white Americans have with African Americans and other Americans of color, the learned views of racial out-groups are usually not contradicted and are thus often stereotypical and negative.

In the data presented in the chapters that follow, we see the many ways that white Americans, mostly white police officers, stereotype, problematize, and denigrate black police officers and other black Americans. We did not interview whites for this study; however, the respondents' accounts of white comments, body language, and actions strongly suggest that many white law enforcement officers share with other white Americans negative views and stereotyped conclusions about black individuals, families, and communities.

Our terms *problematization* and *denigration* refer to the attitudinal and ideological strategies by which whites view and define black Americans as inferior, as people with special social problems, and as people who cause social problems. In this conventional stereotyping and problematizing process, whites imbue African Americans as a group with general characteristics that define black beliefs and behavior as problematic (for example, "deviant") from a white-majority perspective. The manifestations of this perspective involve such elements as comments and attacks that overtly belittle a black person's personality, culture, or biological makeup. This stereotyping can be held in a white mind alone. Yet most such thought often bridges to an array of behavior, including discrimination. Thus the stereotypes may be expressed in discussions or interactions between whites themselves or between whites and those who are not white. Stereotyping in white minds, as we often see in our interviews, likely accounts for the actions of many whites that go beyond verbal attacks to an array of discriminatory behaviors. In chapter 3 we examine this white stereotyping, problematization, and denigration of African-American civilians and police officers, as they are reported in detail in the interviews of our respondents.

Racial Discrimination: Exclusion, Marginalization, and Retaliation

Discrimination, the action component of everyday racism, usually takes place within the context of or in connection with the important social networks of white Americans. Thus, within historically white workplaces, the networks of the whites that have traditionally dominated these work settings are typically central, powerful, and long lasting. Given these white-centered networks, and the racial stereotyping that is usually embedded in them, efforts to maintain these networks and their privileges against racial "outsiders" likely seem normal to most whites. White efforts to maintain their dominant in-groups and networks as comfort zones within workplaces frequently take the form of subtle, covert, and blatant discrimination against the relatively new employees of color. This discrimination typically varies in intensity, character, and location across U.S. workplaces.

Two terms we use in the analysis that follows are *exclusion* and *marginalization*. Acts of exclusion by various whites force their targets, employees of color, away from certain workplace jobs or areas into other, less desirable jobs or areas, if not out of the organization entirely. Acts of marginalization by whites are diverse and, although not excluding employees of color, operate to prevent their full participation in workplace operations, decisions, promotions, and benefits. These two forms of discrimination are common and are perpetrated by whites in most institutional settings on a regular basis, throughout the careers of most black employees and other employees of color.

In this analysis we are most concerned with the workplaces of African-American police officers, but we also discuss the racist incidents in other institutional sites and settings that they report. On the basis of their accumulated knowledge of stereotyping and discrimination, these mostly veteran black officers describe an array of racial barriers, structures, and processes that they encounter in everyday life. Numerous previous research studies have documented the discriminatory strategies developed by whites to exclude or marginalize African Americans in other settings, strategies that often cause their innocent targets great pain and harm. Such discriminatory strategies become more negative in their impact because many white officials and officers view them as inconsequential or normal. They are taken for granted and may be perpetrated by whites half-consciously or unconsciously.[84]

As we detail in chapters 4 and 5, these exclusionary and marginalizing actions and strategies involve many different types of discrimination. They include actions that make workplaces uncomfortable and hostile for black officers, such as the use of racist jokes and cartoons, racial name calling, verbal epithets and related threats, and racialized disrespect and insensitivity. They also include an extensive array of discriminatory actions that reduce or sabotage black officers' chances for specialized training and earned promotions, such as biased evaluations by superiors, discrimination in policing assignments, exclusion from work-related information, and recurring bias in departmental disciplinary practices.

We also document another common aspect of discrimination that faces many black employees in contemporary workplaces, including those of law enforcement agencies. This workplace discrimination takes the form of *retaliation* against those many black officers who protest, or organize against, the everyday racism they face. When African Americans in any workplace fight this routine racism, many in the dominant white group refuse to acknowledge the existence of this racism and instead engage in angry reactions, intimidation, and retaliation against those who assert that racial problems exist in law enforcement workplaces.

Responding to Racism: Black Agency and Resistance

African Americans are not only targets of discrimination, for they often respond to negative treatment by whites with a variety of countering and resistance strategies. When members of the dominant group do not accept the dominated group's pursuit of equality, justice, and power, their reaction is often repression or suppression. Since the seventeenth century and the beginning of their enslavement, African Americans have been theorists of their experiences, as they have made evident in centuries of antidiscrimination efforts, protests, and movements. Everyday encounters with whites are not just stressful for the specifically targeted individuals but often for their family and community as well. Out of this individual and group experience, African Americans have created a culture of resistance—an oppositional culture that underlies individual and group strategies to resist everyday oppression.[85] In chapter 6 we pay specific attention to the process of African Americans' countering and fighting back against the discrimination that they face in law enforcement agencies and in the outside society.

BLACK OFFICERS IN WHITE INSTITUTIONS: THE RESPONDENTS

Very few research studies have ever examined the experiential reality of the black women and men who serve their community as sworn police officers. Previous interviews with officers and autobiographies of officers are not only rare but also lacking in a fleshed-out theoretical framework. Only one such autobiography is of a senior officer who served in a law enforcement agency outside a large northern city.[86] There is also no research examining black officers' situations in towns or smaller cities in any region, or in regions such as the South and Southwest. In addition, the few existing studies of black officers usually do not give serious attention to the situation of female officers, and studies of women officers also ignore the experiences of black female officers.[87] These deficiencies in the literature are among the reasons that led us to undertake this field interview study.

In their classic 1927 treatise using qualitative research techniques, W. I. Thomas and Florian Znaniecki, two of the founders of modern social science, broke new ground in social research by using life histories and other personal documents to delineate in rich detail the lives of immigrants to the United States, as well as to suggest some generalizations about the immigrant experience. Toward the end of their book, they argue that social science "must reach the actual human experiences and attitudes which constitute the full, live, and active social reality beneath the formal organization of social institutions, or behind the statistically tabulated mass phenomena which taken in themselves are nothing but symptoms of unknown causal processes."[88] In other words, social institutions are to be studied and understood by researching their impact on and penetration of the personal experiences of those who must live and work within them. We have drawn much inspiration from this tradition in the research presented here.

An examination of firsthand life accounts of the experiences and perceptions of key people, such as black officers, who work within the justice system can help us as citizens and policy makers to uncover the often hidden features and impacts of the important institutional context, one in which important decisions affecting many people are made every day across the United States. Our approach is a departure from most research on the justice system, literature that mainly examines statistics on, or the outcome of, interactions of the system, its agents, and citizens. We accent and examine the "full, live, and active social reality" of black officers, which lies within the formal organizational framework of law enforcement agencies.

The data for this study were collected from a nonrandom but reasonably representative sample of African-American officers interviewed by the first author in the late 1990s. These individual respondents are representative in the extent to which they reflect the language, understandings, and orientations of their group—in this case, experienced black police officers in historically white police agencies.[89] Our data consist of fifty in-depth, face-to-face interviews with African-American officers in an array of law enforcement agencies. In the interviews we asked about respondents' choice of career, work experiences, and personal goals, as well as their perceptions and understandings of racial matters inside and outside the workplace.[90] Forty-two of the respondents were currently employed as full-time sworn officers at the time of the interview, and eight were retired (five recently). The officers were selected in a snowball sampling procedure. Many black officers have ties to organizations such as the Afro-American Police League and the National Organization of Black Law Enforcement Executives. These organizations helped us by providing the names of officers, who in turn assisted us in generating a list of officers to be interviewed. Fifty-nine of these women and men were contacted and fifty were ultimately interviewed.

Those interviewed represent about 4 percent of all black officers in sixteen different law enforcement agencies located in the South,—in federal, state, county, and city police agencies. At the time of interview, four of these agencies had 50 or fewer officers, three had 51 to 150 officers, and nine had 200 or more officers. Thus, most respondents are from large law enforcement agencies. These respondents are on the whole *very* experienced in police work in these historically white policing institutions. The average total of law enforcement experience is about sixteen years; only eleven respondents have served for ten years or less. Fourteen officers have worked for more than one policing agency (including in corrections facilities) at some point of their career. Because the organizations initially provided the names of experienced officers, there are numerous officers of supervisory and command rank in our sample. In the administrative hierarchy of most police agencies the mission of sergeants is to supervise rank-and-file police officers and their activities, which include patrolling and making arrests. In this book, we designate as command rank officers those whose rank is above the level of sergeant and whose primary functions include administrative tasks and departmental leadership. Fifteen of our respondents are patrol officers, eight are detectives, ten are sergeants, and seventeen are of higher rank than sergeant. Thirty-eight are men, and twelve are women. Five officers have earned only a high school diploma, and six officers did not report their education. The other thirty-nine officers have educational attainments beyond the level of high school, including college degrees earned before and during their police career.

The interviews took place in home settings or officers' offices or patrol cars. The choice was left to each respondent to ensure as much comfort as possible. Here we keep the officers anonymous, as we agreed with them.[91] We explained to the respondents that the purpose of the interview was to examine their life experiences as police officers. Each respondent provided information about his or her background and how it shaped the choice to pursue a career in law enforcement. Also discussed were relationships with coworkers, supervisors, the agency's administration, and the community in which he or she works. We did not raise the issue of race until a respondent began to discuss the subject. Interestingly, only one respondent did not address the issue of race spontaneously in the interview.

The interview instrument included eighteen guiding questions offered in an open-ended answer format. The goal was to cover topics of interest while permitting respondents to control the direction of the interview, to construct a narrative account of experiences with the justice system, and to raise issues not initially included in the instrument. The interviews tried to approximate as much as possible a natural conversation, thereby allowing respondents to conceptualize and share their experiences in their own terms and framing. The researchers Fontana and Frey argue that this type of conversational interviewing "makes the interview more honest, morally sound, and reliable, because it treats the respondent as an equal, allows him or her to express personal feelings, and therefore presents a more realistic picture than can be uncovered using traditional interview methods."[92]

We analyzed these African-American officers' life and work experiences, looking for patterns and shared understandings. Descriptions of events and social dimensions such as location, agents of interaction and discrimination, observers of racism, discriminatory and supportive acts, and racialized attitudes were identified. Of further importance was evidence of a knowledge of racial stereotyping and discrimination, and of the evaluative and comparative processes by which respondents understand particular encounters as discriminatory or not.

We should note two possible limitations to our study. The first author, who was the interviewer in all cases, is white. Some researchers have raised a question as to whether white researchers can successfully interview black respondents. However, the quality of the interactions during the interviews and the depth of respondents' responses on sensitive policing issues strongly suggest that this concern did not greatly limit the data received in most of the interviews. In addition, since many of the interviews were conducted in police departments (e.g., in offices), complete privacy was not always possible. Other officers would enter the room for a time or be nearby. Those in the higher ranks would generally show little concern with interruptions, but some respondents of lower rank demonstrated more concern and often did not continue the discussion if the matter was sensitive. As we see it, rather than being weaknesses of the study, these realities probably demonstrate its strength. If these black respondents' discussions were cautious or limited, then their reported experiences with discrimination and other elements of racism in their workplace and related settings—which here are mostly substantial, nuanced, and detailed—might only be a portion of what they actually experience. In this case, our portrait of their experiences with everyday racism is likely to be a conservative one.

CONCLUSION

The experiences and understandings of these black women and men are revealing, substantial, and quite extensive. As a whole, they provide the reader with much knowledge about the nature of everyday racism inside and outside law enforcement environments. Not all respondents have the same view of their work world, as we see, but there are many recurring themes in their sage analyses. We also see in the chapters that follow that their views and experiences are often similar to those documented in other studies of African Americans by the authors and other researchers.

The chapters that follow are organized to reflect the logic of our sensitizing concepts. Chapter 2 examines the knowledge of discrimination and other elements of everyday racism that have been developed by these black police officers over the course of their career and life. We see how they learn about racism and what they think about it. Chapter 3 examines some of the ideologically racist views and stereotyped attitudes of the whites that these black officers encounter in their daily rounds, views that often problematize and denigrate the respondents or other black Americans. Chapters 4 and 5 examine the broad array of racial barriers faced by black officers as they seek fairness and equity in the workplace. Chapter 6 examines the respondents' views on countering and resisting the patterns of racial prejudice and discrimination. Here we see, once again, that these women and men are not only victims of everyday discrimination, for they as active agents constantly counter and fight back against the racialized mistreatment that they face on a routine basis at the hands of white officials, officers, and citizens. Chapter 7 discusses the implications of our discussion for public policy and the future of U.S. race relations.

Many white analysts, including some social scientists, have argued that the sometimes contradictory findings—usually statistical findings—in existing research studies on racism in the criminal justice system indicate that there is indeed no significant racism there.[93] If this were the case, then the criminal justice system, including the system of policing, would be dramatically different from the rest of the society, where racial discrimination has been demonstrated to be rampant in the twenty-first century. We see in the chapters that follow that this common white view is not only erroneous but remarkably unthinking and naive.

$2.$

Everyday Racism
on the Force

You process information based on your experiences, your education, what you've been exposed to. And if you hadn't been exposed to certain kinds of things, you're going to process information a little bit differently. If you have cultural beliefs, philosophical beliefs that have been ingrained in you for years by your parents, your neighbors, your associations, your school, your friends, your whole socialization process—that makes you who you are and who you are determines how you make decisions and process information. (Black police officer)

Because they experience racism routinely, most African Americans develop a sophisticated and in-depth knowledge of its operation, production, and reproduction over time. Without this accumulated knowledge of how racial hostility and discrimination work, black men, women, and children would have difficulty comprehending their meaning and countering them in their daily life. Reading and assessing our interviews, we see that these black officers' knowledge of everyday racism has several distinct but interrelated dimensions. First, we see in their interviews much commentary on the knowledge acquisition process, which begins in early socialization in collective memories, ideals, and strategies for young black people. We also see in the interviews these officers' understandings and interpretations of recurring encounters with racism in contemporary law enforcement workplaces, as well as their accumulating understandings about the structure of the racial hierarchy and racial discrimination in the United States.

Our conversations with these savvy and articulate law enforcement officers indicate that they, as do other black Americans, regularly use acquired knowledge of racism to interpret and strategize against discriminatory experiences with white Americans. The respondents detail various sources of knowledge and suggest that it is collectively shared, interpreted, and transmitted within their communities. Equally important, they note the cumulative impact of a lifetime of racist encounters with whites on their career, life, family, and community.

ACQUIRING KNOWLEDGE ABOUT EVERYDAY RACISM
Life under Segregation: Lessons for Survival

The United States is, historically and currently, a racially segregated society. From the centuries of the enslavement of people of African descent to the decades of legal segregation following the Civil War to recent decades of informal segregation, black and white Americans have long lived lives separated by the institutional and ideological forces of systemic racism. Residential and other social segregation is fundamental to U.S. society, and its past and present impacts are extensive and long lasting.

The majority of the officers we interviewed reported growing up under *legally segregated* conditions for some part of their life. Most of these women and men describe or allude to the cumulative effects of this segregation, as well as contemporary informal segregation, in their interviews. One officer notes how African Americans have seen themselves as struggling in relation to the social world:

> We, the black race, especially my age group—born in the fifties, sixties, forties—we know how it is to be denied, how it is not to be accepted, and to know how to struggle and that, whatever you get, you have to take it. I mean not by force but, you have to earn it. You have to make a way in life for yourself.

Living in a world of limited opportunities and facing the hostility of whites have forced black Americans to form a collective identification and a sense of solidarity. Most officers speak in terms of "we" throughout their discussions. They speak of how they learn to survive from day to day in the face of racial hostility and how they learn that success depends on mutual support, perseverance, and strength of will.

All major U.S. institutions are involved in maintaining a racial status quo in which Americans of color are generally relegated to a secondary status. However, policing institutions have long been particularly important in perpetuating racial segregation. Twenty-two of these officers explicitly discuss their experiences with white police officers while they were growing up. These often negative experiences have contributed to their understanding of the racialized place of African Americans in the United States, and of the relationship between black Americans and a frequently racist criminal justice system:

> I was, must have been like 12, 13, and I'm trying to play recreational football, so I came out of the theater and I said to myself, "I'm going to see if I can just jog home," if I had the endurance to do it. I got down to right where the old [TV station] used to be, I said, "Gees, I'm not even tired." I was on the last stretch so I picked it up and I really started to sprint when a cop come up behind me, siren on, pulled over, and said, "Get up against the wall, get up against the wall!" The guy says, "What are you running for, what are you running for?" I told him, I said, "Just running, you know, felt like running." I forget all what he said to me.

Most black children learn early that even normal activities for children, such as running and playing, can lead to difficulties because of the way whites perceive them. They thus begin a process of understanding that police officers are often not the friendly "Officer Bill" accented in children's stories and by some elementary school teachers. Many learn at an early age that these white officers play an important role in controlling the lives of those in mostly black communities. Another officer responds, "It just seems like in our neighborhoods, they was always taking somebody to jail. They weren't there to do any good, or what I would call good." Residents of black communities have learned to fear the police and to be careful in their presence. Another respondent remembers, "[Children] would cry, 'Run, the police are coming,' I mean, because they felt that they were going to get beat up and attacked, and stuff like that."

Despite this shared understanding of the police as oppressive, in more recent years police officer positions have often been among the better jobs available to black men. By the early 1970s, as a result of the civil rights movement and the end to legal segregation, there was a push in many police departments to hire at least a few black officers. The economic return from this career choice often outweighed the negative connotations of policing for some black women and men.[1] Most of the respondents, those who grew up under official segregation and those who did not, discuss in some manner the importance of economic benefits in their decision to become a police officer. One man discussed the dilemma he faced in the 1970s:

> After the military, I became married and had a little one. And the jobs that were available for a black man in the early, mid-seventies were manual jobs and menial jobs, and when the job offer of police first came about with the [city], they were paying like $10,500. And I was making probably around $4,000, and I went over there.

Since the 1970s, thus, continuing racial barriers in other sectors of the U.S. economy have pressured many black women and men to consider the local employment options that are available, even if that means working in a traditionally oppressive police institution.

Some respondents explain how the authority granted to black officers is usually not enough to overcome resistance to the idea of black officers among many whites. Opposition from whites is encountered at work and in the neighborhoods that are policed, and this opposition can have a powerful effect on shaping black officers' comprehension of racial matters. Indeed, this has occurred for several decades. Thus, a female detective describes some lessons she learned from the pressure and stress experienced by her father, who was the first black officer in her town. She notes, "Growing up I do remember a cross being burned in my yard and my father moved me and my sisters and brothers and my mother out of the house for a while; we stayed with my grandmother."

Numerous respondents described events such as early negative encounters with white officers and terroristic acts of white supremacists as having a cumulative impact that has shaped their self-image, strategies against racism, and employment choices. Past experiences with racism continually impact the life of those targeted, as well as the lives of other people who know the victims. This commentary underscores our conceptual point that discriminatory acts have a *collective impact* that extends well beyond a particular person's negative encounter with a few whites.

Hard Family Lessons: Past and Present

Many white analysts have written negative assessments of black families, so much so that many nonblack Americans are under the impression that the average black family is dysfunctional, unsupportive of its members, and far from the ideal. Yet this white view of the black family is very stereotypical and one-sided, and it ignores the many strengths of black families, strengths that have been required to allow black Americans to survive, and to succeed, in spite of the brutalities of systemic racism. Indeed, one major disruption of black family life that is omitted from virtually all white assessments is the serious disruption caused by the hundreds of blatant, covert, subtle racist acts that members of a typical black family must interpret and counter each year.

This constant bombardment of black families by racism fosters an atmosphere of learning and of sharing information about the hostile outside world and a black family's place in that world. Two-thirds of the officers discuss how the black family has served as an important context, definer, and interpreter of critical racist and related social events. As one black officer notes in recounting life under legal segregation, this interpretation was frequently developed in conjunction with positive messages:

> Although things were segregated downtown, I never really paid it a
> whole lot of attention because of my mother. We went downtown shop-
> ping, and you said you had to go the bathroom, Mom said, "Okay let's
> go home." And she put you in the car, and she took you home. I never
> used a colored bathroom, OK? You know, that type of thing. And if
> there was a lunch counter there and people were sitting down eating and
> you said, "Mom, I'm hungry," she said, "Okay, let's go home." Put you
> in the car, and you go home and you eat. . . . My parents kind of stressed
> the importance of self-esteem. You know, you're not second to anybody.
> You're not less intelligent than anybody. Just, do the right thing. Always
> respect other people and they'll respect you.

Numerous respondents remark that, despite the hatred encountered from whites, their families taught them a two-part lesson: to have self-worth and *not* to hate those who hate you. Indeed, they stress the fact that their parents did not teach hatred of white people. Instead, they were generally taught how to interpret racist events and how to deal with whites in ways that minimize the potential harm that might come from these interpersonal encounters. One officer remembers his necessarily polite demeanor after he was pulled over while driving through a rural area:

> Well, I had relatives, uncles and stuff who, you know, who I would listen
> to, and they would tell me about, "Hey, when you be out getting older,

watch this, these types of things happen. You know, you have to be careful." So at the time, I was very careful and cool. I listened to the [white] officer, and "Yes sir," and what have you, and he took my license, and I said, "Sir, I'll pick up the money, and bring it right back here. And, of course, I didn't."

Surviving in an overtly and legally segregated society meant that black Americans, young and old, had to learn their lessons about racism well and to share that knowledge carefully with less-experienced others.

However, despite the changes that have occurred since late 1960s in reducing much overt discrimination, black Americans still must help each other understand how blatant and subtle discrimination operates and how to counter it. One younger officer, in spite of his desire to think of racial relations as improved, details with some consternation a conversation that he had with his daughter when she was old enough to ask about racial matters:

This little black kid and this little white kid, and they play together. And as they get older that interaction becomes more involved. The black child can't go visit the white child and the white child can't go visit the black child [pause]. And the reason why when they asked, the parents tell them, "Well I don't want you hanging around those blacks." And they tell the black kid, "Those white people are prejudiced and I don't want you around them." So, now you've created a rift. Being that they're kids, they're not going to look at it that way. They don't understand it that way, but they should. So what they do is they still try to hang out with each other, but the older they get, the more and more the way things are set up separate them more. And it gets to the point where now they're angry at each other and they don't understand why . . . and you have problems, and that's when you get those confrontations. . . . So the way I try to explain it to my daughter. I tell her . . . the reason why is because I think that we create our enemy.

Continuing racial separation and isolation make it easy to reproduce notions of racial difference and perpetuate harsh notions of racial enemies. Once the system of racial oppression and segregation was firmly set into place by white Americans, by the mid-seventeenth century, it developed many complex and nuanced variations across the country's social landscape. Note, as shown here, that those who have been segregated have also played varying roles in countering or reinforcing white-established patterns of racial segregation.

Learning about Racism in Civil Rights Struggles

Much knowledge about routine racism is honed in daily struggles with whites. Yet these struggles are not just one-on-one encounters, for they involve well-institutionalized racist patterns found in every part of the United States. And the social institutions that maintain racial separation and segregation change but slowly. For that reason, virtually all black Americans have grown up encountering discriminatory barriers and understanding the need for a continuing struggle against those barriers.

Interestingly, many of these officers explicitly mention the importance of the civil rights movement, of black peoples' organizations fighting for equality in the face of opposition. Statements such as "I'm a product of the sixties demonstrations . . . and got arrested doing civil rights demonstrations" were periodically enunciated with pride. In addition, numerous officers quoted from or paraphrased speeches and statements by Dr. Martin Luther King Jr. while explaining their understandings of racialized social worlds. Moreover, while we were interviewing, we noticed that many of them have decorated their offices with objects that demonstrate pride in black people's movements, struggles, and successes.

The civil rights movement is not just past history, for, as the respondents often note, there are continuing organizational efforts to counter and reduce discrimination in this society. Many of these officers discuss past struggles in relation to ongoing struggles or future struggles against discrimination, as we see in this commentary:

> I'm talking about the glimpse of what we may have seen, whether it was genuine or not, in the Million-Man March. There has to be a reckoning and a willingness of a group of people to be willing to take some bold steps to make some bold changes. And you know being a product of the sixties and seventies myself, being grounded in the embers of strife and unrest, black people came together because they had to, they had to, they had to! Now they need to come together because they have to. They really do. And we are doing some things that are re-instilling—and I know the values will never be the same because we are constantly changing and moving and evolving—but re-instilling some of those fundamental things that are necessary to work on the conscious of a group of people. It has to happen, it has to happen.

Participation in an unfolding struggle is itself educational. Knowledge is acquired through struggle because involvement provides an atmosphere in which people learn about the social world, the forces that impact their life, and their ability to change the conditions that they encounter. These women and men often indicate that their conceptions of the present and future, as well as their perceptions of solutions to racial and related social problems, are firmly rooted in their under-standings of how these problems were faced by African Americans in the distant and recent past.

The struggle to change a discriminatory social world is not easily undertaken by individuals working in isolation. For that reason, as these officers frequently indicate, the strategies for societal change are shared in families and communities and are, once again, a collective matter. Importantly, working to address the injustices of current racial relations can be a crucial source of knowledge about the operation of everyday racism. Participants in the effort to change society frequently rely on each other for information, ideas, and support:

> I chose a career in law enforcement at the urging and request of the NAACP [National Association for the Advancement of Colored People] because we did not have a black officer in the department at that time. . . . When they threatened to terminate me on trumped-up charges, I always had me a lawyer. When they used to do that, I would go to the NAACP, and I would say what is the problem. The NAACP and the community were 100 percent behind me.

Numerous respondents echo previous research in their discussions of how organizations representing the community actively recruited them to become officers, in part as a strategy for social change.[2] Generally, these organizations have stood by them when they have faced overt hostility from whites in and out of their department. Such critical rela-tionships have facilitated the respondents' acquisition of a sophisticated knowledge of everyday racism in society—by means of recurring inter-action with knowledgeable people intimately involved in working col-lectively to resist racial injustice. Indeed, numerous respondents note that they owe their job, at least in part, to support of black organiza-tions and communities. One officer captures this element of his early years: "My law enforcement generation was from the middle sixties to mid-seventies, the civil rights [era]. We were civil rights officers. If it had not been for civil rights, then probably I wouldn't have been hired. . . . We were like the trendsetters."

Lessons from the History of Policing in Black Communities

Many respondents describe the important sense of responsibility that they have for black communities because of the support they have historically received from these communities. Most are very aware that this officer–community relationship has often been tense or negative. Sometimes, there has been an adversarial relationship with some members of the black public, among whom black officers are, as one officer put it, "viewed almost like the enemy." Significantly, this potentially adversarial relationship between black officers and communities has been a topic of research for criminologists for some years now, and past studies have produced contradictory findings on the acceptance of black officers by the black public. Indeed, a number of white researchers and media commentators have suggested that such an adversarial relationship is evidence that the police occupational role itself is more important than discriminatory police actions in explaining negative attitudes in black communities in regard to police officers.[3]

However, our respondents' discussions reveal the naïveté of many such arguments. White commentators usually look at these police–community matters from a great distance; our respondents see these matters up close and conditioned by much personal experience. They are part of groups and communities in which black Americans are engaged in a continual process of acquiring and sharing information, and they know well the historical and contemporary oppression that has been enforced by white police forces in black communities. As residents of black communities, and often as victims of police malpractice or brutality themselves, these black officers understand very well the adversarial relationship that has necessarily grown out of the shared knowledge about police oppression passed along in black communities. Unlike the naive white commentators, they know well the historical meaning of white-dominated policing practices and understand that black Americans must learn how to interact with white officers in order to survive in everyday life. They do not like this community tension, but most clearly understand it, as we see in a comment by one perceptive officer:

> Well, in my community blacks don't want to interact with you because you're a cop. Well, blacks have had bad experiences all their life. Blacks from my generation have had to run from the police. They were beaten up badly. Some were killed, shot and they just had bad experiences. So,

when I did become a cop, I can see them telling their kids to stay away from cops. "They're no good, they're no good." Because of their bad, negative experiences they've had . . . I can understand why. I can understand why. But, ugh, that's not a good feeling to have when people want to just pull away from you.

Despite these community tensions and the pulling away by some local residents, most respondents explain and defend this community behavior. Indeed, only four of the fifty respondents went so far as to describe this distancing by some community members as a type of black "racism," and they were all younger officers. (This difference may also illustrate how general knowledge of racism is related to age and level of experience with institutional racism.) In contrast, most officers, especially those who had experienced legal segregation firsthand, accent how past—and continuing—racial oppression at the hands of whites clearly influences present police–community relations. Their own experiences with everyday racism are used as the knowledge base that helps to explain the continuing hostility or skepticism of many in the black public toward all law enforcement officers.

Reflecting on the early years when black officers first joined the force and were entirely under the control of white senior officers and officials, a few respondents note that for some time many black citizens even preferred to be helped by a white officer rather than a black officer:

Black police officers were received with less acceptance than white police officers because of how the people felt. They felt that the blacks were sell-outs, and I've been called a sell-out by blacks. I've been called "nigger" by blacks, "Uncle Tom" by blacks. I've been called anything that you can be called. . . . We were viewed by other blacks as being used against blacks, as not giving fellow blacks the benefit of the doubt. . . . In many instances they felt that blacks who were police officers were blacks who were hired to be more oppressive of blacks.

Moving to the present, this officer adds, "Even to this day a lot of blacks still accuse police officers, black police officers of being programmed, instruments of white authority." Although there is still among some black citizens a view of certain black officers as tools of the white establishment, much of the harsher language of the past no longer characterizes such interactions, which seem to have decreased in number and intensity over the intervening decades.

Because of the historically oppressive relationship of the police to black communities, and the expectations of black citizens that the entry of black officers into police departments will reduce abuse, the respondents report that today they must work extra hard to prove their worth as police in black communities:

> We have to live a double standard, and one of those standards is we have to bust our butt and work twice as hard as a white officer to be accepted in the department and make sure that we make it. Then you've got to work three times as hard to convince the African-American community that you're not a sellout and you're truly there to do a job and to do the best that you can to help them; because the distrust of police officers has been there so long.

The last few comments suggest why historically there have been adversarial relationships between black officers and the black public. This adversarial problem is not really explained by black prejudice or by a negative reaction to a generic policing role. Such conventional explanations are contradicted by the fact that *many* black community organizations have pushed, and continue to push, *very hard* for inclusion of black officers in historically white departments and, once they have been included, have strongly supported them. Many black organizations make a point of building strong and ongoing relationships with black officers, recognizing that those officers also face discrimination within law enforcement agencies. Moreover, it seems clear from the detailed accounts in our interviews that African-American officers who police black communities in which they are familiar to community members usually encounter higher levels of acceptance and much less citizen hostility than white officers. Although the shared, and usually accurate, knowledge among black citizens that police officers often oppress black people is so strong that some who encounter unfamiliar black officers may react strongly to them—perhaps unable to unravel the historical contradiction inherent in a black person's being a police officer—many black citizens now seem to be pleased to have familiar black officers who regularly police their community.

Lessons about Racism from Black Religious and Educational Settings

Numerous white commentators have complained of a lack of values and spirituality in the lives of African Americans. No idea could be further from the truth. Research has long demonstrated that religion and spirituality are central and influential in the lives of most black Americans. This spirituality promotes understanding as well as a sense of solidarity and righteousness in the midst of a struggle for rights and equality. Scholars writing about those African Americans who were enslaved have often noted how religion emerged as "African slaves' most formidable weapon for resisting slavery's moral and psychological aggression."[4] This "weapon" has since remained formidable. It was of critical importance in the 1960s civil rights movement and remains very important for the majority of African Americans today.[5]

Many of our respondents spontaneously discuss the various ways that religion and values contribute to their knowledge of and resistance to everyday racism. The message taught in many black churches has provided many of these officers with a will or desire to persevere in the face of continuing racial oppression:

> Well, I guess by, with prayer, support from my family and support from the community, I hung in there. . . . You had to be real strong, real strong. And again I think with prayer and, and you know a lot of times, I hate to come to work the next day because the next day would be worse. Every day would be worse.

Note here the intensity and pain of the everyday exertions African Americans like this officer have made against discrimination at the hands of those whites in the workplace. Numerous officers discuss how their religious faith and values help them to understand, cope with, and survive racially pressurized workspaces. Black Americans have not until recent decades been welcome in most white churches, and many of these churches are still hostile ground for those who are not white. For this reason, African Americans have created their own churches, places where they still feel more comfortable than in white churches.

Numerous respondents note the durability of socioracial segregation as an important reality despite significant societal changes in recent decades. This racialized reality is recognized at various levels of education as well. Many discuss their educational achievements as a source of pride and characterize the racial desegregation of schools as having advanced racial equality to some degree. Still, many grew up under legal segregation and experienced some schooling as perpetuating racism in their day-to-day life. One officer notes the impact:

> We know that every African American did not have the opportunities. I mean, in my short time here I can remember a time when we didn't get the new books in school, and that's in my lifetime. You know, when we look at racism in this country, we're not talking about some deep, dark thing that happened two and three hundred, four hundred years ago. And we know that African Americans did not have the same opportunities education-wise as some other folks.

While recognizing that educational opportunities were and are racially limited, these officers still view education as an important chance for personal advancement and social change. They know that the process of educational desegregation has been full of conflict. Indeed, some discuss their feelings about entering all-white schools: the negative reactions of white students, staff, and teachers, and how these reactions shaped their understandings of racism and of white Americans. For them this learning has taken place at all levels of education. One respondent thus describes the hostile reaction of a college professor: "I remember in college a professor looked at me and said, 'This is a school for whites, what are you doing here?'"

In addition to providing a rich source of experiences through which to hone an understanding of everyday racism, their educational settings have given numerous officers access to black educators whose styles of teaching and messages about racial matters have been decisive in helping them understand their experiences with racism:

> Black people understand other black people. . . . I've taken a couple of classes years ago. I'll never forget this [names black professor]. I took the psychology of African Americans, and that class really helped me understand a lot. It's like if you're not from a certain area, you did not grow up a certain way, a lot of times people don't understand other people's language.

In their extensive interviews, these talented women and men illustrate how the structural and ideological conditions of their youth, and personal and community struggles to change segregated conditions, have provided a framework within which they developed clearer understandings of white racism and means to counter it. The family, the community, the church, and educational settings have all been important centers of socialization on racial matters. In this regard, our findings are very much like those in other field studies of African Americans.[6]

Lessons from Employment Settings: The Importance of More Experienced Officers

Our respondents discuss the variety of ways in which key people in their occupational setting have provided them with specialized knowledge of what discrimination is and how it operates in law enforcement environments, as well as in the larger society. The methods of learning instilled early in life are used over the lifetime to gather the necessary information about the painful racial reality of new settings.

At some point in their interview, most officers discuss relationships with other black officers as essential to their acquisition of effective knowledge about understanding and dealing with workplace and societal racism. This interpersonal process has included looking to, empathizing with, and understanding the racialized experiences of these others. One respondent describes another officer's experience, which, vicariously, has become a vital part of his understanding. He notes that he knew

> the first black officer that was allowed a walking beat downtown before the city had traffic enforcement. . . . While he was walking downtown, this guy [a white man], walked behind him everyday all day long while he was on his beat, 10 to 6, with a big sign, "There's No Nigger Police Downtown." He had to endure that now, and the guy had a right to carry the sign, so. . . . Can you imagine trying to protect [the public] when everywhere you go there's a guy that's got a big sign walking behind you saying, "No Nigger Police Downtown"? He endured that, man, had to do that, but I knew he was a strong character.

This commentary signals just how high the levels of racial hostility can be in this society. Most whites cannot imagine what life is like under these conditions, which persist in both blatant and subtle forms today. Many African-American officers have had to work under extreme racist conditions, which provide severe if not traumatic learning experiences.

Because of the intensity of much hostility from white police officers, the more experienced black officers often become the critical teachers for the newer black officers, providing essential information about the requirements and expectations of the occupation inside and outside the police agency:

> He tried to, you know, wise me to some things. He made me knowledgeable or aware of certain things as to look for as far as on the street and internally in the building. You know, he was a very sharp officer.

Older officers thus provide specific information about how the local law enforcement system works, including its many discriminatory features. Thus, one black female law enforcement officer makes this note about a phone call she got from a newer female agent:

> I just had a call the other day from one of our new female agents. And it was like, "Well I didn't know what to do and." . . She was going, "I got my evaluation." I said, "Wait a minute, before you tell me anything, let me tell you. The evaluation was low 'because you're a new agent and you can't possibly get a high score because that would be different.'" And she's like, "Yeah, that's exactly what they said." I said, "That's what they tell all female agents." She's like, "Oh no."

These respondents' comments on learning from other black officers illustrate the importance of accumulated knowledge and collective memory in black organizations and communities. Once pioneers, these older officers frequently provide a critical network of emotional support, and they are the often the most experienced teachers about the operation of racism in policing. Moreover, as this respondent indicates, they are also the promoters of resistance:

> When I came to the police department there were a couple of older guys, who are both now retired, that I worked very directly with. They taught me about the system, how that system worked. I listened to those guys. So, I got a lot of background information from the older guys. They told me a lot of things like someone said, "Hey you know, you've got a college education. . . . You don't have to take this." And that's what they kept saying. And what I heard in their voices was "We came here, we were the first ones." I'm talking about guys that were the first black police officers. You know, they were getting ready to go out when I came on and they were saying, "Hey, we took all this stuff so you wouldn't have to take it." And that stuck with me. So, I fought that the guys and girls who are out there today don't have to do the same fighting I did.

This respondent makes clear just how the transmission of knowledge from one generation of officers to the next takes place, and how this transmission is consciously noted and fostered. Although these interviewees rely on acquired knowledge of the general nature of racism, dealing with racial hostility and discrimination within a specific institutional setting requires a specialized knowledge as well. Referring to his department, another officer put it this way: "You feel it's wrong. But that goes back to what I was saying earlier, when it is institutionalized racism, you really don't know exactly how to look at it, because you've never experienced it like that." Other African-American officers often serve as important teachers about the racism in a particular department. In describing his responsibility to younger officers, another respondent describes how "I would basically tell him some pitfalls that he would have to look out for. You know some hidden racism. I would tell him to prepare himself, get ready to be disappointed on some avenues, and just give it the best shot." Much routine racism is subtle or covert, and thus it may blindside unsuspecting targets.

Numerous respondents discuss how knowledge acquisition and sharing work together in their occupational settings. They acquire new information and act on it by educating other officers, their own children, other children, and other family members. They also spend time educating the white officers who are willing to try to understand black communities.

Beyond creating one-on-one relationships with other officers, black police officers have developed larger social and organizational networks. These supportive networks take several forms: loose affiliations of usually small groups of officers within the same agency or from different agencies or formal associations of officers across various agencies, the region, or the country. These larger networks help officers share critical knowledge and are often mechanisms through which officers help each other to adapt to, and often succeed in, difficult racialized settings. As we will explain in detail in chapter 6, support is important in these departmental situations because respondents frequently feel isolated and excluded. Often the only ones who can understand their predicament are other black officers, as we see in this comment:

> We encouraged each other to continue on, and discussed how to proceed under certain situations, gave advice to each other. Met each other for

lunch and said, "Do you know what just happened, you won't believe what just happened." So it's good to have a mentor.

This mutual reliance involves an interpersonal process through which officers of color can compare their daily experiences, thereby collectively constructing understandings about experiences and generating ways of fighting racialized mistreatment perpetrated by whites.

Our respondents' discussions repeatedly underscore how they learn about the past and present operation of racial hostility and discrimination in quotidian interactions with white officers and other white people. Numerous officers talk about how the many actions of, or many conversations with, white officers have helped them better understand how whites think and act on racial matters. They indicate how they have listened to accounts and views of white officers attentively and evaluated these white views carefully in relation to their own experiences and accumulating knowledge about racial matters. For example, one command officer explains that in his agency there are some white

> people that just want to sit down and talk about the good old days. I cannot tell you how many times this captain would tell me, "I remember when blacks lived on that side." Then fifteen minutes later, "You know that was the good old days: black cops couldn't arrest whites. Ya'll black cops only had two cars; in order to arrest a white guy, ya'll had to call a white cop over." Fifteen minutes later into the conversation, "You know, those were the good old days."

This conversation provides the listener with historical information about policing during the legal segregation era, as well as insight into how white and black people's perceptions of these oppressive past events are quite different. Virtually no African American looks back on the legal segregation era with a general nostalgia for the "good old days." Only those who have not experienced its deadly brutality on body and mind could keep reiterating such a view of racial oppression.

White officers provide information in yet other ways. For example, the testimony of white officers forced to give information in trials sometimes provides useful information for black officers. One woman describes how such testimony gave her insight into familial socialization. "One of the sergeants that testified at my trial said his parents didn't like black folks. And he can't help it, because he don't like black folks, because of his upbringing." Beyond furthering her knowledge of racism, these white comments serve to legitimate officers' understanding of routine racism. Not only do they themselves learn the how and why of racial discrimination from everyday experience, but they also sometimes hear whites confirm what they experience.

In addition, there are some supportive and antiracist white officers who provide important information about the racial hierarchy and discrimination in their law enforcement agency. One black officer comments, "I've had white guys tell me, the only reason they're [other white officers] doing this or doing that that way is because the guy is black." Indeed, the few relationships with supportive whites can provide some knowledge and emotional support that are essential to surviving in hostile police environments. However, we should note that accounts of such white support are much more rare in our interviews than one might expect given public discussions of the supposedly declining significance of racism in U.S. society.

Lessons from Equal Opportunity Courses and Programs

Over the decades, in many police departments, as in other organizations, one strategy that has emerged to promote increased understanding of members of different racial and ethnic groups is diversity training. Although diversity training's effectiveness is still a matter of debate—and many departments have little such training—several respondents note that such training has provided them with some important knowledge about racial matters in their historically white department. For example, one officer who eventually became a diversity trainer describes issues and interactions in some classes he had:

> They shared some of the things that they were taught in growing up that created a lot of tension. And I kept seeing that in all of the classes—all of the concerns in each group. It would come up again with every class, so I knew that it wasn't an isolated opinion. . . . They're always reluctant until someone says that key word, pushes that particular button, and then that one person explodes and then it allows everyone else to get involved.
> There's always a particular word or phrase that will do that in every class. It varies. Sometimes it's females in law enforcement. Sometimes it's profiling African-American motorists. Sometimes it's why are Caucasian males being blamed all the time, and made out to be the bad guy.

As this respondent clearly indicates, these diversity classes can bring out important issues and thereby provide much information about learning processes, racial and gender stereotypes, and ways in which racial stereotyping operates in traditional policing.

Sitting down with other officers in these interactive settings is a good way to gain knowledge of not only the how and why of racism in departments but also the underlying emotions. Reflecting on some diversity sessions, this officer underscores how heated they were:

> I saw the attitudes of most of the other people that were there, and I thought, my God, I thought that ended a long time ago. Do they really think this way? Things almost came to fisticuffs in these classrooms. It gets heated because you have a mixture, male, female, sometimes homosexuals—people just cannot accept the fact that there are differences, cannot do it. And I don't know, it's kind of hard for a lot of people. The more you attend these classes and are able to talk with these people, you realize that it's something that they've learned, they've been taught. You know, you wasn't born that way. Someone taught you all this, and it's your environment, which you become accustomed to.

As numerous respondents have learned from diversity classes and other interactions with whites, certain prejudices and propensities to discriminate are shaped by the social environment of whites, who usually do not develop their views about racial groups and their propensities without outside influences. Living with racism every day generally leads the black officers to a strong structural and institutional perspective on the operation of the society.

In addition to this diversity training, equal opportunity rules and regulations have sometimes assisted respondents' acquisition of knowledge about discrimination. For example, federal government Equal Employment Opportunity Commission (EEOC) guidelines about the treatment of Americans of color provide a body of information from which the officers can draw. The positive and objective outcomes of these EEOC complaints and discrimination lawsuits generally help legitimize respondents' understandings of racial discrimination in policing. For example, one officer describes how he "filed an EOC complaint against the city in 1979 on the basis of discrimination and promotions for sergeant. The EOC did an investigation and, and their judgment affirmed that discrimination did exist."

In their interviews a large number of officers assess the importance of EEOC guidelines in shaping knowledge of racial discrimination within policing organizations. Thus, five of the officers report that they used the guidelines as a basis for research into the treatment of officers of color within their department. Twelve officers discuss their participation in successful lawsuits, which increased their knowledge of how discrimination works in policing. Commenting on what some officers learned from one investigation, one black officer says: "Oh, rampant discrimination. From the EEOC complaint that we filed in '84 they came back in '88 with a determination that blacks had been discriminated against in hiring, training, and promotions."

Further Lessons on Racism: The Mass Media

These black officers often discuss the media as a reference point in reflecting on experiences that they have had as police officers. About a third spontaneously discussed their knowledge of racism in the criminal justice system by using examples of negative portrayals of black men in movies or on television. They also cite media coverage of prominent court cases like that of O. J. Simpson and of major police brutality cases such as that of Rodney King.

In one way or another, many of these officers discuss how the media construct and perpetuate stereotypes of black men (less often, women) as criminals. One officer sums up the media's negative impact:

> See a car, three white males ride by. We don't think nothing of it. See three black males ride by, you got to look a little harder. Sure, I think that you bring that with you because you look at TV. Everything's telling you, they're bad, they're bad, they're bad. Everything's telling you they're bad, so of course you look harder, you know. When I know any of them could be bad. It doesn't matter. But the perception is, you know, if you see three of them in a car, they look like a gang. Let's face it, you're walking down a street, and five little white boys walk by, you probably wouldn't think nothing of it. Now let the same five black boys be walking by. You do think for a minute, and black people do the exact same thing; the exact same thing. And it's funny, we should know better, but the perception [is there].

The image of dangerous black males is so pervasive that it clicks into the mind almost automatically, often bypassing the reasoning process.

This very perceptive respondent notes that even many black Americans fall prey to such stereotyping, so powerful are the media in constantly creating negative imagery of and fearfulness about black men. The reason for the bias: The U.S. mass media are still mostly white-controlled.

We also see in many of these officers' accounts that a person can process mass media information much more critically if he or she wishes to do so. The problem is that critical thinking is not encouraged either by the media or in other sectors of the society, including many schools and colleges. Another officer underscores the point about not passively absorbing the information that one receives, even from direct experience:

> [It] depends on how badly you want to hold on to what you believe in; it can impact you. . . . For instance, I remember seeing a television show where they had these cops, I think it was in Houston, and these particular white cops were talking about, they had come from places like, I think Oregon, and places like there with very few blacks. They had no experiences with blacks. And the guy said, "When I came to Houston, I wasn't a racist, I didn't dislike black people and stuff, but now I work in this predominantly poor black area and everything I come in contact is pimps and druggies and thieves and all this kind of stuff, and I had this different image of black people." Okay, and everybody says, "Yeah, I can understand that." I didn't, because what about all those black officers he worked with at the police department? Are they druggies, pimps, and thieves?

This respondent digs deeply into the racial understandings expressed by a white officer in Houston. His discussion suggests that, despite the media's power and a person's own limited experience with poor members of a certain community, people can evaluate what they see critically and draw a different conclusion from the conventional white view. In this case, one has to agree, wondering why a white officer did not generalize positively about African Americans from his contacts with the many black officers in the Houston police department—a department that has had many black officers, and indeed some black police chiefs, since the 1980s.

For many of these officers the mass media are a source of knowledge about how racism operates in this society. Unlike many whites, however, these respondents are rather critical not only of media stereotyping of black Americans but also of the uncritical use many whites make of those stereotypes. These officers indicate the often complex ways that they use their media knowledge to evaluate the nature of racial commentaries, events, and interactions in their everyday lives.

In summary, an array of important social settings—families, communities, schools, workplaces, churches, the media—provide the contexts within which black Americans learn what it means to live in the United States, what to expect from whites, and what is necessary for them to understand and do if they are to survive and thrive. An important body of information that black Americans must learn revolves around dealing with everyday racism. This critical learning is derived in part from collectively transmitted information and from personal experience—in interaction with a variety of other people of various racial and ethnic backgrounds. It is individually cumulative, as well as collectively shared. As important organizational and other social settings change, black Americans use not only the messages and meanings that they have learned from the past and from their communities but also the support networks they have developed, in their attempts to counter racism and to create a better life for themselves and their family. Equally important, they develop an interpretive framework—a methodology for understanding—that enables them to evaluate the difficult realities they daily face in a society still intricately riddled with the cancers of antiblack racism.

DEVELOPING AND HONING EVALUATION ABILITIES

Most of the knowledge that black Americans gain about racial hostility and discrimination is obtained through everyday experiences—typically in a great many encounters with racially hostile or discriminatory actions, both subtle and blatant, perpetrated by whites each year. One officer sums this point up eloquently:

> After so many years of overt racism and then watching the change over years from those overt acts to covert acts, I can—and a lot of African Americans have developed an ability to—pick up on certain things. I mean, you can pretty much meet someone [and] within two or three minutes and know if they're sincere. And it's wrong, you can say, "Well that's prejudice, and you're prejudging someone," but the truth is the truth. After you've been treated a particular way so long and heard so many things, pretty soon, they come around full circle and you know what certain phrases mean. You know what certain mannerisms mean,

because you've seen it thousands of times before and you've seen what it's attached to.

The comprehension of discriminatory encounters usually involves the ability of African Americans to explain specific experiences in terms of both a general and a specialized knowledge of racism that is, quite literally for black adults, drawn from several *thousands* of encounters with racial hostility and discrimination over their lifetime. As we have documented in previous research, African Americans develop what they term "second sight" (or a sensitive "antenna") that often alerts them to the reality of white hostility and discrimination that may be less obvious to the untrained eye.[7]

In this section, we briefly illustrate some of the respondents' strategies of interpretation, evaluation, and argumentation. We examine useful examples of how these officers systematically test their specific definitions of situations by drawing on a set of criteria that allow an evaluation of events as racialized or not. The interviews show the importance of racial matters in the officers' workaday lives and how they have developed creative ways of understanding the role that racism plays in recurring events and interactions involving whites.

Developing Insightful Interpretations

The African-American officers we interviewed are nearly unanimous in their view that because of their usually extensive experience they as a rule have greater insight into many racial matters than their white counterparts and that they are therefore better equipped to interpret the racialization of specific events. One officer draws out interesting consequences of facing oppression:

> I really believe that African Americans, because we have always been on the receiving end of a lot of that stuff, that we really have a deeper level of understanding and compassion for other people. I really think it's difficult for whites today to really see even the subtle vestiges of discrimination and prejudices. . . . I'm just saying that I think whites by and large have real difficulty, really being able to perceive and understand people who have to walk through that stuff, day after day after day.

Another officer agreed: "I know what it is to be poor, I know what it is to be oppressed, and I know what it is to have a sense of hopelessness."

Personal, family, and community experiences with recurring oppression provide a tough learning framework within which these women and men develop and maintain the ability to understand and evaluate, usually with high accuracy, the reality and extent of routine racism in both work and nonwork worlds.

Developing Evaluation Abilities

Previous studies have shown that, contrary to the naive assertions of many whites, most African Americans do not quickly jump to the conclusion that a particular person or event is racist. They tend to look carefully at events that could be racist, and often mull on the possibility, before reaching a verdict.[8] Our respondents demonstrate that, rather than jumping to conclusions and assuming that every slight involves an element of racism, they use rules of inference and comparison that usually entail careful evaluations. This example illustrates how one black officer went to the respondent, who had more experience, for advice, and, in turn, the respondent talked to other officers involved to get their side of the story:

> [When] you have an officer that feels like maybe they weren't evaluated properly, or an officer that feels like they are being disciplined because of their race, whereas another white officer wouldn't receive that discipline or the same level of discipline, they may be concerned about that. So they may approach you and ask about it. And so, I have no problems with going up, speaking with the people I need to speak with and inquiring about it. I like to use race as the last thing, you know, typically I don't like [to] cry wolf. . . . I very rarely introduce race into any situation. I eliminate all other factors and then the last thing that's there is race, then it's introduced.

This comment illustrates both the role of mutual support among black officers and their preference to eliminate numerous other possibilities before determining the role that racism played in a particular instance.

Similarly, these savvy respondents demonstrate that they may initially consider racial categorization as a possible factor in an incident but later, after evaluating all factors, conclude that the encounter was not racially linked but occurred for other reasons. Some, like African-American respondents in previous research on other occupations,[9] evaluate events carefully in the process of deciding on the appropriate response:

> If you perceive you've been threatened in some manner, it's better to deal with it right then. If you're so angry that all you can see is red—which I done that before, there have been times when some people just push my buttons, and I—just walk away. And I calm down and I think about it, and I think about all the reasons why this happened. And I try to develop some course of action to deal with it in a professional, peaceful manner. I don't think very good when I'm angry and I may not be very rational.

In environments that are normally conflictual, and in places where black officers generally lack power to alter conditions, they can be firm in demanding appropriate treatment, yet at the same time realize the importance of being calm and analytical enough to evaluate the reasons behind an event.

Another officer discusses the process of interpersonal empathy, of placing himself in the position of another to evaluate his or her actions:

> My partner had bought this Harley Davidson motorcycle. So we meet this [white] sergeant, and we're talking—just a routine conversation about it—and the sergeant says, "Hey, I understand you bought yourself a motorcycle . . . are you gonna let [him] nigger it up for you?" Now he's my immediate supervisor, so it took me a moment to process what he had said. My partner got real quiet because he expected me to explode. . . . "What's his purpose for saying that?" That's what I'm processing in my mind. So he didn't say anything, and the sergeant didn't say anything and I didn't say anything, and then he said something else and we went on with the conversation. . . . I'm assuming, you know, that that type of conversation was common with him, and that he was saying something to see if I would explode, to see if I would react to it, so that he could either tell me, "I just said that to see how you would react. If a member of the public said something like that to you I would correct you and counsel you," and this other kind of stuff. So for him, he couldn't lose making that comment.

After the two officers left to respond to a call, the white partner asked about the incident, and this officer explained:

He either was testing me to see if I was going to just go crazy in the
restaurant because he said that. Or he does have a problem, and he got
off on the fact that as a supervisor he could say that.

This perceptive account illustrates differing reactions of black and
white officers to racist events. His white partner, not accustomed to
accepting overt insults, may have assumed that the black officer would
explode and unleash his fury upon his white sergeant. However, the
unique position of the black officer required great patience, careful
evaluation, and a considered decision about the appropriate response.
It was clearly not the first time he had been baited by a white person,
and so his response was knowledgeable and measured. The respondent
later added that only through an increased frequency of interactions
with this sergeant was he able finally to determine that this sergeant
was, in fact, racially motivated and not merely a superior testing the
responses of his officers. Once again, we also see in such incidents the
ability that those in the dominant racial group—in a highly racist society—have to inflict pain on their targets.

African Americans often process information on what may be racist
events for extended periods and discuss the events with others to make
a considered determination about the motivation of the white actors on
the basis of the evidence at hand. The impact of routine racism at work
is amplified by the need to face racist comments and other actions by
whites in many other settings. Another respondent discusses this
process of interpretation and evaluation in detailing how he and his
wife have attempted to discover why black citizens receive poor treatment at malls:

Me and my wife have had a lot of discussions about it and I attribute a
lot of that to the way a person is dressed, African Americans. I've
observed it; I've experimented with it; and I've found it to be true. And
I've shared it with my wife and she's tested it. You go into a mall or a
store in sweat pants and T-shirts, you're going to be treated with a lot
less respect and attention and probably suspected of being, you know,
the proverbial poor welfare person looking to shoplift something. And if
you go in dress slacks, a nice dress or shirt, golf shirt or something with
a collar on it—things of that nature—I've experienced a lot different
treatment. And so . . . if I'm going to the mall, I'll get dressed and put on
something nice and people are going to say, "Okay, well this one here,

he's not in here to shoplift, he's probably serious about buying something because of the way he's dressed."

This commentator illustrates the often arduous process of sharing information, deciding on an appropriate experiment, carrying it out, discussing the results, and then using the information to guide future behavior. Simple aspects of daily life, such as shopping, are matters of difficulty and concern for many, if not most, black Americans. One must "dress up" just to run to the store for a little while. Note too the sophisticated process of evaluation that is collectively developed and carried out. Once again, we see African Americans' making hard decisions about the relationship between discrimination and various factors, such as racial stereotyping about appearance in this example. In this manner, they further their general knowledge of coping strategies in dealing with everyday racism.

Methods of Analysis Gleaned from Everyday Experience

Given the scale of the everyday discrimination that they face, our respondents have had to develop a complex set of methods for analyzing their difficult experiences. These include evaluations using comparisons of consistency, inconsistency, and consensus. These interviews include many references to personal experiences across similar situations and to experiences of other black people in analogous situations:

> How do you know it's race? If you do a good job, and your evaluations are good, if they begin to nit-pick and bother you. Break it down, and when you can't identify anything else—it's race. It is racism, not education, not class. Look at [names another officer], he couldn't advance here, he was told that he couldn't handle responsibility. Now he is a U.S. marshal.

Again we see that the method for evaluating racial discrimination often involves an iterative process of comparing and dissecting a series of events or incidents to see whether they are racialized, and to comprehend how racialized they are. This is a tedious and tiring process, yet one more example of the continuing costs of everyday racism.

Numerous respondents offer comparisons with past discriminatory practices. In the following comment, one officer notes that his agency was historically discriminatory and that his presence means a certain degree of change:

> Let's put it this way. This district was the first district in the state, and
> you're telling me in the history of this district that we did not have quali-
> fied African Americans in this progressive state, that we did not have any
> qualified African Americans here? I mean to the point of being even, you
> know, a secretary? Unacceptable. And [today], you're telling me that still
> would be the mentality? Unacceptable. I can't accept that. It changed
> when I got here. . . . Okay, I'm here and it's changed.

The respondent's performance in this position not only demonstrates to
him that black officers are capable of doing very difficult jobs but also
gives him an understanding that the reason black officers were not earlier given opportunities was institutional racism. He views the present
barriers as still unacceptable.

As we have seen in previous commentaries, one way of judging consistency in historically white departments involves the comparison of
the results for white and black officers in terms of hiring, evaluation,
discipline, promotion, and assignments:

> Things like that are very subtly done. I guess you just have to look at
> how you are treated. . . . "Is that the way things are routinely done or
> was this done because it's me?" You know, comparing myself to other
> sergeants in similar positions. . . . Perhaps something like having to keep
> more detailed records or statistics to prove that things were going well as
> opposed to just the routine paperwork.

Other research has demonstrated that one of the costs of everyday discrimination is the requirement that blacks keep detailed records when
few whites have to do so.[10] Many black employees in historically white
organizations learn that they must keep these detailed records if they
are to document, later on, the discriminatory treatment that they have
experienced. Otherwise, whites, even sympathetic whites, often see
them as just "paranoid." This record keeping can entail much time and
stress and is one more way in which discrimination over time reduces
the quality of life for black employees. Also, as we will see, among the
major sources of data on fairness and consistency in departmental
actions are outcomes of lawsuits and arbitrators' rulings. These rulings
are important for these officers in developing an understanding of the
differences in the treatment of white and black officers.

In summary, these black women and men develop knowledge about
everyday racism from extensive experience with whites who discrimi-

nate, and from sharing such experiences with other black Americans. In this process they also develop the interpretive tools necessary to comprehend the character, significance, and impact of racial discrimination in everyday events. This sophisticated ability to analyze and interpret racialized events and to evaluate them critically underscores the tragic centrality of white racism in their daily lives. On one hand, they develop a specific knowledge of the operation of discrimination in their occupation and an ability to understand the current relationship between this discrimination and modern policing. In addition, their years of personal and vicarious experiences with racial hostility and discrimination are intimately linked to a cumulative, shared general body of knowledge about racism that they and their social networks maintain.

Learning to Interpret Racial Stereotyping

The white old-boy networks in historically white police departments not only provide social and material support for most white officers but also recycle hoary racial stereotypes and allow one cohort of white officers to encourage the next to discriminate. Indeed, they can be seen as microcosms for generating racial oppression. Many respondents suggest, in one way or another, that there are two distinctive perspectives—one white and one black—with different beliefs, languages, and understandings on critical racial matters. As we have suggested, most whites grow up in and operate within dominant social networks, which provide powerful ways of supporting and viewing the racial hierarchy that is privileging for whites. Black networks, in contrast, are more defensive and oppositional in that they must provide their members with the ability to counter and survive the operation and impact of racial oppression. Because socialization processes in U.S. society mainly involve interaction with family members, friends, and certain others, whites and blacks are socialized to understand the racist social worlds differently.

Not surprisingly, thus, white and black officers often understand and relate to local black communities differently:

> I think that most of the black officers that I know, because of the way that we all were raised, we can associate or we can relate to what most of these people in these ghetto-type communities are dealing with, so we go in there and we understand what's going on. Whereas if the white officer goes in there, he's handling a call, basically. You know, there's no

relating to, there's no feelings, there's no understanding. He's just handling that call and that's the majority of the time.

This officer offers insights into the problems that white officers may
create when they enter and police African-American communities.
Likely to be thinking in stereotypical terms as the majority of white
Americans do, many white officers do not have the necessary knowledge and understanding to police black communities well, and riding in
cars means that they do not interact enough with ordinary black citizens to develop this knowledge. Even in the poorest communities, for
example, *most* people are not dealing drugs or engaging in violence,
they are just citizens and workers trying to survive and provide for their
families. Yet surveys indicate a rather negative portrait among the
majority of whites in regard to black communities, a portrait probably
shared by many white officers.

Interestingly, most African Americans do not suffer from a lack of
contact with white Americans. Most must have contact with numerous
whites in the course of their daily activities. For example, all our
respondents were raised in, or now live in, predominantly black neighborhoods, yet they have often encountered the white world in their
workplace, in education, in shopping, or in the media. For that reason,
these respondents often suggest that they generally have an ability to
understand the black and white worlds much better than whites do.
Some suggest that this enables them to survive in historically white
police agencies while treating members of the black community better
than the average white officer does. One officer provides this suggestive
commentary:

> I think there was a lack of depth of understanding. You had two cultures
> and I think that there was not an understanding of each other, both
> sides, black and white. . . . But when you bring an officer in from the
> community, like myself, I think I had an understanding of both worlds. I
> understood the African-American community and I was beginning to
> understand the police culture. And the people in the community [knew
> me] so well: "I know he'll be here because I know he grew up in this
> neighborhood. He can understand where everybody is coming from."

Since he was raised there, people in the local community know him, and
that familiarity helps to improve police–community relations. Indeed,
employing police officers who were raised in, or now live in, the com-

munities they police has long been a goal of law enforcement reform movements.

About half of the respondents explicitly discuss how racial stereotypes develop as a result of the structural and cultural isolation of most whites that we documented in chapter 1. The lack of equal-status contacts for most whites, beginning in their youth, tends to create a lack of understanding that is often perpetuated through oversimplified notions of "race." One officer discusses the matter rather eloquently:

> You have to really draw the people that have these prejudices, ignorance, out by just reversing the process and letting them see how foolish it looks. . . . The correlation I would draw would be Pee Wee Herman. Several years ago he was caught in a movie house masturbating. How would the person that asked a question of me feel when I reversed the tables and go, "Well, why do white males sit in movie theaters and masturbate?" Now that's about how idiotic that statement is. Or particularly, when you're asked why blacks steal this, as if all blacks do that. Or why the blacks like rap music, as if all blacks like rap music. And so, when you just simply turn the tables, and say well, you just find some embarrassing incident, the person just happens to be white, and flip it around. I think sometimes they see, "Yeah that's not really, okay, well yeah, I, I, I understand" because they can't give you an explanation as to why Pee Wee Herman sat in a movie theater and masturbated. They're white, he's white, but you don't know what was in that person's mind. Same thing goes with a black that might commit a crime, or be perceived of having committed a crime. We don't know what was in their mind or why that, something occurred. I find any time you use the term "all" or use any absolutes, you're showing that you have a prejudice because no absolute questions are correct. You know, all African Americans are not athletic; all African Americans are not well endowed; average males are not well endowed. I mean these are myths and stereotypes that are out there that, you know, if you just took a little time and used your common sense and thought about it in terms of whites and other races, you'll see how foolish they are.

Once again, a respondent sounds much like a social scientist. Here much thought has gone into trying to understand the processes of stereotyping and prejudice. Sharply underscoring the comparison point for a white person caught in a bad light, he explores how it is that whites do not generalize from such events to conclude that white men as a group are inclined to sexual deviance. He also indicates that he must sometimes inform whites, including those who may unintentionally make use of negative stereotypes about African Americans, of their poor reasoning on these matters.

One stereotype that several officers report encountering periodically is the white notion that all black people are essentially the same. Some note how many public discussions refer to "black people" or use equivalent phrasing without recognizing the differences within the group. These evaluations, as do others these black officers make, indicate a nuanced view of racial matters in the United States. Although there is much agreement among the respondents that whites and blacks often have different understandings of racial matters, which are especially shaped by the racial isolation of whites, they do note black Americans are a diverse group and do not necessarily think or act alike, even in regard to issues of racism. One respondent articulates this idea:

> There are blacks in this country; there are blacks in this building that I have nothing in common with. I'm forty-seven, they're twenty-seven or thirty-seven. They haven't been in the military; they haven't been blatantly, openly discriminated [against]. They don't have my same frame of reference; they don't have what is inside of me—my hard-driven attitude, you know.

This officer lists age, military service, and extensive experience with blatant racism as important in differentiating among African Americans. Indeed, African Americans differ in the same ways that white Americans do. Thus, some respondents criticize some aspects of the white police culture as they affect black officers, as this officer explains: "Some of the black officers were just as bad as the others. . . . Black officers become indoctrinated with the system or with racism, and they try hard to prove that they are one of the boys." There is great pressure on all officers to conform to the police culture created and maintained by the white old-boy networks.

These black law enforcement officers generally share a common knowledge of the character and structure of U.S. racism, including an often acute understanding of white stereotyping and patterns of discrimination. Racism is not just an individual matter but rather a matter of structural processes created and maintained by whites acting as both individuals and small groups. Encountering different racial conditions, the racially dominant and racially subordinate groups form distinct cultural understandings and pass these on to others, especially their younger and newer members, through the means of childhood and later socialization. Discriminatory practices become accepted by many whites as more or less natural, and the racial hierarchy is constantly produced and reproduced.

ASSESSING STRUCTURAL FACTORS

What is the structure of everyday racism? What forms does it typically take? Have these forms changed over the time that these officers have worked in historically white police departments? We now turn to these questions, the answers to which indicate that these women and men generally have a sophisticated and nuanced knowledge of the structure and operation of contemporary racism. Virtually all respondents view white Americans as primary agents creating and maintaining institutional racism. One reason is that whites control virtually all major institutions and often exclude or restrict members of other racial groups in regard to institutional access, resources, privileges, and rewards. Whites originally created all the dominant racist stereotypes in regard to "race" and African Americans. Having identified the white-generated nature of institutional racism, these respondents often discuss the factors that shape and structure this racism by reproducing traditional practices or forcing new transformations.

Reflecting on the past and the present, one officer accents certain changes that have occurred since he entered the police profession:

> We don't have the racial problem today that we had at that point. I feel the problems that we do have are pretty much equal with society and are covert enough to where we're not being actually slapped in the face with it the way we once were. . . . Because of hatred and the way that some people are actually brought up, we're not going to ever get past the racial problem, you know, that's not going to ever go away.

Most of these respondents have been officers for a significant period, and thus have seen the nature of racial discrimination transformed. In their interviews most specifically refer to these changes and often discuss underlying factors affecting them. For the most part, however, they describe only modest transformation, not the elimination of racial stereotyping and discrimination in policing. Commenting on the present situation, one respondent says, "Well, when you say 'much better,' no, you can't say that it was 'much better.' It just, in other words, it ceased shortly, but then it started merging in other little aspects."

The transformation from legal segregation to modern patterns of discrimination is noted, and many respondents dissect the modern patterns in detail. Numerous officers describe current patterns of discrimination as ranging from "overt" to "subtle" to "covert," as in this commentary:

> Typically here, you wouldn't encounter racism in the work environment, at least not from your coworkers, not the overt type. Now the hidden racism, or the covert type of racism, exists in everyday life everywhere. You might pick up on some of that. But nobody's going to come to you and tell off-color jokes, and stay here.

Understanding and Evaluating Institutional Racism

In discussing the general nature of contemporary racism, these articulate respondents are clear that racial prejudices and discrimination still exist in many forms inside and outside their employment setting. In fact, only two officers in our sample, both in the same agency, did not view racial hostility and discrimination as having had a recent impact on their workaday lives. Among the 96 percent who do accent the significant impact of contemporary racism, most discuss it as being a *structural* and *institutional* problem, not just a problem of individual white officers. They frequently note the central role of discrimination in police "institutions," the "social system," or "society in general."

As we have already seen, this structurally racist framework provides a context for much learning about how discrimination operates. Reflecting on myriad encounters in which they have learned to comprehend routine racism, these officers overwhelmingly agree that the early and ongoing socialization of white Americans is an important explanation for the continuation of discrimination:

> They are practices that have been ingrained. It has been a part of the system and people are creatures of habit traditionally, and sometimes it's hard to break them. And sometimes they don't even view it as such unless it's thought to be a sin. And it's been a learning experience for me.

This officer clearly implies that because of the way they were socialized, many whites may not understand the ramifications of their discriminatory actions, unless somehow the magnitude of those actions is pointed out to them. Acting on recurring messages they are taught, many whites engage in activities that can be more or less consciously racist in their motivation. The previous respondent also gives an example:

> I have nineteen years in law enforcement. What I've found is that people surround themselves by people who are very similar to themselves, with people who look very similar to themselves. They are with them in social circles and workplace and have a better idea of what these people are capable of doing than they do of these people that they don't surround themselves with in the professional or a social setting.

Again we see everyday experience as a major teacher. He concludes from his experience that whites prefer those like them, a sort of socio-racial cloning process. Interestingly, many respondents have reached conclusions on how racist thought and action are perpetuated that parallel findings of researchers who analyze these matters over large numbers of respondents and across numerous field studies.[11] In this regard, these and many other African Americans become major theorists of their own racialized experiences.

Many respondents argue that whites who have been raised in isolation from black Americans are not used to being with them socially and therefore readily buy into stereotypes about them. Coupled with this social isolation, as numerous respondents underscore, is the white networking that undergirds many institutions and organizations, including police departments: white, or white-male, dominance and control. As one officer notes:

> That was the good old-boys' system . . . they left themselves deniability is what they did. And then you get some like-minded individuals that move up the chain, and then you have the same problem. It reproduces itself. It feeds on itself.

Our respondents are very aware of and frequently name this old boy networking as key to the prolongation of social segregation and many discriminatory practices.

They note too that this white-dominated networking disseminates ideas that legitimate discriminatory practices. By denial of entry to others, not only is an unfair system perpetuated but also racist beliefs are shared among the whites involved, including those initially less prejudiced. In policing, older officers raised under strictly segregated social conditions—who are often central to the old-boy network—can share their racist notions of people of color with new officers. In so doing, they have a disproportionate impact on the perpetuation of racial stereotyping and discrimination in contemporary policing. One officer describes this process:

> Those are the people that perpetuate what racism we have today. And unfortunately, some of those younger people will continue up through their career and maintain those philosophies that have been instilled in their minds by the people they look up to, and then they become those older disgruntled people. And it just continues the vicious cycle.

The Importance of Economic and Political Contexts

A large number of these black women and men view economic and political institutions as having an important role in shaping the contours of racism in the United States. Some of these structuring factors are generally beyond the control of these respondents (for example, the economy); other factors (for example, government) are at least potentially arenas where they might have some impact. The respondents' discussions also illustrate that their attempts, and those of the larger black community, to change existing racial relations can be an important source of knowledge about, as well as a factor that structures, intergroup relations.

One officer's sage comments illustrate how black women and men use their knowledge of the past to extrapolate and understand future possibilities:

> I would say we've made great strides in . . . outright blatant racism, racist practices. There are still and always will be cliques in police departments. There are still and always will be subtle racism. There are still and always will be conspiracies of eating our young, so to speak, but I think we've made great strides. But what I will say is that as the economy goes, it has a direct reflection on the racist practices internally, on racist attitudes here in this agency and all police agencies. . . . Minorities always suffer when things change. You let this economy start to slip, who you think gonna be the first to suffer? Are you going to go across

the street and help some black kid when your own kid needs a job? I mean honestly, you know, if the economy starts to slip, the jobs start to move, start to leave, who do you think gonna be the first to suffer? . . . Yeah, you let a big recession come rolling in here and see what happens. Government can say all they want to say; people are going to do what they need to do to survive.

As other respondents do, this officer recognizes the changes that have taken place in racial oppression over the past few decades. Like a savvy social scientist, he also develops a well-reasoned argument linking cycles in the economy to the willingness of whites to support programs benefiting those who have historically been the targets of discrimination. The implied discussion of how black workers are historically the last hired and first fired suggests that in an ever-transforming economic system, intergroup relations can change for the better or the worse. The latter worsening results from, in part, the entrenched racism that is never honestly addressed in U.S. society and that surfaces as a result of increased competition over scarce economic opportunities.

Another officer acknowledges the importance of the economy for racial relations and then notes how white leaders can structure conditions:

The people that are the king makers, the people that will determine who the sheriff will be or who the mayor will be, or whoever, they're very concerned about that conception [of our city]. And they want to turn all of that around and so we are seeing a change coming around in that way. Because it's not good for the city, and it's not a good image for this city. And if they ever want to do some things to change, to make [the city] look favorable, to make it a first-class city—to attract businesses, to attract different opportunities into this community—they've got to show an image that is a lot more favorable than what it has been in the past. It's essential. For economics.

An ever more competitive world market system affects the nature of local racial relations as city leaders usually find it more difficult to attract outside investments if there is a perception of a major problem with overt racism in the city's institutions.

Other respondents note the importance of white business and political leaders in discussing how in smaller cities, which may not be seeking to attract outside capital, the white elite may attempt to maintain the racial status quo:

> The political powers that be don't want that to happen for whatever reasons. I don't know, I'm just speculating, but they don't seem to want the change. The powers don't seem to want the changes in the community. They want to keep it the same. Status quo. Or keep blacks in their place. They don't want to see any blacks rise to be a political power in their community. They want to keep them in their place. Like what, I'll allude to what I said earlier, this is the South.

In rural counties and small towns the political will among white leaders to change the structure of historical racism may not exist. One respondent in such a town illustrates how the influence of local white leaders extends to the police force: "The power of the town council undermines the authority of the chief . . . no one on council is black." In smaller towns, the police department often is not distinct from the political leadership. The lack of black political representation usually results in the black population's diminished ability to influence policies affecting policing and many other governmental matters.

Understanding Pressures from Black Communities for Change

When white political and economic leaders are resistant to change, the public, especially the black public, can be a force that pushes for a change in the institutionalized structure of racial discrimination. Numerous respondents describe the importance of this pressure. One respondent describes what occurred in his city:

> When public pressure started to build, that public pressure changed City Hall. [The community] had to put pressure on the top people so it could filter right on down to the police department. And as time passed a lot of those older people retired and were weeded out or they left, and things began to change because of a new-generation-type person was brought in with a different mentality and different views.

Public outcries against racial injustice and for changes have, historically, affected the institutional structure of racism in particular areas of the United States. Public pressure can affect the nature of local policing.

Black officers often build ties to members of the black public, but real progress requires some community organization as well.

Understanding Federal and Agency Pressures for Change

Nearly half the respondents suggested that even in communities where black residents are not well organized, local black leaders or police department administrators can take the initiative and push for changes in the nature of racial relations in police agencies. These individuals may help develop initiatives related to sets of rules and penalties that require changes in local police behavior. If they are implemented, as they sometimes are, they can transform the nature of local policing.

Accreditation is one such national process discussed by a few respondents. Accreditation is a voluntary process of self-governance in which accredited agencies adhere to a set of minimum standards developed by the Commission on Accreditation for Law Enforcement Agencies (CALEA). These standards include written policies on the use of deadly force and an affirmative action plan. One officer discusses how national accreditation standards for police behavior and mechanisms of enforcement pressure some white department heads:

> There was some extensive abuse. But now, I think the fear of civil litigation that imputes to the department is causing that behavior to change. I think that's what it was. It's an economic issue now. It's not a moral issue anymore; do the right thing. It's, don't get caught doing wrong because it's going to cost me money, and I'm going to throw you to the damn wolves is what it amounts to. And I think that's what motivated change. I don't think they did it out of the goodness of their heart or anything. Some, I'm sure, did. Some department heads did, but the economic issue alone says, we can't do this. . . . Police officers understand that they can be sued by the individual for that type of behavior.

Fear of lawsuits drawing on national accreditation standards has motivated some change. Moreover, racial hostility in the form of blatant police abuses, such as unnecessary shootings and killings, has declined somewhat, partly as a consequence of the pressure of these national standards.[12] Still, these black officers make it clear that these positive pressures from the outside have not eliminated everyday racism. Their accounts reveal that racial hostility still infects the mind of many whites, and some behavioral manifestations of this hostility have also been transformed out of political or economic necessity: "There's a lot of money being rewarded to a lot of people and when you hit an agency in their budget, hit them in the purse, that sends a strong message. So they had to start addressing those issues. And no, I don't think it was willing; the change didn't come willingly."

Noting that only some manifestations of underlying racial hostility have changed, another officer assesses the economic incentive of whites to control their behavior to ensure job security:

> There is a heck of a problem in most police departments today trying to educate or do something enlightening. What they're doing is they're changing the way they behave; they're not changing their attitude about it. No. They have too much time invested in their careers, and they're not going to leave because of that. And that's a problem.

Some economic and political incentives now exist for white department heads to push for changes in their agency and for white officers to avoid being caught engaging in unacceptable behavior.

Numerous respondents note that the dynamics of police agencies make it difficult for real change to occur in the hidden or underlying patterns of hostility and discrimination. There is considerable agreement that the person at the top sets the tone of the department, but even a positive tone on racial matters does not guarantee that real change will occur. The following respondent discusses the complexity of the process:

> The chief has to say, okay this is what I want and this is how it's done for it to start. But the problem comes [when the] chief is all great for it, but he's hired the wrong people to put it into practice. And so you still have the little inner groups [who say], "Well we don't really have to do it," and the chief doesn't know. Now if you have one who checks back or you have everybody going, "Well you're going to have to do it" and kind of force the issue, then things start to change. If they think it's all just a smoke screen for the public, that they don't have to follow it, then it will never change. . . . The chief and the command staff have to be able to follow it through for any change at all to occur. . . . But even when the command and the chief all say, "Okay, we're going to do this," they get resistance from the troops, but the troops will eventually fall in

line. It has to come from the top, but the only ones who really do it are the bottom. It's always like the top needs this diversity or they need this or whatever and it looks great on paper, but they don't want to have to butt heads with the people who actually have to do the work.

This respondent has a clear understanding of the way in which organizations operate internally. It is not enough for the top executives to assert platitudes about equal opportunity, for they must follow through in actions against racism over the long term. The chief, the command staff, and the informal networks of white patrol officers must agree on what must take place to allow significant changes in police racism to take place. Numerous black officers note the difficulty in getting all levels of an agency in agreement as to how to improve racial relations. Lack of agreement limits the extent of change. Furthermore, the respondents are unanimous in their view that where the agency head is openly racist in his or her thought and actions, racist attitudes and behavior by command staff and officers are more likely to be overt.

Another aspect of leadership that the officers discuss is that the requirements of supervisory level positions often distance leaders from other officers, as well as the community. This can mean that the top officers are less aware of the negative actions of their subordinates. One respondent explains that since becoming a supervisor,

I haven't experienced any overt racism, but I'm not naive enough to think that it's not occurring. [I'm] quite sure. In my position, by me being the boss, I'm going to experience less subtle racism than, let's say, one of my black troopers or female troopers because there's a double-whammy there. One, I'm the boss and I can respond with authority so they're going to be careful not to mess up, whether it's racism or policy violation or anything; and then, number two, that subtleness, from knowing that it's improper from the beginning in guarding against that— those two factors together enhance or make it far more important for the individuals not to be caught engaging in any type of improper conduct whatsoever.

This senior manager has empathy for other officers who lack authority. In a comment similar to previous discussions, he separates white behavior from attitudes to illustrate current forms of everyday racism. Sometimes white actions demonstrate knowledge of the actor that the action is unacceptable and perhaps punishable. Clearly, some black officers are shielded, to varying degrees, from some racist attitudes and actions if they have significant managerial authority.

ASSESSING GEOGRAPHICAL AND DEMOGRAPHIC VARIATIONS
Variations by Location of Police Agencies

Some of these black officers discuss other social and demographic factors that shape racial relations, factors that can have an impact on officers' ability to work well in their agency or community. For example, some posit that those black officers in policing agencies with greater numbers of black officers, stronger organizations of black officers, or organized black communities behind the officers will face less racial hostility and discrimination than those in other agencies.

Arguing that his department is a better place for African-American officers because of years of collective struggle that have culminated in the current strong black leadership, one officer suggests that his department is not the norm:

> It'd be something else somewhere else in a rural area or some other place because I talk to friends that I have in [a nearby] county and you know the stuff that I went through in the seventies, they're going through *now*. The opportunities are just not there, and you know they hired because they have to, or hold on to you because they have to, but you can't go anywhere. You can't do anything, so it depends on where you are, you know. We just have a large department here, and there's enough opportunities for everyone.

Larger departments can sometimes provide better opportunities and support for officers of color than those in rural areas and small towns, though this potential is of course variable, depending on an agency's leadership.

Indeed, many of these officers compare their agencies with other agencies in their state or other states. Their consensus is that black citizens, and black officers in particular, generally face more overt and hostile forms of racism in rural areas and small towns than in larger urban areas. One female officer in a state police agency notes that ill treatment is compounded by gender:

> I investigate politicians or local sheriffs or whatever, in small counties, and you can see the expression when I walk in the door, they kind of stand

back and so they're watching everything that I do. . . . Depending on the county, there's no conflict or they haven't had to move to the twentieth century, I've been called "gal" when I've been to rural counties. Or me and a white agent go, and they only talk to him—and don't realize that at the end, it's going to be my decision. . . . It's the way they talk to you, or the way they hesitate—like you probably don't understand English—or talking down to you because they're not real sure you understand.

One aspect of whites' racist orientation is an inclination to view only whites as those who have organizational authority. Here we see that whites do not expect a black woman to have such authority, and their reactions suggest that they really do not know how to respond. This is a common event, especially for African-American women in authority, in numerous other major organizations.[13] As we move into the twenty-first century, many whites have yet to learn how to interact with African Americans in settings the latter have only recently entered. Clearly, the country's policing agencies have a long way to go in their interpersonal relations.

Variations in Discrimination by Education and Gender

Numerous respondents discuss the effect of their educational level or gender on the perceptions of white officers. For example, education is often seen as threatening by some white officers and can thus affect departmental relationships, as one officer makes clear:

See, the racial problem existed before I got there. And then once they found out that I had an education—for example, when I first got there, the watch commander and sergeant came to me and told me that, if I kept an eye on all of the other blacks, I didn't have "nothing to worry about." And my question was, "If I keep an eye on them today, who's going to keep an eye on me for you tomorrow?" So I said the circle has to stop somewhere. And I'm not going to be a part of that. So that was the feeling. The racial problem was there. It was always there, but like I said before, it was compounded by the educational differences.

Maintaining white domination in police departments becomes more difficult as more black officers are hired, and especially as better-educated black officers are hired. Notice the contradictory nature of the process of hiring for many white departments. White officials often limit the number of African-American officers being hired by creating a requirement that they have a significant level of education. However, when better-educated black candidates apply and are hired, they may use their education to support demands for changes in racist policies, for they often know about the regulations and are more willing to organize or sue. Eventually, some better-educated officers have been able to compete successfully for leadership positions in some agencies and, once promoted, have been able to change patterns of discrimination in their agency.

Another important factor that structures cross-racial relationships in policing organizations is the gender of the officers. Women officers reflect on past experiences with racism and sexism in order to construct understandings of the dynamic interrelationships between racial and gender characteristics in their job as a police officer. One woman discusses how white women are treated better than *all* black officers, but then concludes by examining how all women officers, black and white, share certain experiences provoked by sexism:

> I tell somebody, it's like I've got a double whammy. I'm a woman, and I happen to be black. Because, what was ironic is I used to walk around the police department with this chip on my shoulder. And I have this white female lieutenant; her and I used to butt heads together. And I used to tell her, I used to complain about some of the stuff that they did. And because we didn't talk, we didn't know what was going on, so she told me one day . . . "Oh, that happened to me, too." I say, "You're kidding;" I say, "You mean to tell me all this time I thought they were doing this to me because I was black." "Oh, no, I could have told you they're doing it because we're women." So I think it's more so because we're women, because I know I said that the [white] female would get better preference, but they still treat the men as men.

She indicates that male officers—who are mainly white—sometimes treat her badly, not because she is black but because she is a woman. The women officers in our sample, at different moments in their discussions, vary in their emphasis in assessing how racial or gender characteristics shape reactions of other officers. These African-American women find themselves evaluating whether their racial or gender characteristics, or both, influence encounters with others inside and outside their agency, a pattern that we have explored in previous research.[14]

One woman officer accents this point:

> I guess it depends on what section you are in, who your supervisor is, because there are some people who have no problem with race, but law enforcement being male-oriented, that's what they have a problem with first. Because if I was a black male, I was still a guy and we could do guy things together. And then you have other supervisors or people who don't want to associate with another race period, and a women is just like putting icing on the cake to make it worse.

White male officers and supervisors structure her work experiences. Her comments embody the sentiments of many black male and female respondents: black officers are treated worse in general than white officers, and female officers are treated worse than male officers, so being black and female creates a distinctive and often negative set of experiences. As one female supervisor concludes, "To a certain degree, African-American men face some of the same barriers, and encounter similar problems, but as the saying goes, until you walk a mile in my shoes."

INTERNAL UNDERSTANDINGS: DIFFERENCES AMONG BLACK OFFICERS

In addition to the factors that shape how and when whites respond negatively to black officers, there are differences within the group of black officers themselves that can sometimes affect the character of their job. For example, the social distance that sometimes exists between older black police supervisors and recently hired, younger black officers can generate conditions in which newer officers are not sufficiently socialized by the experienced officers. And new officers may thus develop less specialized knowledge of the operation of racism in agencies than veteran officers do. However, this issue is complex. Because of the distinctive struggles of many older officers in transforming highly segregated policing (see chapter 6), younger black officers are likely to encounter less overt racism today, particularly in departments with a critical mass of black officers. Therefore, the specialized knowledge of the operation of racism in policing changes somewhat as the context of policing and the level of overtness of everyday racism change. Consequently, newer officers may not understand the sacrifices older officers made, as one older officer notes:

> We can't forget that, I don't forget that. In the back of your mind you know that you didn't get here because they waved their magic wand. That was a lot of blood, sweat, and tears that went into it and that made

it better for everybody. The difficult thing is that some of the younger people don't understand; they never experienced that.

Clearly, in many departments and in the larger society, many social and institutional conditions have been transformed since the 1960s and 1970s.

Furthermore, to the extent that forms of racism have been transformed socially, the goals of some younger black officers may not be so intimately intertwined with black organizations and communities as they are for older officers. For them individual goals of advancement, job security, and increased salary may sometimes supplant the collective goals of community betterment. This veteran officer makes some interesting comments in this regard:

> You know what I used to say, and it's the truth. I think if you talk to most guys who've been on, I'd say, over twenty . . . years, we all used to say, man, things are going to get better as we get younger better educated officers out here on the street. In my own personal opinion, it didn't get better. It got worse because it changed from the guy who came from the neighborhood who knew something about me to the guy who has not had the negative experience and don't know anything about it. Nobody's told them about them, and be that officer black or white, there's no connection between these people out here in the streets and that officer. Very little connection, okay? So you, you have a different attitude. See we knew we were part of the community. . . . These young officers don't have that same sort of identity. And I think those [new] officers that we thought—the young guys coming on with better education and raised in integrated schools—knew something about other people, that would make a difference in the way they treated and handled people. And that's just not the truth. Young people, in my opinion, really don't care about other people a whole lot. They do their job, they're not as concerned, they're not as apt to go out of their way to help someone or to see that the job is done properly. They follow the book and the book says, "I go and I check, and I don't see. I drive off." Then that's what they do. So, it's a difference, and I don't think that difference is for the better.

This respondent seems to suggest that younger officers in general, not just younger black officers, are less people oriented than older officers. Clearly, African-American officers draw upon a collective knowledge of racism, but their shared understanding can vary, depending on factors that structure this learning, such as age and experience and forms of discrimination generally encountered.

Several respondents suggest that where an officer grew up can make a difference in his or her job or relationship with local communities:

> Most of your officers now that we are hiring are not born and raised in this community. There's no tie. Go back and look at the seventies and eighties, most of the officers were born right here in this community; they were hired from this community. Now, these people are like transients. They're coming in from other places, and so there's no tie, there's no baseline to start with and say, "Well this is my community; I want to see it get better." And see, people like myself, I was born and raised in this community.

Though fewer in number, African-American officers who worked in the 1960s and 1970s often policed the communities where they grew up. Today, because of an increased demand for officers, black and white, these officers often work outside their community of origin. Some respondents discuss how departmental recruiting often pulls black officers from their home community to a better-paying job in another, often larger urban, community. One result is that the lack of an intimate knowledge of the community and weaker bonds with residents promote a distance between the community and the officer, black or white, who is recruited from another community. Although many of the respondents argue that black officers can adapt more easily than white officers to black communities in which they are strangers, the community of origin is discussed as a factor that structures the relationship of officers to the residents they police.

A number of the black officers also assess the effects of officers' social class on their ability to police their local community. Despite their being black, if they have been raised in a social class that is different from that of those they police, there can be some problems in interpersonal communication, as one officer explains:

> It depends upon the background of that African-American officer. If the African-American officer has came from a socioeconomic background that is out of the mainstream of the black community, they may have problems because they may not understand particularly the culture of the disadvantaged African American. It could be a totally new experience to them, so just because you're black does not necessarily mean that you're going to come in a neighborhood and that you can get along better with

the black community than a white officer. It really depends on the officer, the officer's character, the officer's knowledge of the community and the individuals that they're interacting with.

Because most black officers have a working-class or lower-middle-class background, this problem of class differences is not as great as it is for white officers, who are more likely to police a community that is different from their own. Interestingly, none of the respondents specifically indicates that his or her level of education or class level has had an adverse impact on relationships with the less-educated members of black communities.

In these discussions of age, experience, community of origin, and class, a common theme is that an officer's knowledge about a group of people in a community influences the quality of their interaction and thus of policing. Black officers who have been socialized to understand the general operation of racism in the United States, the respondents agree, generally develop better relationships in black communities. When they lack information about a specific community or class or when lack of experience skews their learning, their relationships with the community can become more difficult or antagonistic.

CONCLUSION: SEEING AND UNDERSTANDING EVERYDAY RACISM

In this chapter we have shown how these black women and men in policing generally share knowledge of the nature and character of contemporary racism as it operates inside and outside their law enforcement agencies. Most view modern racism as involving a complex array of social processes and individual actions under the control of white Americans. Black and white Americans are viewed as different to the extent the groups have been socialized differently in their views of the racial hierarchy and their place therein. Because of collective struggles by African Americans since the 1960s, the latter often view the nature of racism as having been transformed from very overt discrimination to conditions in which there is a continuum of discrimination that ranges from overt, to subtle, to covert. The form of racial hostility and discrimination encountered varies according to an array of structuring factors that operate to shape the specialized nature of racism within a particular institution, a specific agency, or an individual encounter.

The findings of our research are much in line with previous research on the everyday experiences of African Americans with contemporary racism.[15] These black officers possess a sophisticated knowledge about racism that they have acquired through a sustained and long-term process of socialization. Their knowledge of everyday racism is individually cumulative as well as collectively learned and shared. Their discussions suggest the importance of vicarious learning as well as personal experiential knowledge. They possess not only a knowledge of the general nature of racism in society but also, as one might expect, a detailed knowledge of the specific operation of racism in policing.

In their assessments, we can see that these women and men develop and operate from an interpretative methodology that they use to understand their experiences with everyday racism, as well as those of their family and community. This interpretive methodology allows them to evaluate and explain, often through incisive internal argumentation, whether the difficult encounters with whites they face daily are actually examples of racial hostility and discrimination. Drawing on their garnered knowledge, most have formed a penetrating understanding of the current nature of factors that structure and change individual and institutional racism. Although the ubiquitous experience of antiblack discrimination provides the basis for much black solidarity, the officers recognize that differences of age, gender, class, and community of origin can sometimes structure differential experiences for black Americans in regard to experience with racism and the ability to evaluate racialized encounters. At the same time, they have learned that African Americans in all groups face a large array of common problems generated by white Americans.

These officers are articulate in their recognition that traditional accents on individual racism—which are often made in the mass media and in academic disciplines such as criminology—are misleading and insufficient to explain the reproduction of racial inequality in U.S. society. They emphasize the unjust character of the structural conditions that undergird not only the socialization of white and black Americans but also the quality of life for white and black Americans. Their strategies to cope with or combat everyday racism have been related to their understandings of the nature of this omnipresent system of racism. These understandings shape their views of the society's past, present, and future, and of their place within the larger society. Not surprisingly, their involvement in assertive actions aimed at changing the nature of racist relations furthers their knowledge of the complex operations of systemic racism. These insightful women and men do more than acquire this knowledge, for they demonstrate *active involvement* in producing and sharing the knowledge about the operations of everyday racism across their community and the larger society.

Experience with everyday racism generates a deep knowledge and understanding about the future. This experience affects their comprehension of what the future of racial relations is likely to be in the United States, as we see in this sage but pessimistic commentary:

> I would like to think that one day we would have a department where everybody cares about everybody, but I know that I won't be here to see that. I won't; I don't foresee that happening for the next fifty or sixty years, you know, because people are people and that's just the way they are. . . . I mean, in 1997 you've got people that say, "Well if my daughter married a black guy, I'll kill her," and stuff like that. And you see that people in that old-time mentality, and what they do is they teach it to their kids. And their kids teach it to their kids, and on and on and on, and it never stops. There is definitely racism in our department. And I'm not saying it's the administration, but it's going to always be there until you can wipe it out. And I don't know how you're going to do that with generations being taught it, generation after generation after generation.

Problems of the White Mind:
Perspectives of Black Officers

You're looking at a system that's been built up over the years with a phi-losophy that's been built up over the years and it's taught not only in the educational system, on television, in the media. It's all around you, and you either subscribe to it because it's the easy thing to do, or actually it's the natural thing to do. Or you have to struggle with society and once that struggle, once that fever pitch struggle begins and catches on, I think you'll see some progress, but until that you deal with what you deal with. Can you deal with it? You can. Do you really want to deal with it; do you want to live the rest of your life knowing that you're considered a second-class citizen by a lot of people in this country? Many of them you work with or encounter in the community. I don't think that's the way you want to go out. Rather than face those things, you'd rather be respected as a man, as a law enforcement officer. (Black police officer)

Everyday racism is grounded in a hierarchy of racial statuses, as well as in the rationalization of racial difference by white Americans. This African-American officer laments not being treated with respect as a person or as a police officer. Our experiential-racism perspective sug-gests that for discriminatory practices to occur systematically, there must be attitudes and ideological rationalizations that stimulate and legitimize discriminatory practices over the short and the long term. The negative attitudes and images of whites stereotype, problematize, and denigrate black Americans as individuals and as a group.[1] The problematizing and denigrating operate to legitimize and rationalize discrimination against African Americans.

CULTURAL STEREOTYPING

Numerous respondents feel that the continuing structural segregation in the United States constantly produces and reproduces significant subcultural differences between white and black Americans. Understanding these differences is important to understanding differences in the two groups' knowledge and comprehension of everyday racism. We can now examine how these black women and men encounter whites who view black culture as inferior and promote this conception as a justification for the continuing secondary position of African Americans in the society.

Defining African Americans as Uncivilized

In their examination of the role of racial segregation in the formation of distinct white and black cultures and communities, some of these officers suggest how such differences affect the ways whites police many black communities:

> The difference between black police officers and white police officers [is that] we know what goes on in our communities. We know the language in our communities. We know, I know, that black folks hanging under a tree does not constitute black people doing something wrong because my stepfather played dominoes under a tree—because where else were they going to go. They didn't have anyplace to go, so they played under a tree. So if I see a bunch of black men under a tree playing dominoes and drinking, that doesn't bother me, because I know that they're not doing anything wrong; because that's part of our culture. Because we didn't have the clubs, and we didn't have the YMCA [Young Men's Christian Association], and we didn't have these other things that were available to non–African Americans. So that's the kind of stuff that white police officers don't realize. That's their culture differences. And . . . a bunch of us together making a lot of noise is to them disturbing the peace; to me it's not. Like folks getting together and making a lot of noise having a good time. So those are the differences that they haven't been able to deal with.

Drawing on his and other blacks' long experience in communities, this officer offers a sharp sociological analysis of problems in policing com-

munities. Many white officers may perceive groups of black men socializing and playing games in certain public places as exhibiting behavior
outside the societal norm. Yet, they are unable to understand how
extended socioeconomic deprivation has the development of black
communities, through discrimination in jobs, housing, and access to
conventional organizational settings. Instead, as many other whites do,
white officers may focus on what appears to be a rejection of the dominant values of hard work and individual success, when in fact it is the
direct manifestation of institutional racism.

Whites' perception of African Americans as less than civilized can
legitimize unnecessary rudeness, and even the use of force, of prejudiced
white officers:

> You've seen the ghetto blasters? Okay. A white officer comes in on a
> noise complaint, goes in and on first sight his perception is that this is
> crazy; this is out of control. . . . He will, without doing further assess-
> ment of the situation, he will go in and rule this area with an iron fist
> and just be ugly, be mean to the people.

In such settings, white norms about social behavior are extended to the
situations of those who are not white, without the necessary investigation or requisite understandings. Moreover, ideological constructions of
black people as emotional and somehow primitive are related to ideological constructions of white people as serious, rational, and able to
exercise restraint in their attitudes and behavior. A situation in which
there seems to a white person to be too much noise, for example,
implies a lack of restraint and a loss of control—to the point that some
white officers may feel they must restore order by any means and therefore act irrationally themselves:

> Some of these young white officers, you put them in a situation, they
> may panic. They have seen these Tarzan movies and these different, you
> know, African-type movies where natives act a certain way. You get
> these guys and you put them in a situation like that, they may think
> that's the type of mentality they're dealing with and grab their pistol
> and start firing.

White misunderstandings of black culture and communities have long
resulted in injury or death for African Americans.

Defining African Americans as Backward

The black assessments of white perspectives are generally grounded in everyday experience. A substantial number of these officers relate conversations with white officers in which whites' comments define the behavior of black people as backward. One respondent describes an interaction he had with white police officers before becoming an officer:

> I was in the military [when I was] picked up for armed robbery. In dress Air Force blues standing on the street corner waiting on a bus. Police officers pulled up and said, "Get in the car." "What for?" "I said get in the car." "I said what for?" "Nigger, I said get in the car." I wasn't about to go scrapping with two police officers, so I got in the car. They take me back down to a service station no more than a block or two down the street. And the guy looks at me, and I mean he says, "He's not dark enough." Nothing else. He's not dark enough. If I had perhaps . . . been darker rather, I'd probably be in jail. No other identifiers, just "He's not dark enough." And I asked the guys . . . I said, "But do you think that I'd be so dumb that I'd rob a gas station two blocks from where I'm standing on a street corner waiting on a bus? Are you kidding?" I said, "I'd have to be absolutely stupid."

Color coding looms large in this account, and the white officers had so little respect for the intelligence of black people that they could have envisioned a nearby U.S. soldier as the criminal they sought. The respondent suggests that it did not matter to the officers whether he was the criminal or not, showing little concern for the rights of black people. A key aspect of the lives of African Americans is the role of collective memory. By the time they are in their teens, if not well before, most African Americans have had enough bad experiences with law enforcement authorities that they are veterans at interpreting the actions of the latter.

Another officer discussed how he learned that his white counterparts share a perception of black people's concerns as being unimportant:

> We went to a domestic disturbance call. . . . We handled the call. . . . As we were clearing the call, the guy that I'm riding with, he keys his radio and he says, "To headquarters 108," which means I'm back in service or we're back in service, "NR" which means no report, and "TNT." Well I was familiar with the designation "NR," but I was not familiar with the

designation "TNT" because I had not heard, I had now been on the police department about three years and I had never heard anybody use that designation. . . . So I asked him, I said, "What does TNT mean?" and he, he started to blush, and he said, "Oh, you know what it means." I said, "No." I said, "What does it mean?" And then he was not wanting to say anything then and I said to myself, "Something's up." And then I asked him again; I said, "No, no, tell me, what does it mean?" He goes, "It means 'typical nigger trouble.'" Yeah, you know, so I'm on the job, I'm really in the job now three years before I really start seeing the true accepted thing that's occurring in the police department.

The white officer, with one of those numerous racist code words that white officers have traditionally used, dismissed a domestic disturbance in a black community as unimportant. The white officer discovered that his comments were not acceptable. This situation again suggests that whites view their dominant ideas as normal, and that many whites have a tendency to adopt and perpetuate such ideas without critical analysis. The racist ideology is learned and becomes an accepted part of white consciousness.

Another respondent described to the interviewer how comments about the nature of African Americans deeply affect him, even when they are not directed at him. Commenting on racist epithets like "nigger," he explains:

No, they never were directed toward me, but they were directed toward a class of people that certainly I'm a member of. You know, they say "nigger" can mean any low-down person, be it black or white, but I think the reference was an African-American population.

When confronted with their comments, many concerned whites, including white officers, often attempt to rationalize or redirect their comments. Several respondents also discuss how, in performance of their duties, they sometimes encounter cultural symbols of white supremacy or other cultural symbols that denigrate black Americans. These officers discuss the power of statues, signs, stickers, clothing, and flags in reinforcing and perpetuating racist notions, as in this example:

One thing that I was noticing when I was driving down the street is that a couple doors down there is a big rebel flag hanging outside, just down from the station. And you see these flags and other racist symbols, and you're aware that these people who have these flags or hold these meetings, you know that their goal is to build one ethnic group up in America and tear another one down. When you see something like that, I'm not saying that I like it, but I prefer that I'd rather know, OK. I can look at them and say I know exactly what's in your heart; I know how you feel about me.

Evaluation of intent is easier when confronted with forms of such overtly racist behavior. It is difficult for black officers to protect and serve communities of people who adorn their possessions and bodies with symbols that illustrate that they feel whites are superior and blacks are backward and should stay in their place. This respondent is confronted with the Confederate battle flag, which is regarded by many black Americans as redolent with racist meaning, every time he enters or leaves his place of work.

White Accusations of Black Language Deficiency

Numerous respondents further illustrate how defining and stereotyping black Americans as uncivilized or backward are related to processes that attribute to them certain language deficiencies. In the following example, the officer expands upon the theme, developed by many officers, that social segregation has promoted development of subcultures with distinct languages. In doing so, she discusses how some white people regard black language skills as inferior:

> Because I grew up in a predominately, well I grew up in an all-black community, I mean, there were nothing but black people around me. We talk different and a lot of times people from other races say, "Well they don't know how to talk." No, this is the way we grew up talking, and this is just how we talk. And a lot of times they don't understand.

This lack of understanding, promoted by continuing segregation and reliance on stereotypes, frequently is manifested in the way in which white officers treat members of the black community during police–citizen encounters.

Several respondents discuss situations in which white officers, acting on misconceptions of African Americans, adopt what they perceive to be as "black" language styles or forms:

It's just the way that he would talk to that African-American person. He would change his tone of voice, change his lingo or whatever to fit that black person and I just felt so uneasy because you know; he was trying to be black. He was trying to talk black and act black because he was on that side of town and because I was there. . . . And that sergeant walks over there, and has never met this kid before in his life, and starts talking to him like he's known him all of his life. And things like that because he was black.

Once again, a respondent's assessment is grounded in everyday experience. This type of encounter, frequently discussed by respondents, illustrates that some white officers perceive black Americans as having language deficiencies that must be addressed by adopting some type of "black lingo" instead of communicating in the manner in which they normally communicate.

Furthermore, these encounters give African-American officers information that contributes to their general body of knowledge about how whites think about black people. This information about whites and racism is particularly meaningful when language deficiencies are attributed to the respondent, rather than to black people in general. One officer recounts a training incident:

I stopped this guy, and the guy didn't have his driver's license on him. And [the sergeant] said, "We want to write this guy up for failure to carry and exhibit a license on demand." And he asked me, "Can you spell all that?" in front of the guy. I still tease him today about that. And I said, well, and I looked at [him] and I smiled, and I said, "Yes, sir, I can spell all that." And I spelled it, I wrote the guy his citation, and we got back in the vehicle. And I said, "Sarge," I said, "if I couldn't spell it, I sure would have been embarrassed." And we laughed about it. He didn't remember it; I had to remind him about it. . . . And I understood, really. . . . And I love him to death. He's one of the best people and bosses that I can have. He really is; he's a good person, and a good heart. And a lot of people are good-hearted, even racists, really. They are uninformed.

This respondent illustrates how the subtle stereotyping of black Americans is part of a powerful ideological process that many whites engage in without consciously knowing that they are doing so. The event is memorable for the black officer and has shaped his understanding of his supervisor, white people in general, and everyday racism. The white officer, on the other hand, initially laughed at his comment and then forgot about it. It stays embedded in black peoples' memories because it recurs so often across their everyday lives.

WHITE NOTIONS OF BLACK CRIMINALITY

Clearly, thus, many whites, both officers and civilians, attribute the problems that African Americans face to an array of cultural factors that are viewed as conspiring to keep the latter in subordinated social positions. Historically, the ideological problematization of African Americans was rooted heavily in whites' justification of black subordination on the basis of asserted biological inferiority to whites. Today, only a modest minority of whites still openly assert this notion that black Americans are intellectually inferior because of their biological makeup. Most whites now interpret racial differences in more or less cultural terms. Significantly, notions of cultural backwardness remain central to much white thinking about African Americans.

Numerous officers discuss the forms of this ideological-racism process and its significant impact on their life. They frequently discuss the ways in which they encounter being problematized as deviant or criminal in firsthand incidents, or from vicarious experiences shared with them by friends and relatives. For example, one savvy officer indicates that she frequently witnesses racist notions arising in her planning meetings with certain white officers:

> I have been in meetings where persons, white officers, have been describing an event that happened. And they'll say, "Well the black male grabbed the white female, and then he dragged her down the street." But then if it's two blacks, you don't hear, "The black male grabbed the black female and dragged her down the street." You hear, "And then the man grabbed the woman and dragged her down the street." Well why do you think they say the black male grabbed the white female? We're sitting in the meeting; see it's so natural. . . . And they're still doing this because it's just, they don't even realize it anymore. Why do you think they say that? God, because it creates such a horrible picture; it gets everybody all stirred up to say, "That black male grabbed that white female." Now everybody's all "My God."

White people tap into traditional racist ideological messages concerning black men and white women, often unconsciously, and promote the notion that black-against-white crime is particularly horrible. Black officers in attendance are treated as if they automatically share the understandings and are treated as "overly sensitive" if they point out how such conversations reproduce racial stereotyping.

The Impact of the Criminality Stereotype: Action in Public Places

Stereotyping often leads to discriminatory action. We see numerous examples of this process in our interviews. Indeed, these officers pepper their discussions with examples of incidents in which they felt that they themselves had been viewed and treated as criminals. A few mention specific incidents in their agency, and many others discuss negative treatment that they have experienced in public places while they were out of uniform. Often this mistreatment has been at the hands of white police officers.

One respondent describes how ill treatment by white police officers before he became an officer has had a lasting impact on his life. He first describes being with a friend who had a dispute with management in a restaurant. The police were called, as he continues this account:

> I was grabbed, put in a police arm-bar with my hands behind my back. The guy had my hands so far behind my back that I felt my collarbone. I felt like he was going to pop my arm, and you know I never said anything verbally wrong to him. I mean, it was unmerited, unwarranted; OK? And basically he held me there and he kept applying pressure to my arm, and asking questions, "What's my name?" And, you know, I mean I was in serious pain the entire time, and they did all that just to get my name and whatever. They trespassed me from the establishment, but that was fine with [me], but for him to just grab me like that, it just stuck in my mind. It still does.

Again, this officer, judging a past encounter with police from his current knowledge of police practices, finds that the level of officer response to the situation was excessive. Furthermore, he illustrates that these types of police–citizen encounters can remain in one's memory for long periods, again illustrating the cumulative impact of everyday racism.

Events that accent negative stereotyping by whites can shape not only African Americans' understanding of racism but also their self-image and self-worth, as another officer made clear:

You get perceived that way. And that's disheartening at times. I remember I went to Church's Chicken once. I was a cop, but I was off duty. I remember that I had on a tank top, and the lady was sitting in a car. And I assumed that was her husband in there buying her chicken, and I walked by her car. I mean, I'm clean cut; I'm a clean-cut guy. Not thuggish at all . . . I just got out of my car; I drove a nice car. Actually, I was driving an older Mercedes. I pulled up next to her. She was sitting there; I got out of my car, and in a second, [she] locked all of her doors. Now, you can either be insulted by that, or you have to understand. I don't know what experiences this lady has had with black males. But should I be judged? Or should everybody, should all white males be judged because of [Timothy] McVeigh?

This respondent, as do most others, searches to find meaning in such negative experiences with whites. He even tries to see the situation from the point of view of the white person, and that is more than she did. Black officers are frustrated and insulted by their treatment, particularly since they perceive themselves as responsible citizens who work to maintain public order. However, in situations in which they are not protected by the authority invested in their uniform, they are frequently misperceived as threats to order.

One situation in which our respondents have, as many other African Americans have, periodically encountered this stereotyping is in stores while they were shopping:

You walk into a department store, and you know language is not universally verbal. I mean you just get that [body language] in that sense. That somebody doesn't want you, or they don't trust you, or they fear you or something, you know. [They] talk to you in one tone one moment, and the person behind you walks up and, "Sure what can I do for you?" And you see that kind of stuff. You know, you can't do anything about it, so you don't let aggravate you or anything like that, but . . .

Here again we see an example of woodwork racism, the type of recurring insults that range from subtle to blatant and form part of the everyday experience of African Americans over a lifetime.

Some respondents report as well on their attempts to do something about this type of routine mistreatment. They sometimes seek the shelter provided by their occupational status, such as by confronting the perpetrators and letting the latter know that they are, in fact, police officers rather than criminals. For many respondents, it is a painful decision to emphasize their occupation in order to counter discriminatory actions. Although they are not likely to change the ideological construct in a white mind, they can at least address affronts to their self-image, as this officer notes:

> My nephew and a couple of guys went into a mall. I know this goes on. The security, we went in there, we were looking for something. And we were talking and just walking around. And we were dressed casually. Finally, we notice—we didn't initially pay any attention—that everywhere we went we were being followed. So finally, hell, I just asked them. I said, "Are you doing what I think you're doing?" I said, "Ever since we've been coming in here, you've been following us and everybody else is standing around. We've got money. We're police. We're going to pay for what we get." The guy was so embarrassed. I hated to do him that way, but I know his boss had told him to do that, so I really can't blame him totally. I blame the system that's in place. Because if you're African American and you go into a department store, they're going to watch your butt; and I know that.

This searching comment reflects this officer's well-documented understanding of racism as structural and institutional and as likely to extend beyond the personal attitudes of one white employee. He recognizes that African Americans will continue to face this treatment in stores and will continue to be bothered by this form of recurring racism.

Another situation in which these respondents frequently encounter white stereotyping in public places occurs while they are driving from one point to another. African Americans often call this the problem of "DWB," that is, "driving while black." One study of citizen self-reports of traffic-stop encounters with police officers found that police officers make traffic stops more frequently for drivers who are black and male. Black and Latino respondents were also more likely than whites to report that a stop was not for a legitimate reason or that the police officer acted improperly.[2] Many of our respondents discuss their knowledge of police policies for stopping black motorists, and, most important, many note that they too have been stopped while driving out of uniform:

> Every time I'd go through there I would get stopped, and the excuse was always "You were speeding a couple miles back down the road; you

mind if I look in your vehicle?" It was, you know, it was the same old line, "Go ahead, look, so I can get on." They looked through, search around and, "All right, I'm not gonna write you a ticket this time; go ahead on." So, you know, I'm not even sure that I may not have been stopped by the same officer several times who didn't recognize that I'm the same person that they're stopping every month or so whenever I got an opportunity to go home. But it was constant.

This form of discrimination becomes a regular part of many black officers' lives. As most other African Americans are, they are forced by everyday realities to recognize the possibility of being stopped and questioned at any point by white officers. As a result, they often have developed an awareness of the steps they must follow in order to control the encounter with a white officer and to prevent it from escalating.

One respondent illustrates that he has rationalized being stopped as almost routine even though he maintains the treatment is unfair:

I have a '86 Chevrolet Capri, which is a highly stolen-type vehicle, usually associated with [drug dealers], but that's not fair to me or any other citizen because, you know, my preference of vehicle is of no evidence to the type person that I am. That's where it's stereotypical thinking that should be done away with. If I were to have anything that would imply that that was my lifestyle, or frequently visit high drug crime areas, something associated with it that would send off extra signals to officers, then I would have no problem with it. But just because I drive that type of vehicle, and I'm a black male, that just doesn't cut it, and that's what I found myself faced with predominantly on weekends after midnight. . . . In three years I would say I've been stopped probably six times with no traffic violation.

Suggesting how commonplace these events are, this respondent calmly discusses what most white people never imagine—the possibility that at any moment, without provocation and without resulting a citation, they could be pulled over and questioned, if not manhandled, by police officers.

Another officer illustrates how white perceptions of black Americans as criminals and their subsequent responses to those perceptions extends beyond shopping or driving to such matters as interrupting recreational activities:

I mean we're just literally at the beach, just talking among ourselves. You know, kids joking and stuff like that. And [two white men] came up thinking that we were selling drugs, that this is why we were there. That happened this past summer.

Misperceptions of criminality are clearly part of the ideological process that legitimizes white repression of African Americans. The respondents suggest that this criminal stereotype plays a role in staff meetings designed to plan departmental policies, as well as in white officers' and civilians' treatment of black citizens during everyday encounters. We see the intrusion of this view even during activities that most white Americans take for granted. Black Americans are constantly reminded of their secondary place in society in such encounters.

DENIGRATION OF BLACK PERSONALITY AND PERSPECTIVES

Stereotyping of black culture and knowledge is not the only form of denigration that African Americans experience at the hands of whites. Drawing on personal experience respondents explain clearly just how whites often attribute certain personality problems and failings to African Americans as a way of legitimizing discriminatory treatment. In this manner, societal problems created by discrimination are directly blamed on the targets of that discrimination, and not on white actions or on the broad processes of white-generated institutional racism. Indeed, racial discrimination is removed as a causative reality, and the perspectives of those who experience racism intensely are routinely dismissed.

Negative Images of Black Officers' Abilities: The White Public

Some of the respondents report that a negative perception of blacks' abilities extends beyond the organizational boundaries of their police agencies and that members of the white public who are not trained police officers treat black officers as though they are incompetent:

You have to deal with the white public thinking that you're not competent enough to handle the call, they almost want to walk you through it to make sure you're doing it right, and make sure you know how to do it. And then you have to deal with the different departments in which you work, and not necessarily my department. I'm talking about the whole, and I know a lot of black officers. And then you have to deal with the department scrutinizing you and wondering, can you and can you not do this or that or the other. So you really, you're almost in a shell by yourself, so to speak.

This officer notes facing underestimation of his abilities at all levels of the agency—by peers, supervisors, and command staff, as well as by citizens. Although well trained, after many years of service as an officer he still routinely encounters challenges to his intellectual and professional abilities.

Significantly, these officers also report skeptical responses when they have attempted to aid white citizens, as in this case:

When I went into some white communities. "Ugh, mom there's a 'nigger' policeman coming up." Is there a problem here? "No, no, no, there's not a problem here." And as soon as I got in my car, there was a call for service at the same address.

Although the white public has become more accustomed to black officers in many towns and cities, the perception of racial difference and an overemphasis on that difference are still encountered by these officers. One officer underscores this point:

There was a disturbance, I got on the property and it was an older white female. The house was an old cracker-barrel-type house, the wood and so forth, had dogs in the yard, and a fence around it. She had a problem with her niece, and it was a personal family thing. And I came and she told me to get off her property. That she needed a real deputy, that I was black, and so on. And she tried to sic her dogs on me. . . . Oh, she was furious. She could not understand that black people had progressed so and could be deputies. And she had the old mentality that black people were below and beneath them.

This type of encounter was reported by several officers, especially those working in rural areas and small towns. It seems natural to white citizens that when they encounter the police, they should encounter white officers.

Some African-American officers report that better-off whites sometimes have the tendency to treat them as servants. One notes, "In their eyes, all black people still are lesser than white people are, and I have been told by people to go to the back door before!" Such overtly racist reactions instill in African-American officers an understanding that they are not regarded merely as police officers, but as police officers who are *black*. A deputy chief suggests that this form of racism is prevalent, yet so subtle that often only those who have experienced it can understand it:

> It's been my experience that if I'm with a white officer, and somebody comes up to ask assistance, if it's a white person, they go to the white officer. They automatically go to the white officer. If it's a black person, they tend to go either way unless it's a black person who does not like whites. But the average black person, they'll approach the first police officer they can get to. But invariably in dealing with whites, what I have observed, and I observe it now as a deputy chief—I'm in situations where I was in charge of patrol operations bureau . . . and it's the largest bureau in the department. I had 4 captains reporting to me, I had 11 lieutenants reporting to me, I had about 24 sergeants reporting to me and 280-plus police officers that I was responsible for. So I would go out when things were happening of significance, you know, a robbery or something like that, and I would see people defer to people of lesser rank if I'm standing there next to a white person and again, I'm saying part of that is people not identifying the rank structure, but generally speaking when you're dealing with whites, they tend to do that.

This practice of assuming that whites are in the superior position has been reported in other studies of middle-class African Americans, such as those who work in corporate settings.[3] For many whites, blackness is linked to notions of inferiority, and for that reason many black officers are treated, subtly or overtly, as if they are less able to perform their jobs than lower-ranking whites. Despite repeated attempts to evaluate and understand other factors involved in the behavior of white people—such as in the mention of rank structure described in the preceding interview—many respondents conclude that racism is the persistent and determining factor. A female respondent explains how racial characteristics often supersede gender in the white public's overemphasizing of racial differences:

> Two of us go up on a call. And you're white. The call's mine; I get there first. They're going to come right past me and talk to you. . . . What they'll do, though, say if it's two females, they'll go to her, invariably go to her, every time.

Another female officer discusses a more complex interaction of racial and gender characteristics in creating perceptions of difference. Traditional notions of policing as a male occupation foster an overemphasis on differences between male and female officers despite research that shows that female officers perform as well as or better than their male counterparts in policing. Combined with white constructs of black inferiority, male notions of women as inferior have the effect of maintaining low numbers of black women officers or blocking their advancement through the policing ranks:

> In general, if they have to choose working with somebody black, they're going to choose a black male. Oh sure, over a black female. I always tell people that I'm the scum of the Earth as far as the world is concerned. I'm not only female; I'm a black female.

Black female officers note that negative treatment at the hands of white (and occasionally a few black) male officers is detrimental to the formation of a positive sense of self-worth. Both they and black male respondents discuss feeling that they have to perform their duties at a level above that of white male officers in order to receive full recognition of their competency and their superior achievements.

Allegations of Personal Unreliability and Inferiority

Common white stereotypes include the notion that African Americans are incapable of intellectual advancement and that they have a weak work ethic and a weak drive to succeed. Whites often view the failure of black Americans as proof of the inferiority of their personal and community values. In contrast, whites often view the success of some black Americans not as a sign of their intellectual prowess but as as exception or as evidence of favoritism through affirmative action. From this white perspective, there is no serious antiblack discrimination left in society.

Half of the respondents discuss the tendency of whites to overemphasize differences in people based on their racial characteristics. Their experience is that whites often react to black officers with a "Who are you?" response, as though these whites have a hard time understanding how blacks can occupy positions of such responsibility. When black officers first entered policing in significant numbers during the 1970s, they frequently encountered white officers who refused to acknowledge that blacks could and should be police officers:

> Well, [white] officers didn't want to go. They canceled you on the calls when you were going to assist them or something. They'd cancel you before you'd get there and they would never meet with you, and that sort of thing, and yea, those were some eye-opening moments.

Rather than accept important support from a fellow officer, white officers would act as if the black officers did not exist. Male respondents report this form of discrimination occurring in the 1960s and 1970s; female respondents discuss similar experiences occurring well into the 1980s.

Commenting on the contemporary situation, nearly half the respondents mentioned some form of white underestimation of black abilities. For example, one officer discusses why a former boss decided to hire him:

> See that's still judging of a black person [pause]. A manager there, he gave me a job and I worked there for a while, and I did good and everything. And later on I found out that he gave me the job because he wanted to prove to the owner that he could train a black person to sell $300 shoes and $1,500 suits. That was the only reason he hired me.

The perception of black Americans as not competent to perform required tasks, as here in the case of a clothing salesperson, is further manifested in the occupation of policing. One respondent laments, "There were a lot of guys that were great police officers, black guys. Man, this department really overlooked their ability." Black officers are often not recognized as capable or smart enough to fill sergeant or command slots.

Discussing their police department in the past and in the present, numerous officers explain that whites there periodically view them as unreliable in job performance. For example, one officer discussed the general distrust of black officers that was common in the 1970s in spite of his, and other black officers', high level of everyday performance:

> I've actually testified in front of the U.S. Senate twice as a crack cocaine and illegal alien expert and worked narcotics for 12 years and have been renowned nationally with some of the techniques that I use. But because they didn't want me—at that particular time in the seventies, blacks weren't trusted with the money, with the dope—I was denied the position of narcotics detective.

In this period of overt, often hostile treatment of African-American officers, they were perceived as not being reliable enough to be trusted with
cash or drugs in the performance of their job. This perception legitimized exclusion from promotions. Although this officer's agency eventually relaxed such restrictions, another explains how the white
perception of black officers still has negative effects:

> I tried to push for more African-American training officers. And the
> response that I was given was that they were questioned. [But the whites]
> thought they were playing favorites. I'd be lying if I told you that there
> were not two standards at this department. For blacks, you're either
> excellent, or you're no good; nothing in between. For whites you're
> either no good, you're OK, or you're excellent. You know, unless you're
> one of those African Americans that's outstanding, that's above reproach,
> you get shafted.

White training officers can significantly limit the number of black officers
in law enforcement agencies. This officer discusses how a white image of
black training officers as incapable of impartiality serves to legitimize
blacks' exclusion from these important training positions. Questioning
the integrity of black officers in this manner legitimizes white perceptions
of African Americans as inferior. Note too the insightful point that whites
tend to place black employees into just two categories, as not good or as
excellent, and do not recognize that large category of average performers
that they do recognize for whites. Mediocrity is probably the norm for
many if not most employees in most institutions, yet it appears that it is
only when black employees are average, or mediocre, that average performance becomes a much-noted issue in workplaces.

Assessing the contemporary situation in their departments, numerous officers assess white stereotyping about black officers' abilities and
achievements. These stereotypes can have a serious impact on their
career advancement. For example, white decisions not to place black
officers in specialized assignments are often justified by stereotyped
conceptions, subtle or blatant, of black intellectual inferiority. One officer notes the problem of stereotyping in assignments:

> There may be a misconception or perception that blacks may not be
> doing as well and may not be qualified to do certain things; that's a per-
> ception out there. . . . I've experienced it, where I felt that individuals
> had a different set of goals. Supervisors came to me and provided me

with the information, and told me, "This is what you need to do." In other words, that made me feel like they were trying to make it appear that I was incompetent.

For black women officers, underestimation can be a function of both racism and sexism. For example, one officer comments, "In general, if you come on this department, I have told females—and I may be wrong in my perception of things—but they don't particularly want you here anyway, because you're black. Because they feel you're not qualified." Because policing has traditionally been a male-dominated occupation, many male officers and supervisors regard women as not capable or not physically and emotionally strong enough to do the job.

Working Harder to Disprove Stereotypes

Underestimation of abilities means that both black women and black men must often work harder than whites in comparable roles to prove their abilities. Elaborating on sexism in the police academy, one female officer notes the extra striving required:

> For women it's harder, because you're there with all those men and men never want to admit that women are just as good as they are. So you have to strive just that much harder to do as good, if not better than, you know, the men that you're, you're going to the academy with.

Women officers report facing notions that, as women, they are inherently less capable than their male counterparts. This means not only that women officers feel they have to prove themselves but also that a few women press too hard and try to perform their occupational functions as if they are aggressive men. One female officer discusses what she sees a few women do in her agency:

> You have the small woman effect. You've got that female that whether she's black or white, she's always got to prove something. And she escalates the situation wherever she goes because she's so busy trying to prove to the males that she can handle the job. And she's going to get somebody killed, or herself.

Most respondents have concluded that they have to be better at their job than whites. Many make comments like this officer's: "As black police officers you have to be twice as knowledgeable about the job in order to get the same recognition." White constructions of black intellectual inferiority and incompetence are so frequently encountered by these officers that they begin to see that many whites expect them to fail or at least to perform a task poorly. This is likely linked to a very old stereotype of African Americans, which goes back to the days of slavery, as not competent to do historically white jobs.

Being successful means much more than just doing one's job competently, for it also requires overcoming notions that black employees are incapable, as another officer explains:

> We would have to be more professional. We have to make sure that we conduct ourselves—I would say that we would—we would have to carry ourselves in a different way. We're being watched as not only an officer, but as black officers. We have to show that we can be professional, we can do the job, and that we're not as maybe uneducated as people think we are.

Beginning from a position in which they realize that they are regarded as incapable forces respondents to work harder to prove that they personally are competent. One officer sums it up this way: "Black officers give that second effort. They expect you to give 110 percent while white officers can only give 50 percent and get as much credit as you for his 50 percent as you do for your 110 percent. It's that way." Frequently viewed as less able by white officers and supervisors, these black officers feel that they are often scrutinized more than whites and that more is expected of them. As a result, they also feel a constant need to push themselves to meet high goals that they know they may never meet.

As rank-and-file officers do, black supervisors also experience being regarded as less competent than white subordinates or counterparts. Respondents such as the following officer give numerous examples of how whites indicate that black officers are not deserving of positions they hold:

> That's the slave mentality that I got to prove myself to white folks. I know, like it's again I said before when I got my job as a lieutenant, I knew that I was qualified, OK? Now I knew that I qualified. Now do I have to go spend my time to go try to prove myself to the majority of the white guys who think I got the job only because of affirmative action? Admittedly, common sense tells me affirmative action was a, was a cata-

lyst behind me getting the job, but nonetheless I'm qualified. Now does that mean I got to spend the rest of my tenure as a lieutenant trying to prove to all these other people that I'm qualified?

Note the white interpretations that constantly recreate a relational hierarchy of ability in which "white" is perceived as superior to "black." These officers understand that they must continually prove themselves to white officers, to members of the communities they police, and, ultimately, to themselves.

However, although this form of racial stereotyping is directed at all African Americans, these officers maintain that they face added responsibility. The actions of one black officer are often seen by whites as a reflection on all black officers, if not on all black Americans:

> But you know, [I] make a mistake, now you may make the same mistake, but for some reason my mistake carries a great deal of weight as opposed to [yours. It's] a racial and social statement. If you make a mistake, it's just you making a mistake. There's no aspersion on the rest of white society; it's just you making a mistake; you're just a dumb white who made a mistake, you know. I make a mistake and all of a sudden all black people are called into question because I made a mistake or, because I'm stupid, you know. And that's crazy; that's crazy.

These black officers reveal an awareness of their treatment as being distinct from that of white officers in similar circumstances. For that reason, they must have a constant awareness and self-surveillance that white (male) officers generally are not required to have. The awareness of this white perception of African Americans and the consequent scrutiny that they receive because of it add pressure and stress to their occupational role:

> If a person of another race, primarily a white, had moved up at the same rate that I had and then made a mistake, that's not going to affect the rest of the whites that might be promoted. However, if I, a minority, having moved up as quickly as I have moved up, make a mistake or do something that's improper, it could taint any other blacks or minorities that might have that opportunity in the future.

Our respondents' insightful discussions show that they conceive of underestimation as a shared racial experience, which is usually more than just a matter of their treatment by a few individual whites. It is a rather widely held ideological construction that serves to justify the limits placed on black participation in many aspects of U.S. society and is used to justify the primary position of white people in the racial hierarchy. For example, one respondent illustrates how the underestimation of black Americans is historically related to the overestimation of white Americans. He provides an example in which, during a meeting to decide who should be hired, his boss maintained that a white seventeen-year-old store clerk was comparable to a black man with military experience and four years of college. He felt frustrated by this meeting and concludes, "Just because you're white doesn't mean that you are qualified." Rare, indeed, is a meeting that is held to discuss or debate the lack of "qualified white applicants" for positions in an organization.

Civilians also question black officers' abilities. As do black Americans in other interview research studies, these respondents point to white assumptions of unreliability and inferiority outside their own workplace.[4] For example, one respondent discusses her treatment while she was purchasing a home:

> I had no problem out of the loan company whatsoever getting the loan. . . . When I went to closing, an attorney made a statement to me that I would never forget. He stated, "If you miss your monthly payments, I get to make your life miserable." And I thought that was extremely unprofessional.

Without warning, African Americans often face comments from whites that incorporate images of blacks' being untrustworthy. Because these encounters are commonplace, African Americans regard such comments not as flippant statements made in jest but as commentaries signaling the negative conceptions that whites, on some level, hold of black Americans. These respondents, and their family members, hear such comments repeatedly, and for that reason they often remember them and the meanings attached. When African Americans protest such comments, uninformed and inexperienced whites tend to regard their reactions as overly sensitive or even paranoid.

WHITES' QUESTIONING RACISM AND AFRICAN AMERICANS

In addition to the array of blatant and subtle stereotypes and prejudices directed at these black officers, they must sometimes endure a certain distancing and detachment response that whites often use in interaction. Several respondents discuss the form of personal detachment from history that some white officers engage in as they try to demonstrate that they have no responsibility for the country's racism. One officer summarizes comments frequently made by white officers during multicultural training sessions:

> You know, if a person says, "Well I wasn't here 200 years ago; I never owned any slaves; why do I have to suffer?" Good question, you know, because the slavery was 200 years ago. As I said, in my lifetime, I can still remember . . . separate and not equal. And because of the sins of the past, we are attempting to get to the level where we should have been, or could have been, had it not been for the sins of the past. And unfortunately, no, you were not living in that time, your daddy didn't own any slaves, but my grandparents, my great grand's and great-great-grand's, just happened to have been slaves. That philosophy, no, I might not have been a part of it, but believe me, it's been passed down to me.

She then explains from a sociological perspective what the long-term costs of earlier oppression are for African Americans like her:

> When I look back in my history, I can't see many professionals. You can. You know, where are my mentors? They were somebody's slaves because they weren't given the opportunities. That's why . . . we have been the underprivileged. We didn't ask for it; we didn't ask to come here; we were minding our own business. You can't just wave a wand and say, "Okay, no more racism," and believe that because the laws have changed, suddenly everything's going to be okay. I mean, you know, it'd be nice, but it just doesn't happen that way.

African Americans like this woman have learned from contact with the everyday reality of racism that it has a history and a long-term and ongoing impact. Her comments indicate that most whites are able to detach themselves from a role in racial injustice, as by arguing that the injustice is rooted in some apparently distant past. Yet, slavery actually ended less than 140 years before these whites made such comments. As this respondent suggests, most whites making such arguments conveniently ignore the material benefits that they and other whites have accrued over generations from repeated racial discrimination and other racial oppression. The lasting effects of racial oppression are seen in the denial of educational and occupational opportunities to some thirteen generations of African Americans. Historically, this unjust enrichment of whites, and the consequent unjust impoverishment of blacks, created an entrenched racial hierarchy that is difficult to overcome because of white resistance to surrendering ill-gotten gains. As African Americans pass down knowledge of the operation of racism from one generation to the next, white Americans pass down the fiction of racial superiority and the myth that their societal position is solely the result of hard work—and is not linked to past and present oppression.

In addition, whites, as we see throughout the chapters of this book, often see the contemporary racial situation in the same distancing way. As the dominant racial group, whites do not face institutionalized racism and thus are able to detach themselves from its everyday realities. Shared understandings of the world from a dominant perspective become the norm, making it very difficult for the white majority to see the world from the viewpoint of those who are continually reminded of their color and subordinate position. Indeed, whites develop "sincere fictions," mythological understandings, through which they interpret what they view as whites' positive role in racial relations.[5] Most downplay or ignore the realities of everyday racism. To the extent that whites are able to detach themselves from this racist reality, they do not see themselves as responsible for the barriers and impoverishment experienced by African Americans.

We should add one final point here. Yet another manifestation of detachment noted by these respondents can be seen in the emphasis many whites place on being unable to "understand black people." Consequently, many whites expect black coworkers, such as the respondents, to be the interpreters of the behavior of yet other blacks, to be "spokespersons for the race." As one African-American officer notes, these whites "assume that all black people think alike, but that's not the way it is." Indifference to black experiences and barriers results in whites' treating blacks such as this officer as "spokespersons for the race":

> As an example, someone will come up to me and say, "Why do blacks do this?" Okay, and I am not an expert on blacks. I'm an expert on [me] and I happen to be black and I'll tell you what I do or the blacks that I know do or what their opinions are that they've expressed, but I'm not expert on being black.

Exaggerating the differences between black and white Americans and maintaining that the two groups cannot understand each other help to legitimize the color hierarchy in which whites are defined as normative.

CONCLUSION

> I'm riding with another guy, a white male, and he was closer to my age, but he had been on the police department, you know, six years at that time. And we're passing by an apartment complex, and I'm sitting in the passenger side of the car. This guy's driving the car, and he looks over at these people. We passed some black people who were out in the yard of this apartment, and he goes, just out of the blue, he goes, "Now, those people there, I would consider them 'niggers.'" I said to him, "What are you talking about?" He goes, he didn't think that I would even take exception to it. "Well, you know, guys like you and these other guys on the police department," and he named some people in the community, "I don't consider them that way, but people like that, drinking and all, I would consider them 'niggers.'" I said, "Let me tell you something." I said, "I'm a black person," and I said, "I don't need you or anybody to tell me what you think a 'nigger' is." I said, "Now if you think that they're 'niggers,' that's fine. But as long as we're riding around in this car, I'm not getting into that." He goes, "Okay man, okay." But he took it like it was not a big deal.

The accounts from experience presented in these officers' interviews show that many white attitudes and images problematize and denigrate African Americans. In so doing, they generally operate to produce and reproduce an ideological climate that fosters discrimination and the continuation of racial injustice in the United States.[6] The African-American officers' knowledge of everyday racism in the United States, and more specifically of racism in policing, allows them to understand well the role of racist ideology in reproducing a hierarchy in which African Americans are defined as inferior. This ideology rationalizes the exclusion of African Americans from many societal rewards and legitimizes the discriminatory practices that exclude them.

For white Americans, the attribution of biological, personality, and cultural shortcomings as the explanation for African Americans' secondary status in society links closely to the notion that racism is no longer a significant causative factor in maintaining this condition. These discussions reinforce themes discussed by the respondents in previous chapters. Racism is usually discussed as societal, not as the actions of a few individual whites. Outside the relative protection of the occupational setting, the black women and men frequently encounter overt forms of everyday racism. These respondents constantly illustrate our earlier point that racist encounters are remembered and shared among black people, whereas whites often dismiss such encounters' importance or forget them. A great deal of pressure and stress result from an understanding of the necessity to excel in tasks in which most whites hope they will fail.

4.

Racial Barriers in
Police Departments

White stereotypes that problematize and denigrate African Americans often lead to discriminatory actions. In this chapter and the next, we examine an array of specific discriminatory barriers as these African-American law enforcement officers regularly experience them. The various forms of blatant, subtle, and covert discrimination in the workplace reflect and reinforce the persisting racial hierarchy common in historically white institutions. Although in recent decades some societal and institutional changes have permitted some advancement for many African Americans, most still encounter significant racial barriers that indicate that they are stereotyped and unwanted by many whites in both historically white workplaces and other important societal settings.[1]

Very few previous research studies have paid any serious attention to the discrimination that African-American officers face in the workplace. One rare example is the recent analysis by Samuel Walker and his colleagues, who note briefly that black officers experience employment discrimination in three areas: recruitment, promotion, and assignments.[2] The black officers whom we interviewed discuss these areas of discrimination in great detail, as well as numerous other areas where they face discrimination in their workplace. Generally speaking, they discuss the various methods by which white officers and civilians seek to marginalize them or exclude them from sharing in the rewards and benefits of the workplace, as well as from participating fully in the larger society. Reflecting on the difficult occupation of law enforcement officer, these black women and men discuss or allude to racial barriers they encounter more or less *daily* in their agencies. Reflecting on contemporary experiences, these talented and articulate officers explain how many racial barriers remain blatant and intentional, while others are more subtle, and even unconscious or unintentional. Many white Americans do not see these barriers; often they view them as illusory or as part of the natural order of things. In contrast, African Americans can see the true nature of these racial obstacles because of long-term experience with racism and because of the shared knowledge they have garnered, typically over many years, from family and friends.

WHITE NETWORKING IN THE WORKPLACE

The persisting and damaging system of racial segregation in housing, employment, and other major institutions was created by whites from the first decades of European settlement in North America. For nearly four hundred years now, this segregation and separation have had many serious consequences, not the least of which is the fostering of important networks with which and along which whites pass critical information about employment and other important issues, exchange critical resources, make important decisions, and provide social support for one another. As we have documented in chapters 2 and 3, when they move into historically white workplaces, black Americans have usually found entrenched old-boy or buddy networks, fully operational and generative of an array of racial prejudice and discrimination. These white-centered networks in turn generate black resistance in the form of counter-networks and organizations, an issue to which we return in chapter 6.

Research on U.S. workplaces shows that the informal networks of existing employees determine much of workplace operation on a day-to-day basis.[3] When one analyzes workplaces like those of law enforcement agencies in which our respondents work, it is important to attend to the operation and impact of the old-boy networks. These are the social contexts within which much negative stereotyping and many discriminatory actions are generated, tested, and reinforced. Historically, police officers have created within their law enforcement agencies strong informal groups with a distinctive police subculture, the famous "blue curtain." In most contemporary police departments, whites control the dominant informal groups and culture, a culture often entailing an "us" versus "them" view of the world, substantial isolation from civilians off duty, a tough-male crime-fighter image, and a strong loyalty to fellow officers. Given that most white officers were raised in, and now live in, more or less segregated residential areas, it is not surprising that many have learned the usual antiblack and related stereotypes from family or friends and have had little or no sustained equal-status contact with African Americans or other Americans of color, especially outside the workplace. In addition, because they often deal in their work with street criminals, often disproportionately members of groups of color, these negative encounters seem to harden rather than to challenge their stereotypical views. Today, as we see in the reports of these black officers in earlier chapters, many white officers still hold to negative views of African Americans and other Americans of color, which make it very difficult for black officers to do their job, to get promoted, and thus to integrate fully in today's police agencies.

Several earlier studies have examined the isolated situations, other discrimination, and stress that black officers face in white-dominated departments and police cultures. One 1970s survey of black officers in Washington, D.C., found that most rarely socialized with white officers, and two-thirds reported that as a result of their experiences they trusted few or no white officers. Black officers reported being isolated by the white officers and discriminated against in many areas, including hiring, assignments, evaluations, rewards, and discipline.[4] In 1997, another researcher interviewed several dozen black and Asian officers in England and concluded that there were strong pressures, stemming from the police occupational culture, on officers of color to conform to white-determined racial categories that inform relationships within police contexts and with the general public. These categories maintain a hierarchy in which white, black, and Asian officers understand their "place." Because the discrimination and pressure to conform are considerable, many officers of color in England and in the United States develop strategies of resistance, which include humor, group organization, and lawsuits.[5]

The "blue culture" is usually very strong and thereby creates a pressurized environment where conformity to the white-determined informal norms is highly valued. In the process of adaptation, many black officers conform to the informal norms of this occupational culture. Their lower occupational status, coupled with a desire to maintain a positive self-image as a good professional officer, can lead them to the conforming view "Blue is blue."[6] Yet the degree of conformity varies greatly among black officers, and most manage to maintain some independence in thought and action. Indeed, research studies in the 1990s cited former black officers' reports that extended police training pressures the new and young black officers to conform to the white-normed traditional police role in order to receive good evaluations. Thus, highly conforming black officers guard their position from other black officers and often hold back on critiques of discriminatory white officers and department policies.[7] In this way, racial oppression is translated so that it also affects some interpersonal relationships even among black officers themselves.

Old Boy Networking in Law Enforcement Agencies

Our respondents note in various ways how they are greatly affected by the orientations and actions of whites who form informal groups and networks. Their experiences with the old-boy and buddy networks often involve racial hostility or discrimination. These informal workplace groups and networks facilitate favoritism for white employees and discrimination against black employees. Such support networks have been especially important in historically white agencies in the Sunbelt, as one officer makes clear:

> This is still the South, and blacks have a certain place. And the white
> establishment wants to keep those blacks in their place. And they do that
> by enacting certain policies that keep the good old boys in the system
> and keep the people that are a threat to them out of the system. So. And
> they're doing it quite effectively.

This comment echoes similar reports in many of the interviews. Despite their strong desire to advance, and tangible transformations in the general nature of racism that they have catalyzed and witnessed over two or so decades, these women and men frequently note that major racial barriers still exist because of entrenched networks and traditional white-normed ways of interacting, hiring, and promoting. These obstacles often restrict blacks' entry into policing as well as their advancement once they have entered.

The continuing physical separation of racial groups promotes racialized behavior that is often not seen as such by the whites engaged in it. Thus, most whites in agencies seem to prefer to interact with one another and thereby to exclude those who have relatively recently entered their institutions. In this white viewpoint, their actions seem right, natural, and comfortable despite their isolating and marginalizing consequences for most black Americans. One savvy officer points out the recurring and interactive social matrix that is commonly involved:

> Because it can cost you in the pocket, it is not so up front. It is very sub-tly done, subliminal. For example in this department, the [white] chief of police makes all decisions concerning hiring and promotions. We'd like to think that we have some input in these decisions, but the fact of the matter is that they're his decisions. He's not going to make a lot of changes, because with changes often come problems and resentment. He wants to do his job without a lot of problems and go on to the next job. The [white] mayor, who appoints the chief of police, is going to appoint somebody that she is real familiar with, and that she can identify with, that is most like her in the ways that they think and idealize alike. And that means if you are very different than she is, then she doesn't really understand you. . . . She doesn't know the African-American deputy chief. You know, he doesn't get invited to her house, his kids don't go to school with her kids; they don't work together. With the exception of a few community events, they really don't get to understand what we do for the organization over here.

The social segregation of U.S. society pervades not only the political and policing institutions but also the informal socializing connected with workplaces. Despite the best intentions of some white leaders and officers to improve their department, they frequently reproduce general patterns of segregation to the extent that they themselves are separated from, and unable to get to know on a sustained basis, local black citizens. Afforded protection from the reality of racism by their segregated residential life, they may choose to act as if black Americans do not exist.

Maintaining Social Segregation

To most whites, segregated socializing and in-grouping probably seem normal. Yet they are rooted deeply in age-old patterns of informal seg-regation in housing, education, and workplaces. Oddly enough, in spite of much evidence to the contrary, a majority of whites seem to feel that the 1960s civil rights movement and legislation eliminated the last ves-tiges of serious discrimination in these areas. Our respondents, how-ever, well know that this is not the case and cite much evidence from their experiences with continuing racial mistreatment and segregation, in the past and in the present. Some note the continuing lack of integration of residential communities, as in the case of this officer:

> I also tried to buy a house off [ABC] Boulevard, and they talked to me over the phone, and for whatever reason did not pick up on the fact that I was black. But when I showed up in the neighborhood, the picture changed. That willing salesman said, "You know, as much as I'd like to, you know, I'd be blockbusting my neighbors, and I'd hate for you to come home one night, and something has happened to your family." . . . I said, "I'll be damned. I want to buy a house, and someone's going to make subtle threats. So if I have to go through all that, I'll take my down payment back, you keep your house." . . . So, I bought in a black neighborhood.

Today, African Americans still face much overt discrimination in renting or buying housing, one of the most fundamental of family needs. Not surprisingly, such experiences add to the fund of knowledge about racism, and they are accurate readings because of the researchlike comparison often at hand—as here, the dramatic difference in treatment over the phone, in which blacks are acceptable if they sound "white," versus the openly discriminatory treatment in person. Notice too how dominant group members work hard to keep African Americans in restricted places, such as segregated housing areas where it is more difficult to build up the large housing equity, the family wealth, that whites have used for advancement over the generations. In such cases, an enforcer of the law has no effective laws on which to depend to prevent whites from threatening the life situation of his family.

Another officer notes some of the consequences of this (mostly) white-enforced segregation in U.S. society:

> When you look at 1997, you still have a great deal of African Americans living in, I wouldn't say segregated neighborhoods, but you would say that they are living in neighborhoods that are not greatly interracial, okay. So you still have a sort of culture; and it's the same with a lot of your white communities . . . you just look at where your population lives. You'll find that we are still not a totally racially integrated community.

For most African Americans, the still substantial housing and other physical separations are not of their own choosing. Our respondents generally agree that distinctive perspectives sometimes result from this separation and segregation, perspectives that can reduce the ability of both groups to understand each other. This lack of understanding is usually most stereotyped and abstract for white Americans, because on the average they are much more isolated from African Americans during the course of daily life, than most African Americans are from whites. Because they are a statistical minority of the population most African Americans have many contacts with white Americans in the course of their daily or weekly rounds.

Ideological conceptions of differences among whites remain difficult to overcome when whites lack direct contact and experiences with black Americans, especially equal-status contacts. These experiences could help whites identify and overcome the contradictions inherent in their stereotypically racist notions. Some officers comment on the segregation of religious organizations in America and what this says about the society. In contrast to their professed messages of love and brotherhood, many whites have maintained very segregated religious institutions that serve to perpetuate and reinforce the racial division in society. One officer underscores this point:

> America's still a very segregated society, you know. Look in the churches. The churches are still very primarily segregated. The social clubs are still segregated. There's a little bit of seeds of diversity, but we are still a segregated society. And because of that there's still misconceptions and misunderstandings of each other.

Another perceptive officer adds that black and white people are

> quite different and . . . in numerous situations, quite segregated. Probably the most predominant barometer will be on Sundays when you look up and you see who's at your church. They're still predominant—and although there are a lot of blacks that live in upper-middle-income, white, predominantly white neighborhoods, they go back to the black churches on Sundays. . . . I quote from a Zen acknowledgment that people are the summation of their life's experiences . . . so if you're unfortunate to be caught up into a little vacuum, then you are what that vacuum is.

As patterns of segregation in housing, in churches, and in most formal and informal groupings are persistent, the white racist ideology flourishes and whites acting on this ideology continually reproduce patterns of segregation through their quotidian actions.

Given residential and social segregation, and the isolation of most whites from sustained equal-status contacts with black Americans, it is not surprising that black employees face stereotyping and discrimination within their workplace. In an earlier chapter we cited data that demonstrate how widespread discrimination is in U.S. workplaces. Now we can turn to the accounts of our respondents about specific racial barriers they confront and counter within law enforcement workplaces.

RACIAL BARRIERS: RECRUITMENT AND HIRING

The civil rights movement of the 1960s had a great impact on racial hostility and discrimination in police agencies. For example, numerous respondents, in assessing their agencies, cite the impact and importance of equal employment opportunity guidelines and goals. These provide a standard against which officers can judge how much marginalization and exclusion remain as workaday problems. Most are aware of, and in agreement with, the view that police agencies should reflect and be representative of the local population. They frequently discuss the representation of black officers in their law enforcement agency in terms similar to those in this comment:

> [The] African-American population in this town is about 28 percent, depends on who you talk to. It would just behoove the department, it would behoove the community, to be reflected. So you wouldn't want to have a department with 50 percent blacks, nor would you want to have a department with 4 percent.

To the extent that departments are not representative, these officers argue, racial hostility and discrimination are still factors that routinely operate to set limits on the number of African-American officers.

Not Actively Seeking Black Recruits

Half the respondents discuss the countless ways in which continuing racism impacts the ability of police agencies to recruit members of the black community to serve as officers. Some discuss the oppression of black communities by police agencies and the knowledge that black people accumulate about their relationships to police. One officer notes the problem of the traditional lack of recruitment of black officers:

A police department is not a profession that African Americans have beat the door down to get into. Now, but if any city is committed to hiring African Americans, you go get them. And the reason that I think African Americans don't beat the door down in police departments is because when they grew up in their underprivileged neighborhoods, the only time they saw the police [was] when they came in to arrest their mother, their father, their brother, their sister, their grandmother. All of their experiences, or at least most of them, have been on negative terms. So they were never going to beat the door down at the police department. But you go get them. I think most of the very successful blacks on this department, the department went out and got.

As with most historically white occupations, active recruitment is essential to desegregate police forces, and in this process black communities have to be convinced that the local white authorities are serious about changing the racial discrimination long embedded in local police institutions. Indeed, "affirmative action" often works best in opening up recruitment networks to Americans of color, networks that were traditionally white. All these respondents understand that, historically and in the present, African Americans have been severely abused—even lynched and killed in the not too distant past—by white officers in southern police agencies. They are aware that for this reason policing is not generally an occupation that most African Americans have been eager to pursue.

Numerous respondents indicate that the persistent ideology of racism within police agencies often impacts whites' willingness to recruit blacks as well as their ability to do so successfully. Agencies have representative numbers of black officers only to the extent that they design appropriate recruiting strategies to attract them and provide career paths with advancement. These respondents suggest that recruitment strategies must include input of black officers to improve recruitment strategies. However, there are still relatively few African-American officers in most police departments in positions central to recruiting efforts, as one respondent indicates:

They didn't use black policemen to recruit black police officers, so they wasn't getting any. Because . . . nobody that he relates to can tell him about the police department. They know that there's not a whole lot of blacks down there and there has to be a reason for that, okay. It's just common sense, if I have a choice, that I'm not going where I'm [scared] of the way that I may be treated.

Low numbers of black officers in general, and in specialized positions, perpetuate the impression in black communities that police agencies are still very discriminatory. The lack of representative numbers of African-American officers now will make it difficult to attract representative numbers in the future, as potential recruits perceive that they are not wanted.

Members of black communities share information about continuing racist practices in local police agencies, information that contributes to the view that policing is not an attractive occupation. If potential recruits perceive training in agencies as still unfair, they are unlikely to pursue policing as an occupation. One officer discusses community awareness of unfair practices:

> I was in a meeting about . . . two months ago, for the concern with where are the African-American police officers? Why, you look all over the state, there's none. . . . It's really hard to get somebody in [this city] because we're getting a bad reputation in training. I mean, we can train, but we're getting a bad reputation [in the community] when it comes to African-American officers being trained.

Developing police agencies representative of the general population is an ongoing struggle. The goal of increasing the number of black recruits often clashes with realities that create social contradictions that agencies must overcome to achieve a reasonably representative police force.

Other Hiring Barriers

Even when law enforcement agencies intentionally recruit black candidates, racist practices can operate to make sure that most are not hired. The majority of the respondents enumerate various hiring barriers in their organization. One respondent describes how the complex nature of police administration operates:

> The sheriff goes out and he says, "Well, you know, we want to do this minority recruiting and hiring." And I really believe him because I'm on the recruitment board and the hiring board as well. But then you have those people in between him and me. They make sure that person that I may have gone out there and recruited doesn't make it. They have a weed-out system in between. He doesn't pay enough attention to that to realize that, hey, there's a problem. I know he's busy, and has a lot of

other things, but that also comes with understanding and sensitivity that people will betray you and people are racist and discriminatory and will discriminate regardless.

Despite the best intentions of some department chiefs and some recruiters, prejudiced managers below them still have the ability to limit or prevent the hiring of black recruits. This is an example of *institutional racism,* for it is the bureaucratic structure here that restricts a concerned chief administrator. Because of the way that most departments are organized, black officers and other members of black communities usually lack the proof of where and how this weeding out of black recruits takes place within that bureaucratic structure.

For that reason, black officers typically rely on their experience and the use of comparisons to evaluate whether racial hostility and discrimination are factors in managerial decisions not to hire black applicants. One officer discusses cases that he has concluded were discriminatory:

> African-American guys that I had known that were brilliant, none of them could pass the entrance exam. . . . I thought that don't sound right. I knew a guy that went to the Air Force Academy and became a fighter pilot, and he went and took the exam, and he flunked it. And I knew some [white] boys that passed it, and I thought there's something wrong here, buddy!

To the extent that discretionary options are in place, which allow subjective interpretations of white managers to determine whether black recruits are hired, the stereotyping of these managers can impact routine decisions. African-American officers have sometimes sued and successfully challenged such practices, but often the corrective solutions still allow substantial subjective input by white managers in hiring.

For example, one respondent discusses how polygraph tests have been unfairly used to check the background and habits of new recruits:

> The person that does the polygraphs is friends with the chief and the deputy chief. We would have officers come from another police department, and they would fail our polygraph, go someplace else, and pass the polygraph and get hired. And we're not hiring any black police officers because they couldn't pass the test, they said. Most of them would pass the test. Most of the black Americans that we were getting in, that we were actually going out and recruiting, had degrees. So they couldn't say

that they couldn't pass the test anymore. They were weeding them out in the polygraph. So, but they would go to another police department and get hired.

According to this account, white managers in some departments fudge polygraph results to exclude black applicants who easily pass polygraph tests in other departments. As long as whites with prejudiced views of African Americans are in positions of authority and decision making that involve subjective input, they will be able to screen out many black applicants. Many of these officers describe a perpetual struggle to overcome discrimination in the recruiting and hiring practices of law enforcement agencies. Often, once a policy or program is determined to be racist and dismantled, new policies and programs that still allow racist attitudes of white managers to have an impact on the ability of agencies to recruit and hire black women and men are developed.

Educational and Other Barriers in Recruitment

Other factors, such as level of education and a record of minor criminal offenses, are also cited by these respondents as contributing to lower numbers of black recruits in some communities. The area of education illustrates some of the racialized problems in recruiting:

> It's hurting us because a lot of minorities cannot afford to go to college and get a two-year degree. And if they do, you know, law enforcement is not something that a lot of them want to do if you get a two-year degree. I mean, if you go to college and get a degree for something, from an African-American standpoint of it, why would you want to go up to be a law enforcement officer?

Being in a racially subordinate position in society means fewer financial resources with which to pay for a college education, and those without some college education are usually not eligible today for police jobs. Yet, those African Americans who have a college education generally wish to pursue an occupation with greater rewards and less stigma or danger. Nonetheless, one interviewee discusses how he was able to develop successful strategies to recruit black officers:

When I went to the recruiting section [we had] a total of twenty-seven blacks in 1987. I felt lonely in the department. When I left after three years, we had 107. They told me it couldn't be done. . . . Straight "A" black students on campus do not want to be cops. . . . I got "C" students. You don't need to be a Rhodes Scholar to be a cop; you just have to have good common sense. They went up here, and when they went to these colleges, they didn't bother with these people. And in essence what they were saying is, they didn't look at this as discriminatory, that black males, in order to be equal to a "C"/"B" [white] student, had to be a straight "A" student. That was bullshit. . . . You know, you never get enough, so you have to constantly keep recruiting; you have to constantly provide upper mobility career paths for these people. And you're not doing anything for them that you are not doing for a white officer.

Notice in this account that there is *no* bending of the qualifications to recruit black students into policing—despite the assumption of many whites. Instead, the situation is the opposite: black candidates were expected by white recruiters to have higher grades than white candidates. Traditionally, a type of "affirmative action" set for blacks has favored whites. This officer's success in recruiting is uncommon in the interviews.

Despite research studies that show moderate improvement in the representation of communities of color in large urban departments, our respondents provide evidence that most police agencies are not racially balanced,[8] particularly the rural and small town agencies. Numerous respondents discuss the reasons why, including financial barriers:

The young people that want to be police officers have to pay between $700 and $1,200 for the [academy] class. Now, a lot of African Americans don't have the money to do that. [So] the sheriff now is actively recruiting African Americans from other police departments. They did it some in the past, but not as heavy as now because we see that shortfall from those classes. So, the thing is, we've got to get guys out there to sell this department for a guy to leave another department. And you got some of these police department guys who don't even make $10,000 a year. So, to come here and start at $22,000, and then within less than five years you're up to about $35,000, you know. See, that's a good chunk of money for a guy. [Other departments] can't keep officers, because they train them, and the next thing you know, they're gone. They'll come to work here.

It is costly to take the police classes, and many working-class people cannot afford them. This problem may lead to one law enforcement department's stealing officers from another. Inadequate recruitment and development, coupled with the recruitment of black officers from poorer-paying agencies, tend to keep the total number of black officers, as well as the number of those with supervisory and command potential, rather low in many law enforcement agencies.

RACIAL BARRIERS: TRAINING AND PROMOTIONAL BARRIERS
Bias in Field Training Programs

The African-American officers interviewed generally view police academies as fair and objective. Even those trained in the 1960s and 1970s note little experience with overt racism in the police academy programs they attended. However, this is not true for the Field Training Program (FTP), a program designed to improve the quality of officers. Rookie police officers are usually assigned to a field-training officer (FTO) after completion of the academy. The FTO's job is to reinforce instruction in topics covered in the academy and to evaluate the rookie officer's suitability for police work. FTO evaluations are crucial in determining who continues and advances in policing institutions.

Many respondents see this program as frequently furthering racial divisions in agencies. Rather than improving the quality of officers, the FTP is described as an important weeding-out point in which subjective decisions of white FTOs disproportionately impact the new black recruits. As in most specialized positions within police agencies, there are typically few black FTOs. Black officers are therefore removed from making decisions that affect the quality of officers in general, and of racial representativeness within law enforcement agencies.

One officer discusses how, by comparison, she concludes that mediocre white trainees generally pass the FTP, whereas black trainees are too often "washed out":

> In training at the academy, everyone is together and getting the same information and you have to pass a test, objective training, they do fine. But when they come out and go into Field Training, where they ride with officers, and some officers have different standards, [there is a problem]. Some [trainees] may have passed the training, but that doesn't mean that they are good officers. A lot of those are white males and some white females.

Several respondents stress the importance of racial characteristics in this process over and above other factors. The consensus seems to be that whites in training positions often share notions that black people are not fully capable of performing required policing tasks or that black people should not be allowed to be officers. The result is that disproportionate numbers of black trainees wash out during this period of white-controlled field training.

Interestingly, a black training officer describes the racialized processes she has seen as an FTO:

I've trained white women, and I've seen white women pass the FTO program that no-way-in-hell should have passed. I've had white women that I've wanted to fail, and they've actually come to me and told me I couldn't fail them. No, my administration has told me that: That I couldn't fail them.

Although the power of individual white FTOs to judge rookie officers and make subjective decisions that affect the racial character of departments is reported by the respondents to be extensive, discussions such as this one also point out how agency leadership can influence FTP decisions. White officials sometimes step in to ensure that below-average white trainees pass the program.

Another respondent explains how her agency leaders act to limit the number of black and female trainees who pass:

These officers are told to weed certain people out of the program. Sometimes that black officer or that female officer just says, "To hell with it, this is not for me." And it's because of how they're being treated in the program. They believe this to be true, so they just flunk out.

The shared knowledge in black communities in general, and among black trainees specifically, of the discriminatory treatment of trainees has the effect of reducing the number who complete the program. Black trainees do become disillusioned and drop out rather than persevere and suffer. Another respondent notes the impact of educational differences on the subjective decisions of white training officers:

I see our biggest problem, we lost a lot of black officers during training, but . . . we very rarely lose a white officer in training. They may have the same problem as the black officers, but sometimes [white field-training officers] may use that paper and pencil to basically express why a black officer shouldn't be on department. . . . Ninety percent of black officers on the department have bachelor's degrees. Now you take them and you stick them in a car with a training officer that's probably has no more than a high school diploma—and maybe post–high school police academy and may have a couple of hours in junior college or something—and you cast them out training somebody with a bachelor's degree. Sometimes those [white] guys feel threatened . . . I think they feel threatened. . . . We're having guys with no education, with high school education and maybe some limited college baiting somebody with a bachelor's or master's degree.

The problem of African-American trainees' being weeded out in the field training by biased or threatened white officers is indeed a multi-faceted process that operates to reproduce traditional patterns of inequality within police agencies.

Not surprisingly, a low number of successful black trainees translates into a low number of black officers within police agencies. This, in turn, means few black officers in specialized positions such as field training. One perceptive officer sums up this less obvious but still racist cycle:

I know that racism is there. However, it is not the type that you will be able to draw [a] direct correlation, draw from [one] line to the other. Nobody's that foolish. And so, when they present a case on a field trainee, it's one that's very little room for interpretation. . . . The only thing that you can do to address some of that would be to have more African-American field trainers, and there's a paradox in that. You have to get more African-American police officers in before you can have more African-American trainers.

In addition, a recurring problem in paramilitary agencies such as police departments is that the new black officers are often required to undergo more surveillance and probation than new white officers.

Numerous respondents note that a persistently problematic aspect of field training is the addition of differential requirements. Although each of them ultimately passed such a training program, they often had to fulfill requirements beyond those that most white trainees were expected to fulfill:

When I first started here, I was going through a one-year probation. And for nine weeks you're assigned to a training officer, and after going through my nine weeks, I wound up with one last training officer. And I didn't have any problems with any of them, and that last week, he released me to go solo. And for some reason, this one particular FTO, who doesn't work here anymore, apparently, I heard, put up a fuss about it for some reason. And I was assigned to her again, so they extended probation. And no one could really say why. During that time I stayed with that FTO for another month or two.

Using FTPs for screening provides an easy way out for many historically white departments. They can screen out black applicants with subjective criteria implemented by FTOs whose past discrimination has guaranteed employment primarily of white officers. Those who are not weeded out in this way often find their career path impeded by the demand that they meet additional remedial requirements.

Although noting a lack of direct evidence of racism, one experienced officer underscores the personal, administrative, and economic waste generated by having an unjust training program in agencies:

I [don't look] at the motives. I [look at] the results. In fact we have a great deal of [trainees] in the program and a lot of them are being weeded out, and they happen to be black. Either there's something wrong with our recruiting program or there's something wrong with the training officers, because why is it that we are hiring so many people that can't make it through the program? . . . I think, again to look at the results. It may be racism; it may not be racism. . . . You've hired them. You've interviewed them. You've done background checks. You've tested them. You've sent them to a training at police academy. And now they can't make it through, and that's almost like, I guess five or six months of work, and now you bring them to the police department, now they can't make it, something's wrong. So, I would say, hey, you need to, we need to look at our recruiting process or we need to look at our FTO process.

Biased Evaluations of Training and Performance

Building on the theme that discriminatory practices permeate police agencies, numerous officers explain how biased training and performance evaluations can limit the ability of trainees to become police officers, or

limit the opportunities of those who become officers to advance within
agencies. One officer suggests that police training should be realistic
about tensions that are present and work to teach effective policing:

> During training these guys get nervous, they may misspell a word,
> they may leave out a word. Give them an opportunity to go back and
> correct their problem. Don't just sit there and say you can't write a
> police report. . . . I had my sergeant tell me this long time ago, "Write a
> police report, put it over your sun visor and then come back and read it
> after about 30 minutes. You'll find all your mistakes." And I tell my
> recruits that. . . . When you start talking about, evaluating people's
> report writing, all that can be . . . subjective; it's all subjective.

Most of the respondents indicate that at times their white superiors
closely monitor their actions and look for errors that can be blown out
of proportion and used to impede advancement. Significant job insecurity results from the fact that assignment, specialized training, advancement, and salary are influenced by evaluations by key whites, who often
harbor stereotyped images of African Americans like those of a majority of whites.[9] Most black officers indicate that they feel they are subjected to more scrutiny than most white officers and spend more time
under a microscope.

These usually well-educated women and men periodically refer to
the huge amount of energy that African Americans like them must
waste in attempting to deal with this extra scrutiny and related discrimination, while trying to do their job well. One respondent sums it
up this way:

> Everybody second-guesses us. And . . . it still happens when I write a
> report. It's, "Why don't you charge them with this instead?" You know. I
> was in a situation, this is what I felt, and this is what I render. Nothing is
> ever good enough. Instead of saying, "Well you did a good job," you
> know, "Well why didn't you do this?" or "Why did you do it that way?"
> . . . You've got to base it upon what you got; you're there. And it's amaz-
> ing how people judge you.

Our respondents are often perspicacious in their comments about
the process of acquiring knowledge about racial hostility and discrimination. They are thoughtful and articulate about the nuanced character
of everyday racism. For example, they are aware that some white offi-

cers have similar experiences with problems of unfair evaluation. Indeed, many whites respond to black complaints of discrimination by suggesting these problems are related to bureaucracy and not to racism. One respondent discusses how the recurring reality of discrimination inside and outside departments influences understandings of blacks about the evaluative process:

> So, there's, again, there's a psychological problem. I don't think most whites face it and they're not aware of it. And what I often try to share with most people is when you get a black and a white in a training mode, and the white person is in a superior mode and they're evaluating the black person—and I can only speak for a black person because I don't know about the other minorities—but the black person, especially when they're criticized, the question always comes into their mind, "Am I being criticized legitimately or am I being criticized because of a racial mode?" And that's extra baggage. You see, I can't look at the issue and say, "This guy's criticizing me in a direct objective way." It's always in the back of my mind that I got to deal with, "Is it really objective or is it racist?" And that's an extra level, a filtering screen that I have to go through. And sometimes it's to my own detriment, because it doesn't allow me to look at myself objectively. . . . Whereas, you, as another white guy riding with a white guy, if he evaluates poorly, it may be that he doesn't like you specifically, but it's never gonna result to: All the white folks don't like you. . . . So you don't have that baggage; you're going to look at [the situation] and say, well, "It's me, I need to do something here or maybe it's a personality conflict between me and this guy," but it never goes to the point that this guy doesn't like white males.

This respondent is referring to the long experience that most African Americans have had with discrimination and to the shared knowledge they develop to survive. The U.S. racial hierarchy has a counterpart: its psychological manifestation in the minds of black employees, who must constantly judge whether the mistreatment they face is indeed racial or is nonracial. This is yet another energy cost of everyday racism. As long as institutionalized practices within policing that are not objective exist, the potential for subjectively racist decisions by biased white officers will continue to reinforce existing racial divisions and inequalities within law enforcement agencies.

Bias in Departmental Disciplinary Practices

Previous research has found discrimination in the disciplinary practices of historically white law enforcement agencies. For example, one study of Detroit officers found discriminatory practices that were subtle and well disguised, yet numerous.[10] Nearly half of our respondents spontaneously discuss how many disciplinary decisions are subjective in nature and operate to reproduce racial inequality in law enforcement agencies. These women and men note that in the past and today there were "two standards there, you know, there were some things that a white officer could do that a *black* officer couldn't dare do, and get away with it."

These articulate respondents discuss how popularly projected notions of "blue" unity within the police ranks unravel in the face of the glaring contradictions in the manner and extent of black officers' disproportionate disciplinary penalties. One officer lists certain recent examples in his agency:

> On the surface, I'm "blue." They say, "Well you're not black; you're blue. Now you're part of us; you're on the team." But in the real sense, I'm not treated like I'm on the team. . . . Just recently we've got a [white] lieutenant who got caught in the graveyard having sex. They fired him; he's coming back to work here. A black guy was just talking to a white female; and they fired him. Okay. They had a white officer taping a black male talking to a white female; they fired the black male because he was talking about sex. But they didn't fire the guy that wiretapped him. They found in an investigation that that was an illegal wiretap; they didn't fire him. He's still working here. We had a [white] police officer that got caught stealing twice. Petty theft the first time, grand theft the second time. Still working here. . . . He's still working here. But blacks are being fired for policy violations, which are less—these are criminal charges that these [white] guys are doing. They're still here. Blacks are fired for policy violations—going out on his own, talking on the telephone, not answering calls properly. You know, this kind of thing. Blacks are being fired for these kinds of things. But these [white] guys are still here . . . because the disciplinary action for blacks has been very harsh, more so harsh for lesser offenses, than for whites.

In spite of the police ideology of shared "blueness," there is no multiracial team in many such departments. According to the respondents, African-American officers often receive disproportionately harsh penalties for offenses similar to, or more minor than, those committed by whites. Knowledge builds on this matter as African-American officers share their experiences, discuss such events, and observe the different treatment of black and white officers.

Even when white officers are disciplined, they are more likely to be allowed to make amends than black officers. One respondent mentions a white officer who faced an issue of money:

> If an African American had of committed that violation, he'd be out
> the door. A white male would get maybe a week or two suspension,
> demoted, but still allowed to work as much overtime to make up for the
> economic loss. You know, they might have lost the rank, but they still get
> the money. The buddy system: their buddies receive better assignments
> and they go to bat for them.

Once again, we see the importance of the buddy system within historically white departments. As we have seen numerous times, such networks are operating centers for contemporary racism.

Biased disciplinary decisions are especially significant because current practices within many police agencies limit the number of African-American officers employed, and especially limit the number of African-American supervisors. When black supervisors are absent, black officers may well feel that there is no one to monitor and influence the decisions of biased white supervisors. One officer makes this pointed comment about the problem of supervisors and discipline:

> Mainly because the majority of the supervisors are white, you know,
> that's just the only way you have to look at it. The majority are white so,
> therefore, you find some of those guys, and I'm being honest about it,
> who are very fair and go out of their way to do the right thing. But
> you're always going to have some who are not. And there's still a few of
> them around because I've seen instances where black officers were
> involved in minor incidents, but they paid a higher price than whites
> who did the same thing—or sometimes even more severe things.

Unfair evaluations and disproportionately harsh discipline have a significant impact on the work life of black officers because they create an impression that those officers can never be good enough for advancement within their law enforcement agencies.

Bureaucratic Discouragement of Promotions

Several respondents indicate that white-dominated agencies, usually through whites in important departmental positions, attempt to marginalize black officers by trying to discourage them from advancing through the ranks. One officer relates evaluations to this type of discouragement: "And our reports I think were scrutinized more so than the white police officers. So my reports would come back and theirs wouldn't . . . so, I think it was just their way of trying to discourage us." Hidden behind the scenes in bureaucratic procedures, this form of discrimination is difficult to measure.

Several officers note the historical and contemporary use of discouragement to limit advancement of black officers within agencies. A command-level officer discusses how he felt when white officers informally attempted to discourage him from advancing beyond his patrol position:

> I began to desire to be a supervisor. And we take a promotional exam every year. And then our exam score's good for one year. So the year I was going to take it, I told some of my zone partners—of course I was the only African American in that—I was riding the rural north end of the county and when I told them I was going to take the promotional test, they all burst out into laughter. And they were really sincere about that being funny.

The glass ceiling to promotions here was expressed by laughter. Evidently, these white officers could not see the situation from the point of view of an experienced black officer.

Although this discouragement can still be overt, the respondents indicate that often it is manifested now in a more subtle form, such as in the recurring lack of incremental rewards and recognition. For example, one officer describes how she has experienced practices that serve to discourage her and other women: "Sometimes a female might have done a good job, and they ignored her. Or, 'you did a good job.' But never rewarded [her] in the form of letters of commendation." Another respondent similarly notes the hurt of being excluded from sharing an award that his white partners received:

> Two years ago, I think, they started up the awards recognition program, and I was assigned to a certain detail with four other officers. And the year that they gave out those awards, I was promoted to this position,

but those [other] officers were still in patrol. And that night they received recognition for putting a dent in crime on campus, and I was left out of that recognition. I don't know if it was oversight by their supervisor, but someone should have seen or recognized my being one of those four. . . . That kind of bothered me for a while.

Numerous officers report feeling alone, left out, and unable to achieve certain career goals. We see too how they develop knowledge of racism by regular comparisons with what happens to fellow white officers. Comparing their experiences with those of whites who receive less discipline and greater recognition causes black officers to feel that white officials do not care about what happens to them. One respondent describes this recurring isolation and estrangement: "Oh yeah, I'm pretty sure that if my neck got on the line that I wouldn't expect my supervisors to come to my rescue. I know if I got in trouble I'm on my own."

Exclusion from Key Promotions and Positions of Authority

Many of these officers report that lack of acknowledgment of the qualifications and contributions of black officers often serves to exclude them from positions of greater authority. They express concern about the manifold barriers to advancement. Thus, they discuss how the subjective evaluation of candidates has served to limit promotional opportunities. Many recount overtly or subtly racist practices that have excluded blacks from supervisory and command positions. One respondent comments, "I've had supervisors say, 'I don't know why ya'll black guys take this test anyway because if you pass, we're not gonna promote you anyway.'"

In some areas, lawsuits by black officers have forced law enforcement agencies to remove some of the traditional barriers to promotion to higher ranks. For that reason, many white officials argue that current promotional practices are fair and color-blind. However, our respondents discuss various ways in which they are still differentially denied promotion and other advancements. For example, one respondent who works in a small agency discusses the difficulty of being promoted despite superior performance:

We had a promotion exam. I don't want to be given anything because I'm black. But I don't want things to be taken away from me because I'm

black. I scored the highest on the written exam. I scored the highest on
the oral exam. . . . And still it took my ex-chief longer [to promote me]
than it took him to promote anybody.

Several respondents note that they have been officers for more than
twenty years and either have *never* been promoted or have not been
promoted in a very long time.

One common reason for this discrimination is that these officers are
outspoken about issues of racism in their agency, in policing generally, or
in the larger society. One officer describes his experience in this regard:

> I've faced a lot of opposition toward promotion. I've been up for lieu-
> tenant eleven times, and I've been passed over even though I've passed
> every exam. I have been denied transfers. I was just recently transferred
> back to [an old post] where I have people who are my junior, people that
> I had recruited that have been promoted and that are now my supervisors.
> They have less education, they have less time in grade, they have less
> experience as an officer, but now they're my supervisors. So, I've faced
> much opposition, simply because I'm very outspoken. And I deal with all
> the issues in society; I deal with a lot of issues involving police and race; I
> deal with a lot of issues involving police and black male conflict.

When whites control organizations, they control promotional procedures. Repeatedly, in these interviews we see how little truth there is to
the white notion that U.S. employment settings typically have meritocratic norms. Most historically white law enforcement departments are
not meritocratic but instead operate more or less in terms of old-boy
networks and their whitewashed norms about a range of racial and
policing matters. Black female and male officers are often remarkable
in their courage and willingness to stand up for justice and fairness
against these powerful networks in policing and in society.

The subjectivity of white officers has an impact on the promotional
process. One solution to discrimination in the promotional process is
the creation of assessment centers that use a multistage process of determining officer suitability for promotion. However, at least one of these
assessment stages often substitutes another form of subjective evaluation by whites for the older subjectivity, as this officer notes:

> We eliminated the evaluation, and just started doing [a process] where
> you take the test and then go through the assessment center. But the fact

is, at the assessment center . . . [white] sergeants ended up pretty well being the graders of everything.

Our respondents report that black officers who do well on written exams are often hurt by the subjective evaluations of the white sergeants who screen in the process. In addition, extradepartmental factors have an impact on the ability of some African-American officers to prepare for the intensive police exams, as we see in this report:

Another problem I have with the assessment process is that if you don't spend a lot of money, you don't make it. My brother spent $1,000 on the last one, and I spent $800 just for a two-day course to prepare for assessments. And you have to spend money. . . . I've got friends that have done very well on a written exam, but they've got three and four kids and a house, a car. And they can't afford to fork out $3,000 and $4,000 for a sergeant's exam.

The importance of black officers' staffing supervisory and command positions, and the lack of black officers in these positions, are topics of concern in some police agencies and in most black communities. Often members of the black community push for greater representation at the command level. Whites inside and outside the departments often respond that promotional criteria are objective and fair, and that only the best officers can advance. Yet, as we have seen, this is often not the case. This reality of continuing barriers can negatively impact black officers, who may, after repeated attempts to advance, lose motivation. Indeed, in many areas the white command officers and supervisors are in difficult positions, as they are required periodically to justify unfair promotion processes to outside critics.

One respondent's discussion illustrates the complex nature of his promotion and the great importance of outside citizen pressure:

When I got promoted to detective . . . the city was under duress because of the inequity of numbers of people that they had. Now granted, I was qualified for the job, but they would not have looked at me for the promotion without the outside pressure. They would not have looked; there was no need for it because again, they had at least ten white guys who were just as qualified for the job. And so unless there was something to make them look at me, you know, consider me, I wouldn't have gotten that promotion. And again, too, I had only been in my slot for like I think three or four years, and as I said, I'm not a fool; I mean, the only reason they looked at me was because of the affirmative action; they were looking for someone, the community was raising sand about inequities of the disproportionate numbers of minorities they have in these management positions and so they look around. They said, "Well, we need to promote somebody. It just so happens that [he] is qualified, he's doing a good job, hasn't caused anybody any problems and da-da-da-da," and so there he is.

Although well qualified, this respondent notes in his interview that past discriminatory practices conspired to limit his advancement. Now, in a promotional pool with officers of equal qualifications, there would be no special reason to promote him. He is thankful for community outcry and pressuring policies such as affirmative action that have at least given him the opportunity for advancement.

Other respondents discuss how sometimes past racist practices and present affirmative action policies can combine to limit advancement of African-American officers by creating what are white-maintained quotas effectively favoring whites. For example, a woman officer notes that

you have a list of people. . . . If you have a promotion, my name is on the list. . . . And I only get looked at when you need to promote an African American or promote a woman. You've got to be looking at me every time you look at that promotion list. That's the way our system, our department is geared. I mean there is a promotion list; everybody's name is on it . . . but I know past practice has been where you were put in a category over here and pulled out when there was a particular need. If no woman or no black retired, then you might not necessarily get that promotion because they're saying there's no need to replace. You're looking at numbers; there's no need to replace one who left because nobody left. And the qualities that really matter about the person are secondary.

Black or female officers often are promoted only when a black or female officer retires or moves up. In this way, artificially low numbers of black supervisory or command staff are maintained. This type of quota favoring whites or white men, interestingly enough, is virtually never the target of criticism in the white-controlled mass media.

Furthermore, many agencies make promotional policies far more difficult for the first promotion to sergeant, further complicating a promotional process dominated by whites' subjective evaluations and informal quotas. One respondent describes how this process operates at his agency, in this case with union complicity:

> But only with sergeants is this prohibition in here that says, "Oh no, you've got to pick from this group or that group." The consequence of that is you won't be a lieutenant, and you won't a captain if you aren't first a sergeant. So you have to first get that first promotion, and the way the system has been implemented in these agreements between the union and the city, so there's a 50/50 partnership there. It has allowed the promotion for sergeant to be the hardest promotion to get for anybody— and the preeminent, hardest promotion for blacks or Hispanics to get by its design.

The enhanced difficulty in being promoted to sergeant thereby limits the numbers of black or Latino officers who can be promoted to even higher positions. In most agencies, white administrators are generally in control of who is promoted up the ranks.

One major effect is to limit black leadership in law enforcement agencies. Many respondents express fear that the future of black leadership in their agencies is threatened by the present lack of black sergeants: "I have expressed this with my bosses. I find it totally unacceptable that in 1997 there's only seven I think, seven or eight black sergeants. In 1985 there were five." This struggle for the limited number of supervisory and command slots has an impact on black officers and on the future of policing. Respondents in thirteen of the sixteen agencies included in this study describe a slow or nonexistent growth in the number of black sergeants in their departments, and they also note how few black patrol officers are currently eligible or ready to take the sergeant's exam. This translates into limited numbers of black sergeants who can later be promoted to command positions. Numerous respondents note, therefore, that the gains in the numbers of black supervisors and command staff made since the 1980s are now at serious risk. When older black leaders retire, there will be an even greater lack of black leadership in law enforcement agencies.

Because of the fact that upper law enforcement positions are typically appointed by the current chief or sheriff, and are not under civil service regulations, a change in sympathetic black or white leadership at the top could wipe out a number of black officers currently in such positions. One officer notes,

We've got a black sheriff now. The most he can serve is one more term. I don't know if we'll have a black sheriff next time. So, with a new sheriff—all of these are appointed positions—so [it's possible] that in an election, they'd all be wiped out.

In addition, a few respondents report that some law enforcement agencies intentionally promote underqualified black officers to command positions. This action reinforces white notions of black inferiority by ensuring that those promoted will likely fail. The damage to that black officer extends to other black officers by reinforcing notions of incompetence in white minds and thus legitimizing barriers to black officers' advancement. One respondent puts it this way:

My thing is that if you're going to do a promotion you want to try to promote the best-qualified individuals for the job. If there are African Americans that are included within the process, yeah, that makes you more of a diversified agency. But when you start just going and just pulling one. . . . You're going to need someone who's qualified. You're going to need someone who can make the right decision out there in the field, and I think you're doing a greater disservice.

Other potential results of the limited ability of many black officers to advance within their agencies may be more competition and less solidarity within the group. Given the limited number of positions and rewards, it is not surprising that there is some competition. One female respondent describes her impressions about another black female officer this way:

I felt like she was a threat to me; I was a threat to her. First of all, we don't have many African-American females at all in our department. I think that only four, well one got terminated just a few months ago. So there's really only three and one lieutenant African-American female. . . . I'm a threat to her because, believe it or not, it's reality, I would probably get promoted before she would and that's what she was thinking.

Discussing a related problem, another respondent describes the way in which some black officers who do make it up the occupation ladder do not reach back to help other officers move up:

> In the black neighborhoods, they call it "crabology," the crab effect.
> When you put crabs in a bucket and one tries to go up to the top,
> another crab will pull it down. But, you know, if you look at a crab in its
> natural environment, if you put crabs on the beach, they would spread
> out and go different ways. . . . The black person that makes it over the
> wall, should reach back or throw the rope over. But what happens, they
> throw the walls up higher. Yeah, they want to stay the kingpin because
> they're scared somebody else will pass them.

Shifting her discussion, she then notes that in her experience women
police officers, who are mostly white, have not been very supportive of
each other:

> In law enforcement I have seen very few women that back other women.
> They are more prejudiced and biased than men. You have just a few that
> will back each other, support each other, because they're so busy trying
> to move up the ladder and get the blessings from the guys that they step
> on the other females. They create confusion. . . . They forget where they
> came from. They think there's not enough room there.

Persistent racist notions and practices serve to limit the promotion
and advancement of black officers in various ways. Despite some gains
from collective action by black officers, lawsuits, and affirmative action
programs, still the future of black command staff, particularly black
female command staff, is tenuous at best. Those who have advanced to
high levels also face numerous problems, including constant critiques of
their abilities and the possibility that they may be replaced after the
next election.

RACIAL BARRIERS: ASSIGNMENTS AND AUTHORITY
Discriminatory Policing Assignments

The failure to acknowledge the qualifications or contributions of
African-American officers takes various forms in contemporary law
enforcement agencies. The majority of these respondents discuss continuing patterns of discrimination in assignments within their department. Numerous respondents discuss how officers of the same rank and
experience are differentially assigned by racial characteristics. For
example, one officer notes a distinctive category of this discrimination:

Assignments in where you worked, even little things. Like this [white] guy and I were working the same section of the town, and he wanted to work in the black part where I was working at, because the girl he was getting ready to marry, worked for a trucking company that was in my area. And so he wanted to be closer down that way. . . . He wanted to switch and he asked me, and I said, "I don't care." . . . Because you know, you're everywhere anyway, but you're just assigned to a certain area. You know. And he was told by the watch commander that if they allowed me to move up to an area that was 50/50 white and black, then that would be like giving me a promotion. Moving me out of an all black area, 99 percent black except for the whites who worked at the different companies in that area.

In this officer's experience, not only was the area of assignment based on *his* racial characteristics but the *prestige* of the assignment was determined by the racial characteristics of the population of the area policed. These black officers periodically underscore the point that law enforcement agencies punish officers by assigning them patrol duties in certain predominantly black communities. Assignment to a patrol position in a partially white area is thus a rung further up the prestige ladder of policing, which can thereby affect the possibility of future advancement.

Another officer emphasizes the importance of racial characteristics in determining local policing assignments. She accents racist and sexist obstacles:

There's still a difference between white women and black women. As women as a whole, we catch hell when it comes to promotions, when it comes to job assignments, when it comes to the way we're treated. But white women are still treated better than us in the police department. Don't get me wrong; white women are treated like shit now, but I'm still saying compared to the way they treat black women, white women still get the better treatment. If I apply for a job assignment, and a white female applies for it, a white female is probably going to wind up getting the job. Absolutely she will, over an African-American male. Oh, absolutely. The white woman still is going to be treated different than us. In terms of job assignments, in terms of the way they're rated on their evaluations, in terms of the way they're treated by their white male counterparts.

Although white female officers are often treated badly compared with white men, at this agency they are treated better than all black officers. The racial hierarchy that is produced and reproduced in all historically white police agencies examined in this book places white men at the top and black women at the bottom. Depending on the collective strength of black officers at a particular agency—and the views of departmental leaders at the top—the position of white women and black men varies. This applies to assignment within one particular division, as well as assignment to more prestigious divisions within the same agency.

These officers also discuss the periodic exclusion of African-American officers from specialized assignments within the law enforcement agencies. As previous discussions have illustrated, African-American officers are often excluded from important specialized assignments such as FTO positions. One respondent comments on the depth of racial divisions that exist in his law enforcement agency:

> It's easier for the black officers to go to drug-related units than, say, homicide, which is like an exclusive position on the police department. One other unit I would say is a barrier for this agency is canine positions. I don't know that if ever in the history of this department we had a black canine handler.

The exclusion of black officers from these positions allows the racial hierarchy to be reinforced in multiple ways. Exclusion is a form of discrimination that becomes ever more important over time, because new black officers thus lack experienced mentors who help them understand their difficult position in agencies. It has a further impact on people in black communities, who, for example, have to deal with white dog handlers who may be too aggressive or white detectives who are too aggressive or fearful.

Another problem of differential and exclusionary assignments is the fostering of exclusionary cliques:

> We've got one canine black officer. We have none in homicide, none in marine patrol. We have certain areas that are just not attractive to blacks. . . . Where that unseen clique is there that not only does the black not have the experience, he doesn't want to pursue it because he knows it's a closed door. And he wouldn't be embraced if [he] were selected, all right, and there's no way, as an administrator, that you can change the way that people think. For instance, I get selected to go into homicide,

but the guys don't talk to me, and Sergeant comes in, "You got to start speaking to this guy," and they say, "Oh, hello [officer's name]," and then that's it. So it's those kind of things, and there's really nothing you can do about that.

As other black officers do, this respondent notes the informal segregation of various divisions in his agency. Virtually all such organizations operate along informal lines, and in some critical ways not according to their formal organization charts. Even white administrators with reformist intentions often cannot control subtle discrimination that acts as a barrier to advancement of black officers, because of this power of entrenched white-normed networks.

In the past African-American officers within white policing institutions were generally limited to positions set as "black" positions. Before the 1970s, almost all African-American officers were allowed only to police black communities and to arrest black citizens. Older officers describe a time when they were not allowed to arrest whites, and many can easily recall the first time a black officer in their agency arrested a white person. In their interview, numerous officers discuss how, although the most overt racial barriers have been overcome, the process of assignment by racial characteristics *persists* in their agencies. One respondent thus maintains, "It's no accident that probably 98 percent of the black officers in patrol are assigned to the black communities. That means it's no coincidence."

In general, most black officers are better able than most whites to understand black communities because they often grew up and were socialized in such a community. However, our respondents argue that this fact should not limit them to patrolling black communities for most of their career. Racialization of job assignments by white supervisors seems to be rooted in an overemphasis on white–black community differences. This view fails to recognize that white officers can be trained to work in black communities and black officers can be trained to work in white communities—a desirable goal in a democratic society. Furthermore, this assignment practice limits black officers to certain areas of policing and can thereby restrict their advancement in an agency. Promotion, salary, recognition, and feelings of self-worth are usually compromised. This can mean fewer (or no) African-American officers in higher-level positions in an agency, which in turn means fewer mentors for younger black officers. This process also reinforces racialization in white minds. Racial discrimination is also seen in the whites-only assignment of other positions, such as K-9 and marine patrol units. These are areas that black officers have rarely been able to penetrate in most agencies.

The racialization of policing tasks occurs in other areas as well. One officer argues that, at least in his community, black officers are often dispatched to more dangerous calls than white officers:

> I can lay in my bed at night and listen to the dispatcher. White officers are dispatched to certain calls, and black officers are dispatched to others. If it's a situation where they think one may get hurt, injured or something of that nature, they're going to send that black officer first. Especially if it is out in the boondocks, they'll give the black officer a far enough lead on . . . white officers so they can say, "Well you need to go as backup." Making sure the black officer gets there first, so if there is hostility he is going to catch it first before the white officer arrives.

In addition, women officers frequently report genderization in policing assignments and tasks. Gender roles in the society are reproduced in policing, as women often are assigned to positions that are supportive of male officers or that are limited to work related to women's issues. One female officer describes this process and discusses how people internalize it:

> It's male-oriented, male-dominated. If you're a woman, you can only work certain jobs. When you defy that, you're seen as masculine or some other type of problem with you, power-hungry. If you're not sleeping with everybody to move up and do it on your own merit—my education and so forth—you're also seen as a problem. That's from the male's perspective. From the women's perspective, you're just not capable because you're not a man. You could have more education, more training, but you'll never be good enough.

In many departments, women officers are supposed to fulfill tasks perceived by men as appropriate for women and no others. One respondent notes the irony of this process that has historically marginalized women in most occupations, and now that they have entered policing, seeks to create genderized policing roles within law enforcement agencies:

If a victim is a female and it's a sex crime, they call me or they call [names female officer]. They haven't had one in 25 years up here, so what did they do when the other ones came, and we weren't here? They've forgotten.

Exclusion from Specialized Positions

In the process of legitimizing the oppression of African Americans, white Americans have created an ideology that places whites and a white-dominated sociopolitical culture at the core of U.S. society. This means that from the dominant white perspective Americans of color are often more or less peripheral in importance. For example, most of our respondents note that in traditionally white-controlled police institutions they are often considered outsiders. Ironically, experiences of advancement within agencies often allow them to understand better the nature of racism in policing, as we see in this typical comment:

> I was the first black female person to go to the D.A.R.E. [Drug Abuse Resistance Education] unit. I was the first black female person to go to internal affairs. I was the first black in sex crimes. I had an opportunity to go to robbery; I would have been the first black female there. I've been asked because of the way that I do my work and investigate my cases; I've been asked and turned them down. I've turned down a job in homicide, and I would have been the first black there.

She has had many opportunities, yet we see her sense of being alone as well. Many of these officers share similar experiences as the first black person in an all-white agency or department within an agency. Indeed, this reality is so commonplace that numerous black Americans refer to themselves as "the only," a situation in which the adjective becomes a noun.

Gender discrimination works together with racial discrimination to exclude black women from the positions within police agencies that some black men are allowed to fill. As these respondents move through their agency, most have become increasingly aware of the rarity of black female and male officers in various positions. The normative character of whiteness periodically translates into negative perceptions of black capabilities, as another respondent illustrates:

> I was the first African-American female sergeant, so there had never been one. So no one even knew whether there was anybody who could do that

particular job in this department. So I felt like, at the time, the administration was just sitting back waiting to see how successful I would be, not as a new sergeant, but as an African-American female sergeant.

Historically excluded from certain positions of authority, black employees who finally do occupy supervisory positions are often scrutinized. They have to demonstrate to white authorities and peers that they can perform the required tasks. If they fail, their individual case may be generalized to the capabilities of other black employees and thus serve to reinforce the ideology of white superiority, again legitimizing whites and whiteness as the norm. Yet, African Americans who succeed do not necessarily pave the way for others, and may instead find themselves singled out as "exceptions to their race" and used as examples that other blacks should follow, or as evidence that there is no racial problem in an agency.

An additional area in which qualifications of African-American officers are not acknowledged is in the differential placement in training programs that prepare officers for specialized positions or general advancement. One officer discusses how her agency excludes officers despite their petitioning for inclusion:

> The white males and the white females would get to go to training, and we African Americans didn't get to training. . . . They would say "no funds." Most of the time they would ignore your memorandums. You would send them upstairs, and you would never hear anything about them. And training positions, we didn't have any blacks in training positions, working as trainers. And we still don't have any blacks working as training—so, that's till fifteen years later.

As of the date of this interview, this agency had allowed only one black woman to enter a specialized training program, and no black officers had been promoted to trainers. This illustrates the dual nature of such discrimination—few trainees and trainers.

White in-groups determine or influence many discriminatory decisions about assignments and training. Another officer links this problem in training to omnipresent old-boy networks:

> The supervisor may have had a long-term friendship with this individual. They may feel comfortable talking like that around them, and [when] these opportunities arose for them to send someone to special training

classes . . . these special schools, they would send the people that they've known all their life and were comfortable with. Then here are these African-American and female troopers over off to the side going, "Same old system, good old-boy system, they're not sending me because I'm black or because I'm a female" or whatever the case may be. And that's clearly the way it would appear, clearly the way it would appear.

As we see throughout our respondents' comments in this and other chapters, the informal white-dominated networks are commonplace, and the underlying social foundation, in all historically white law enforcement agencies. They are usually central to everyday operations and in many ways shape the allocation of rewards and privileges within an agency. The racial separation of these dominant networks from those who are not white can reinforce ideological notions of "racial others" that make discriminatory practices seem natural. Since white male officers are accustomed to being around other white men, they may arrive at decisions that are, intentionally or unintentionally, exclusionary:

> Leaders choose those that are most like themselves. There are few African Americans in decision-making positions. Therefore, African Americans don't get specialized trainings or positions. Experience helps promotions: The more jobs you do, the better able you are to understand the questions on exams and get a better score.

It appears that both intentional and unintentional discrimination by white law enforcement officials reproduces the racial hierarchy within agencies. The inability of black officers to be admitted to specialized training programs and to work in more prestigious and specialized positions inhibits their opportunity to gain necessary experience that would allow them to perform well on promotional exams, or otherwise limits advancement within agencies. In turn, the lack of black command staff and supervisors means fewer mentors for new black officers. It is these black supervisors who would likely be more willing to assign new black officers to specialized training and assignments, which would in turn prepare them to be future leaders.

Limiting the Authority of Black Officers

The history of black police officers is one of discrimination-generated contradictions, contradictions that become clear when one examines the authority vested in the police occupational role. Black officers often have much less authority than white officers. Numerous respondents discuss experiences at some point in their career with this form of discrimination. In the 1960s, for example, white supervisors routinely counseled African-American officers about the limitations on their authority. One veteran officer recounts what was said to him:

> "Boy, now I want you to go out there and do a good job, but I don't want you putting your hands on no white people out there. Now, you call another white officer in there. I don't want you putting your hands on them. I don't want no problems," is what the old chief said.

The patterns of segregation prevalent in U.S. society were recreated within police agencies, and on a daily basis. The effects on black officers included providing them with more insight into how racial hostility and discrimination work and teaching them that they were expected to remain in a subordinate position to all whites. Black officers who did not internalize that message were taught the error of their ways, as in this report:

> It bothered the heck out of me when I caught a young white man in a black community turning donuts and driving in a careless manner. I stopped him, wrote him several tickets, two for careless driving and all that. He called someone. . . . I was directed to go back out and pick up the tickets and tell the young man that I apologize for giving him those tickets and apologize to his family when I was right. Now that, that one got me.

Such experiences were embarrassing and lowered black officers' status in the eyes of the general public.

Whether in the past or in the present, the ordinary stress of the police occupation is multiplied by such humiliations and often results in problems with self-esteem. Some comment that they have begun to wonder whether they can be leaders and whether subordinates will respect them. One officer discusses why he has never pursued advancement:

> I'm not sure I would be seen as viable or have the same opportunity. I look at the fact that because the majority of the agency will be white males . . . they may not cooperate with me if I were a supervisor.

Black women entering law enforcement agencies, most since the 1980s, have faced similar concerns about their ability to lead. One female officer notes, "There are still some males that do not believe that females belong in law enforcement; there are people that do not want to be supervised by women nor do they want to be supervised by a minority." Racial status and gender can interact to limit the authority of these officers further.

Other respondents' accounts illustrate that the fears of black and female officers, unsure of whether they would be accepted as leaders, are usually justified. Many describe patterns of disrespect, insubordination, and attempts to undermine their authority. One senior officer makes this acute observation:

> [The other officers] under me would circumvent me and go around me. Their reports would come late and [they would] take it and turn it into another sergeant or turn it in to the lieutenant. They didn't want me checking their paperwork—some of them, not all, I would say . . . well a squad's fifteen, so I probably have three, four that would go somewhere else.

Some white subordinates, likely well versed in dilatory practices, go out of their way to demonstrate to their black superiors that they do not recognize their authority. Respondents such as this officer see that whites' not following orders is racially motivated when they disregard such orders:

> Their actions, more than just words. You can tell when they do things. I have worked side by side with some other officers whose supervisor was white. And he'd tell him to do it, and he'd go right on and do it. OK? But when I became the leader of this tribe, I could tell the same officer to do something and he would take his time about doing it, and say give me a little bit of time, I've got to do this and I've got to do that. But basically he wouldn't be doing anything; he'd just be trying to show me up.

Such reactions are often more than the actions of a few white officers with strong prejudices. In the experience of numerous respondents, their own white superiors often accept or prolong the problems of insubordination that they face from their subordinates. For example, one black officer recounts how the actions of his captain undermined his ability to discipline his men and ultimately culminated in his being disciplined:

I wound up getting a letter of reprimand in my jacket for failure to supervise my men properly and that—they say that was another straw that hurt me when it came time for promotion, not being able to supervise your people. How can you supervise your people when people are not working with you to supervise your people?

A constant problem with discrimination in many organizations lies in the unwillingness of those at the top of the bureaucratic structure to reign in the discrimination by their subordinates. When those up in the ranks wink at the discrimination below, those suffering from such discrimination have little recourse.

Tokenism and Pressures to Be the "Good Black"

Tokenism is a major strategy used by many historically white institutions to create the appearance of significant social change without the reality. Sometimes, black officers who move into positions normally occupied by whites receive public attention disproportionate to their actual function within an agency. Indeed, a sizable number of the respondents describe how they are used to presenting the impression that their law enforcement agency is progressive and attempting to address racial injustice:

At the time, I was the only black female at the sheriff's office. . . . I was the only one to do black perspective, black female perspective. Interviews, everything fell on my shoulders. And they used me royally. So, but you know, there's a positive when you're being used; people start recognizing your name and you gain power, and that becomes a problem.

Gaining power as a black individual within a police agency is most difficult if one is outspoken on important issues, especially racial issues. Many, if not most, white-dominated agencies seem to be careful in choosing which black employees are allowed to enter visible positions usually occupied by whites. As one officer aptly put it, they "want a black that is safe." It is common for white officials to screen and monitor the token black officers who advance to these visible public positions. Part of this process of control requires that whites define a particular black person as "good" and "trustworthy." This procedure serves the dual function of legitimizing existing racial barriers in the light of the one successful black person—she or he alone is capable—

and attempting to pressure the black employee to think that she or he is in fact better than other blacks. One respondent describes his experience with this definitional process:

> The classic term you used to hear all the time for blacks when the whites would want to credit a black for being somewhat intelligent or more than what they expected, "Well, you're not like the rest of them."

This attitude of whites reflects the old white-racist strategy of describing black Americans who succeed, or appear to conform to and cooperate with whites, as notable "exceptions to their race."

This white approach involves an interesting array of interpretations and responses to interactions with coworkers. Evaluating the comments of a white sergeant, one officer reflects on the white fascination with skin color:

> I remember once he was telling me, he says that, "You're not black." He's talking about the literal sense, you know, and he says, "You're brown." Now I know I'm black as most; I'm black. As a black person, I'm probably darker than the average black person. . . . In his effort to be complimentary, he was saying to me, in a sense, like there should be something ashamed to be, that I am black. So he's trying to say, "Well you're really not black; you're brown." Well, my remark to him was, "You're not really white; you're tan," you know. I mean after I had his shirt because in those times the sergeants used to wear a white shirt, I said, "You're not the same color as that shirt; I mean, you're not." But that was his effort of trying to, you know, come to some grounds of familiarity, friendship, or so forth. And I've had experiences like that.

This white sergeant, when confronted with a black officer he found to be capable, apparently attributed that quality to the tone of the officer's skin and thus defined him as "brown." Apparently, for this white officer the degree of racial inferiority can be measured by tonal variations in skin color.

In their interview several officers note that the negative definitional process is sometimes extended to certain white employees, in the attempt to make sure that all people in an agency are ideologically in accord with notions of white superiority. They note that there are white officers who are supportive and who sometimes fight against overtly racist practices in their department. However, their department also screens and monitors white officers to make sure that those who express sympathy for employees of color are to some degree marginalized. One respondent puts it strongly:

> They see a lot of good white officers coming through there, and right away they got to figure out a way to get rid of them . . . that's the mentality, and that's where the racism comes in. See, you got to find that certain breed that's going to stick with the Klan, you know . . . this guy that we know that's going to follow the so-called tightrope, the Gestapo-type guy, they want to keep him.

Many historically white departments, especially in smaller towns and rural areas, are oriented to a certain type of white officer, one who will fit in well with prevailing views of policing and of African Americans among the majority of whites in the area. Many whites rationalize and reinforce the existing hierarchy by defining whites and blacks as different and then maintaining these differences by excluding blacks or whites who challenge the rationalizations. As with black officers, liberal white officers may face a complex process of redefinition and resocialization designed to force them to conform or quit. One respondent discusses how certain white officers who ride with black partners find their jobs more difficult:

> Actually the people who had the problems were the white officers who said, "Okay, I agree to ride with you." So they became "nigger lovers." Whereas, hey, as soon as I performed my duties, I went home to my black neighborhood. I didn't have the problems, but he had to go back and live with his friends.

As members of the racially dominant group, most whites are generally able to detach themselves from empathy with black Americans, dismiss their experiences, or overgeneralize the differences between black and white people. Defining themselves as normative in society, while redefining and punishing those blacks and whites who challenge this situation, the dominant group is able to maintain the racial hierarchy.

DECEPTION AND ISOLATION
Forms of Deception

In addition to supporting the actions and attitudes of insubordinate white officers, white officials can undermine the authority of their senior black

officers in yet other ways. Numerous respondents discuss how withholding of information and outright deception are used to weaken
them in their agency by undermining their ability to lead. One respondent, who echoes the experiences of numerous senior black officers,
underscores a common form of withholding information: "They
would have a meeting there with me and then they would have the real
meeting."

To survive, these black officers note that they learned two key lessons. First, they must not trust white officers without checking, because
they are not always who they appear to be. As one officer notes, "One
thing that we knew, and that I learned right off the bat, is white officers' conduct was different when you were around than it was when
you weren't." A second lesson is to be careful of what you say:

> That's why part of the reason there aren't many African Americans in the
> department. They don't know who to trust. I don't know who to trust.
> We live in a dog-eat-dog world, and information is the thing that is used
> to accomplish certain things. And we very much have to watch what we
> say. You might feel a certain way, but the truth will not help you out.

We have made the point previously that the key white in-groups within
law enforcement agencies pass information along their networks, information this officer notes that "is used to accomplish things." In many settings, information is the key to good decision making and performance.

Thus, those who naively believe in the fellowship of police officers
and feel that "blue is blue" lack the knowledge of racism in policing
that is necessary to survive in it. The older, more experienced black officers report efforts to teach and guide younger officers. They note that
experience, if one survives, opens the ears of younger officers and
allows many of them finally to understand what the older officers have
meant. One respondent recounts a nearly career-ending experience:

> I had an experience that hurt me so, and I just couldn't believe that
> things like this could actually happen. Now you read about things like
> this; and you see things in the movies, but when these kind of things start
> occurring and happen to you, you know, personally, that's when you say,
> "I don't believe this; how could a person lie and say some of the things
> like they were saying." To give an example, I was a detective working at
> a homicide and robbery, and I thought at that time I was doing an ade-
> quate job and my end-of-the-month statistics showed that I was surpass-

ing a lot of the white detectives and was doing a good job. A white detective from a different division came up with a scenario that I supported a known felon or criminal, drug addict in the robbery, and he went forward with this. And he got enough people's attention that they really thought that I had done this, and they investigated me as though I was a criminal. I was exonerated from this; nothing ever happened to them. But now if I had done something like that, they'd have probably put me in jail or fired me.

According to respondents, such cases demonstrate the efforts that some white officers will make to undermine the authority of black officers and destroy their career.

In addition, many respondents discuss or allude to ways they are reminded of their subordinate position in their agency by their inadequate equipment and facilities. They describe receiving outdated tools, worn-out cars, and offices in the corner of basements where no one will see them. One outspoken officer describes how poor facilities are spatial manifestations of white officers' notions of their superior place:

> If you notice the location in this building, it's in a hole, no windows, no doors; it's like a closet. You've got to come all the way to the back of the place to find it, to the back of the police department to get here. OK, they ostracize you, isolate you, separate you from the general public. They don't communicate with you—the flow of communication to me is nothing. They always want me to go up to them and communicate, but they don't bring information back down to me, so I'm at a loss. If I didn't hear anything from other people in other sections, I wouldn't have any information at all. Because my superiors don't talk to me; you see what I'm saying; they won't even talk to me.

Here again we see the critical role of white networks, and of information carried therein, and these social webs are linked to such apparently innocent relations as physical location.

Being Ignored by Whites: Isolation Inside and Outside the Workplace

Numerous respondents note how whites who encounter blacks in certain social situations often turn a cold shoulder. This white reaction is usually more than mere indifference, for it communicates to African Americans "that they should not have been in the situation and that they are going to be treated as if they were not there."[11] About a third of the respondents specifically note experiences in which they have encountered this response from white people. One senior officer comments thus:

> [I'm] generally well accepted when it's known that I'm a law enforcement administrator, well accepted. Now if I go somewhere and do not identify myself or go just as an African American, then I get the normal semi–cold shoulder or, you know, a good degree of less attention than I get if I identify myself.

Without the uniform or his assertion of his status, whites treat him as the generic black person, making clear the continuing importance of racial characteristics in society.

Even in occupational situations with fellow white employees these officers sometimes experience such treatment. One officer describes the overt behavior of a white supervisor who went to great lengths to demonstrate that he did not want her in his section:

> I was the first black female assigned to commissary and accounts in the division of corrections and I got along with my coworkers very well, but I had a lieutenant that was used to an all-white department, and I felt that he didn't treat me fairly because I felt that I did a very good job in there. He never addressed me by my name. He would come in, and he would basically speak to everybody and he never would talk to me. . . . I was in the position for two years. He would come in, and maybe mumble something. And I can always remember how he would address everybody by name and then he would refer to me as "what-chama-call-it." And you know, I didn't feel respected that way. I felt that as long as I did my job then he should respect me.

Once again networking among whites effectively excludes the "racial other." This form of isolating action is not innocuous, for it communicates to black employees the place they hold at work, as well as in larger society. It also disrupts their daily life by making them constantly aware that whites view them as outsiders. It serves as a great source of worry and stress, particularly if the person ignoring them is the supervisor responsible for evaluating their performance and determining their advancement.

Whites' Avoiding Contacts: Maintaining Social Distance

A related problem specifically noted by about half the respondents is the way that white fellow employees maintain social distance even though they work together and rely on each other for assistance. The view that all officers are "blue," asserted by many scholars and commentators implying group solidarity, is dispelled repeatedly by the accounts of these black officers. As this officer does, they explain that in the streets all officers may be blue to those policed, but in their agencies officers are *white* or *black:*

> So, that was a real eye-opener for me. And after being told in the academy that all the officers are going to be treated the same, and the job was one that once you put the uniform on you became "blue." And then, when you get out there and you find that, first of all, there was not a lot of socializing between black officers and white officers. As a matter of fact, I probably went about a year at one time without ever speaking to one other than in a working sense. They went their way, and we went ours and that was about it.

The official view of socialization in the department turns out to be rather different from the actual reality, that most whites are not interested in socializing with black officers. This is the case even though the occupational nature of policing, with its odd hours and stressful working conditions, tends to generate an interdependent camaraderie and networking among most (white) officers.

In the larger police agencies, especially those with greater numbers of black officers, the respondents note that they have other people to talk with and rely on. The presence of a critical mass of black officers gives them the ability to create their own support network to counter their exclusion from the dominant network. Thus, the lack of socializing is perhaps most serious in agencies where there are few black officers. In such situations, black officers generally describe difficulty:

> But then for years you get a guy [who says], "Let's meet, let's go fishing, let's do this." All of these guys were doing so much together off duty, when I didn't have no one to do anything with. Not in a working relationship. And I would like ride around for hours and the other guys would talk on the radio and meet somewhere, and you know, the only way they'd call me is for backup. And these are experiences that I'm

talking about. They are not complaints. This is not to judge any of these people. This is just what happened. So, if you put yourself in that situation for about ten years, it can wear on you. It really can.

Racially enforced isolation and marginalization have *serious* consequences, especially for those working in a dangerous occupation such as policing. There are costs to those who are targets of everyday racism. That many white officers are not accustomed to black officers, do not want black officers in the agency, and do not know how to have an informal conversation with them indicate persisting patterns of white-directed discrimination and segregation.

Recounting a question from a white female friend in her department, a black female officer describes similar experiences:

> There's a very good friend of mine—we're both from the department—and she asked me one day, "Why do they always bother you?" And I just looked at her, and it just dawned on me she had no concept of why they bothered me, because it doesn't happen to her. You know, they go out and eat lunch together. You know, like buddy-buddies, and they're not going to ask me out to lunch. And this is a female. The difference is between a white female and a black female, and she has no concept of why. And that's my answer to her. Because I am [black]; and that's it. . . . The sarge would ask her—she and the sergeant would go out regularly. They wouldn't ask me. I don't mind, because actually I prefer being by myself anyway. But if you ask me, I could possibly go on occasion. But it would never occur to them to ask me. . . . That was a revelation to me, though, because she just doesn't understand. I thought as a female she would understand. But, I keep forgetting I'm a black female.

Again the internal networking is white-centered, even cutting across the gender line, and a black female officer is constantly marginalized. Although all women officers face sexism in police agencies, black female respondents continually note the differences between black and white women officers. Despite having the same gender, this respondent feels left out in a way that is impossible for her white female counterpart to understand, because of the differences in racial experiences. Thus, when white officials and officers daily ignore or avoid most social contact with black officers, they isolate and marginalize them within their department.

Indeed, black women respondents generally note the gendered

racism they encounter, yet typically comment that racism is a more important problem in their life than sexism. Their comments generally suggest much in common with the experiences of black male officers with white views and perceptions, a point summed up well by this female officer:

> Just like we are affected by what we see and experience and our backgrounds, I would think certainly a system that is run by human beings is also affected by their life experiences, their perceptions and, and their beliefs. . . . Certainly I think [policing is] not infallible because it's run by human beings whose values and perceptions and beliefs certainly enter into decisions that are made.

DISCRIMINATION IN PAY AND BENEFITS
Pay and Benefits

The subordinate position of African-American officers, including those few in command staff positions, is reported by numerous respondents to be reflected in pay and benefit differentials. Older respondents discuss how receiving far lower pay and benefits for the same work was common when they began work in the 1960s and 1970s:

> [Another black officer] called me and came by my house and took me to his house, and he told me there was a black salary for police officers and there was a white salary for police officers, and it was going to remain that way. That was a Saturday and the very next week I went and asked for an appointment to see the chief, and when I went up there I said, "Chief, I hear there is a black salary and white salary for police officers." He didn't deny it at all.

Outright discrimination was commonplace just a few decades back, another signal that the hurdles for continuing in law enforcement agencies were then very high.

Because of the collective organizing of black officers and policies enacted to formalize pay standards, most respondents indicate that today this differential is only occasionally a problem. Still, a few from rural agencies maintain that salaries reflect racial characteristics. Even lower-ranking white officers earn more than they do. One discusses how he understands this pay differential as a manifestation of racism: "When they demoted me from police chief back to patrolman, they were giving the person that they put in the position more money . . . as a patrolman than I was making as police chief . . . and you think that's no racial motive?" This racially motivated demotion reduced his salary and made it harder for him to support his family. This finding is consistent with other scholarly findings, which suggest that smaller, or rural, police departments are more likely than larger ones to have priorities and a style of policing influenced by key whites in the local community. As a result, local police officers tend to police in a manner acceptable to those with power in the community, lest they be dismissed.[12]

Another perceptive respondent discusses how an injury was evaluated as not job-related and cost him a large percentage of his pension, even though a local white firefighter suffered a similar experience yet received more of his pension. He concludes that had he been white, the result would have been different:

> I got injured in the community relations part where I was trying to bridge a gap between the community and the police department . . . if you don't want to accept that, I really don't understand what your problem is. You don't want to accept it because it's me. And based on my attorney, I kind of listened to him. Now he was . . . a specialist when it come down to going up against the pension. He have had all kind of cases against white officers where you felt that he would lose, and he won. He had never lost a case against the pension board, but mine he lost. . . . And the same ruling that I lost on, there was a white fireman—I got the documentation and all that—[he] was granted his 65 percent for the fire department, but I was granted . . . 32.5 percent from the police department, and the cases were identical.

Even a veteran and specialist lawyer could not overcome the apparently discriminatory treatment in pension awards.

Clearly, pay differentials in salaries and pensions, as well as loss of pay resulting from disciplinary actions, can work to undermine black officers, marginalize them in relation to white officers, and reinforce their subordinate position in a variety of police agencies.

Pressures for Early Retirement

The end result of the myriad barriers to the advancement of African-American officers is often early retirement. Ten of the respondents spontaneously explained that their law enforcement agency has had increases in the numbers of black officers who retired earlier than necessary for reasons associated with their racial experiences:

> All the black officers that left the police department in the last sixteen to twenty years were either terminated or forced to resign, or they tried them. They tried me too, but I always got me a lawyer. After I got my time in, they tried to put the threats on me. They brought me on the inside to do work. They knew I didn't like the work on the inside so they brought me inside, and I sat right there and did the work. The white officers, if they wanted them to resign, they would go and give them a twenty-five thousand dollar [buyout]. They would take the twenty-five thousand, and their retirement, and run. Black officers, they would always try and put some pressure on them and say, "We got this one; we got you." You have black officers that have resigned with twenty years experience . . . that is a waste of taxpayers' money because you have trained them. In the last five years, [there are] eight black officers that has retired, and they are not forty years old yet.

The differential treatment of white and black officers often culminates in black officers' leaving some police agencies; then the discrimination continues in often substantial differences in pensions.

Another respondent discusses the detrimental ripple effects of this phenomenon on his agency's ability to overcome a history of racial injustice:

> Over the last couple of years we've lost eight of our black officers to retirement. So 50–60 percent of our black workforce has less than five years. So we don't have but one officer eligible to take the sergeants' test this time. Hopefully, in two or three years we'll have some that'll move up in the ranks and move into command staff positions. Although we haven't hired any African-American females in the last three years, now compare that with the number of white females and males.

As this respondent implies, early retirement creates a shortage of black officers, as well as supervisors and command staff who can represent the views of black communities. In addition, younger black officers have no mentors to teach and support them through the first formative years of service, a point another officer accents:

> Now I think there's a major problem for most of the younger Afro-American officers. [They] don't have anyone to go to, because most of

the senior officers pretty well retired. And from what I can gather, you know, I was talking to one of the rookie officers about two weeks ago, and he's already contemplating leaving because he feels like the problems have worsened down there.

Many insightful reports from these officers do not paint a picture of improving white–black relations within most of their police agencies but illustrate instead the point that racism, whether subtle or blatant, is persistent, complex, and still institutionalized. This is true at both the beginning and the end of their police career. Many of these officers agree that only through continually pushing for fairness within histori-cally white agencies, such as by means of collective black associations, can the persisting nature of racial mistreatment and inequality be sub-stantially transformed.

CONCLUSION

Responding to those who argue that racism in policing is now a myth, one respondent describes how black officers talk about her particular agency: "We say, 'That's the police department that's ten miles down the road and fifty years behind times.' Nothing has changed." In fact, these officers' interviews provide a great deal of support for the con-clusion that racial exclusion and marginalization are still fifty years behind the times. The black officers' experiences with a panoply of sub-tle, covert, and blatant racial barriers have enabled them to understand deeply how contemporary manifestations of racism work, and how unimportant and unwanted African-American officers often are in his-torically white law enforcement agencies.

Most respondents are very much aware of the ideological justifica-tions for the advantaged white position in the omnipresent racial hier-archy, and of how both the advantaged position and its ideology are continually reproduced in the routine operations of most police institu-tions. Encounters with everyday racism enable these black women and men to understand how whites learn about their superior place relative to blacks and how much of this racism is accepted as normal by most whites. It is clear from their discussions that discrimination is often not recognized as such by white officers, supervisors, officials, and civilians even though it is manifested in their own attitudes and behavior. The perceptions and concerns of black officers and civilians are frequently dismissed, and the majority of whites disavow any significant responsibility for the negative conditions still faced by African Americans, and indeed many other Americans of color. Numerous African Americans who make it up the policing ladder are often seen as token exceptions to the hierarchical rule, as "good blacks." Moreover, although white officers sometimes ignore their authority, officials may also use these promoted black officers as evidence that racial discrimination is no longer a significant barrier in these law enforcement agencies.

These officers often note one important factor that undergirds and fosters the persistence of racist thought—the continuing physical segregation of racial groups in the larger society and in specific police agency settings. Societal segregation not only makes it difficult for members of different racial groups to communicate and mutually uncover contradictions inherent in racist practices and thinking but also limits the ability of African Americans to advance the material conditions of their family. The difficulty in getting jobs and the lack of earned promotions mean less family income and wealth, which in turn often result in less ability to get an adequate education, adequate medical care, and adequate housing for family members. This, in turn, underlies the daily reproduction of black subordination throughout the society.

Racial discrimination in policing institutions creates many barriers that thwart the ability of African Americans to enter the profession and, once there, to advance freely into specialized positions and up the ranks. These black officers cite continuing problems that African Americans face in being recruited, hired, and trained in contemporary departments. As traditional racial barriers that weed out black women and men are identified, attacked, and transformed, yet new subtle and covert barriers that perpetuate the exclusion or marginalization of blacks in historically white agencies have been developed. Black officers disproportionately face unfair evaluations, discipline, and promotion decisions. Despite the gains made in the 1970s and 1980s, these officers posit that it is becoming increasingly difficult to achieve racial representativeness in their agency because of agency competition for black officers, because of high turnover rates, and because of early retirements stemming from discrimination within law enforcement agencies. Most fear that significant changes in existing equal opportunity guidelines or in the currently modest affirmative action programs will be a serious setback for African Americans within the policing arena.

In interviews, these perceptive officers suggest that although many forms of discrimination exist in most places, such practices are more frequently experienced as covert or subtle in agencies with more black officers and are more overt in rural or smaller law enforcement agencies that have limited numbers of black officers. Much overt racial hostility and discrimination in policing seem to be linked to the extent to which subjective decision making by white officials is coupled with the lack of a critical mass of black officers in agencies. The white old-boy networks are most effective when there are not enough black officers to create countering organizations. Here again we see an argument for developing a critical mass of African-American employees in every historically white police department, as well as every other historically white institution in the society.

5.

A Hostile
Racial Climate

National opinion surveys indicate that a majority of white Americans believe that serious racial discrimination in most areas is a thing of that past. From this perspective, overt racial hostility and discrimination may once have been problems, but now African Americans have societal access and opportunities at least as good as those of whites. For example, one recent survey asked whites whether they thought that the average black person had health care access, education, wages, and jobs equal to or better than those of the average white person.[1] Some *70 percent* of whites held to the erroneous belief that black Americans were at least as well off as whites in one or more of these major areas. On a general question, some 71 percent of whites felt that black Americans had societal opportunities *equal to or better than* those of whites, and just one in five felt that black Americans still faced "a lot of discrimination" in society.[2]

Actually, as we have documented in previous chapters and in other books, the evidence against this naive white view is overwhelming, particularly in regard to historically white workplaces and other major economic, political, and social institutions. And it is certainly true of law enforcement agencies. Although our respondents sometimes suggest that certain overt forms of discrimination occur less often in their occupational setting today than in the past, they make clear that even overt racism has by no means ended. In addition, they demonstrate with many experiential accounts that numerous forms of subtle and covert discrimination now operate to block, exclude, and marginalize them in their career and life.

Discriminatory actions by whites are generally buttressed by negative attitudes and ideological constructions. As we saw in earlier chapters, these attitudes use a variety of disguises, ranging from images of black Americans as lazy or incompetent to defensive ideas about the character of discrimination and remedial programs such as affirmative action. Previous research shows that racial discrimination often operates in a context in which many whites deny that it exists at all and, therefore, that black Americans who complain about racism usually do so without justification.[3] The ideological constructions of whites maintain conceptions of white and black people as opposites in perspectives, values, and cultures. Stereotypical notions of these differences are reflected in racist talk, jokes, and cartoons that belittle and humiliate black Americans while reinforcing their subordinate position. In this chapter we continue an examination of the way in which stereotypes and prejudices shape the discrimination that makes the everyday lives of black Americans so painful and difficult.

Here we pay particular attention to the way in which various types of racial hostility and discrimination create a hostile work climate. In workplaces with hostile racial climates, a variety of techniques of control and intimidation, such as racial insults and even physical violence, are employed by whites on a more or less regular basis to thwart or slow the advancement of black employees beyond their current position. When black law enforcement officers address the racist attitudes and discriminatory behavior of white employees, our respondents indicate they are frequently perceived of as threatening. They may face from white colleagues and supervisors a range of responses, not only resentment but also retaliatory actions that seek to contain them and that often result in emotional or physical harm. In the second part of this chapter we examine what happens to black officers who resist discrimination and hostile workplace climates.

HOSTILE WORKPLACE CLIMATES: WHITES PLAYING THE "RACE CARD"

Conventional white notions notwithstanding, racially hostile workplaces remain common across the United States, not only for black employees but also for many other employees of color.[4] Yet, in spite of the extensive evidence of continuing racism, many white juries and judges often have trouble seeing or remedying this discrimination. For example, in one recent California Court of Appeals ruling, *Etter v. Veriflo Corporation*, white judges concluded that the use of frequent racist epithets against a black male employee (Etter) was not "severe or pervasive" and did not require a legal remedy. The target of the epithets reported that a white supervisor used racially derogatory terms such as "Buckwheat," "Jemima," and "boy" and mocked blacks' pronunciation of words. However, in its decision the court played down the frequency and significance of these terms and ignored Etter's own account and painful experience.[5] Thus, although white judges and juries have become willing at least to listen to black accounts of everyday discrimination, as they did not do in earlier decades, they often find it hard to understand and credit fully the accounts of African Americans about discrimination.

Racist Talk, Jokes, and Cartoons

Half the respondents explicitly discuss encounters in which whites use racist language in conversational settings to refer to them or to other black people. The fact that encounters with these derogatory terms are experienced frequently demonstrates the extent of racist stereotyping and prejudiced thinking of many whites in historically white institutions. Such racist thinking and commentary have often been reported in research studies.[6] Supported and generated within white social groups and grids, this explicitly racist talk and terminology help to promote white solidarity through creating an outside "racial other" that is constantly derided.

Some older respondents note that racist talk was very commonplace when they first joined their law enforcement agency:

> When I first started it was nothing to hear the word "nigger" on the [police] radio. I mean, that was common, because everybody hadn't gotten the word, apparently, that there were some African Americans listening now. Then they went from that to a term that some guy used when he referred to a car with more than two blacks in it as a "load of coal." The first time I heard that, I thought, "Why that son of a bitch; I know what he just said." . . . And a lot of that went on. And then if they realized that I was working, they'd come to me and tell me, well we didn't mean you. And I thought to myself, "What a damned asshole, you meant me."

Although white officers may have altered the terminology according to their needs, the shared negative meaning and intent of this racialized terminology have remained more or less constant. This example illustrates an important point stressed throughout many respondents' discussions of the 1960s and 1970s: although overt forms of racist behavior have become somewhat less visible, the attitudes of many white officers have not dramatically changed. We have previously noted how some white officers have used terms like "TNT" on the police radio (see chapter 3). And in the famous trial of the officers who beat Rodney King in Los Angeles, there was some discussion of police radio terminology for black Americans, including the phrase "gorillas in the mist," although a white officer denied that this term had a racial connotation.[7] In the preceding account, the white officers' awareness of the repercussions of their language alters the language to cover their intent, and then they apologize. However, drawing on the totality of his experiences, this respondent understands that they were referring to him.

Another black officer recounts how white officers talked about him as if he did not mind being insulted:

> Well, take for instance my first day. I reported and was told that I'd be riding with another officer who was going to show me around. There was another trooper in the [highway] median and as we, he pulled over into the median to see that trooper to talk, he looked over and saw, you know, that there was another new trooper there. And he said it as a joke, but it wasn't funny at the time. He used the word "nigger." "Oh, that's just what we need, another fucking 'nigger,'" you know, and laughed, and they laughed and carried on. And I looked, and they could see I wasn't laughing. . . . But I knew they were accustomed to saying that and telling jokes that way, and felt comfortable with it and thought that it was not going to be taken offensively. But, in a period of time, that became taboo, and we really made a lot of progress. . . . Other than that, it's just been, you know, vibes and hearing things from another office when someone doesn't know you're there, and stuff like that.

These reports indicate that numerous white officers are comfortable with racist talk, if nowadays mostly out of the hearing of black officers. They do not seem to care that their joking hurts black officers. Once changes began to be made in departments, racist talk around black officers declined, yet often it continues behind closed doors, as what some researchers call *backstage racism*. With the decline in publicly expressed racist attitudes across the country, many analysts have argued that there is now little racist sentiment in the white community. Yet, studies of what whites do and say just off the public stage, as well as often on the public stage, indicate that this is a greatly mistaken view of racial change. In settings where they feel comfortable, such as with family or white acquaintances, many whites still make blatantly racist comments and perform discriminatory actions that they might not do in public.[8]

Another officer indicates not directly encountering overt racist talk, such as comments using epithets, yet knowing it goes on backstage and behind his back:

> Not directly, indirectly you got those names. What I mean is behind your back basically. . . . You would probably hear them talking about you, or another black officer as you passed by an open door, a cracked door. Or you may have been standing nearby a crowd of white supervisors or white officers, and you would hear that word.

Racist talk just off the public stage takes place as whites vent their anger and frustrations in regard to changing racial relations. It often occurs when whites are gossiping and in private conversations, when whites often let their guard down. One officer notes that:

> I've experienced some of the things that I consider to be racism. I was standing there talking with a sergeant. And one of the relief guys who happened to be white—and the sergeant was white—and I was the only black guy there. But you know, how you get accustomed to talking to people and you forget their identity, their culture. . . . It's just a person you're talking to. So he and I were talking and this white guy came up and says, "Sarge, where do I go on my relief duty?" And the sarge, without hesitation, he says, "You got the back fence over there, but the only thing you got to worry about is them little nigger boys trying to climb through the fence." And he looked over at me and he says, "Oh, I'm sorry; I didn't mean to say that." I said, "Well, I know how you are; it's all right." And I did know how he was, you know. I knew his bent; I knew his bent.

Note the comfort level here: these whites understand and employ, usually without thinking, racist constructions to converse about daily occurrences. Often these black officers describe being torn between anger at the insulting nature of the language they are subjected to and some pity for white officers who try to maintain a facade of innocence, only to be revealed as they really are in these everyday moments of routine interaction.

These black officers are quite concerned about the racist jokes and cartoons that are often shared and copied among white officers. Such joking and cartoons serve to denigrate and intimidate black employees and to reinforce the sense of white superiority. Many of the respondents spontaneously discuss how whites in their agency have incorporated jokes into departmental routines. The following account from a very perceptive respondent illustrates how roll calls have served as settings for racist jokes. This ritualistic telling of "the joke" promotes white officer solidarity, reproduces a shared understanding of the subordinate position of people of color, and informs black officers of how many whites still perceive them:

> We had roll calls where everybody would meet at whatever the designated time was for you to start work. . . . There was a long-standing tradition that someone would have the joke for the night. . . . All the ones I've heard, about a month's worth of jokes for the nights that I worked, were all racial jokes. And I didn't like it, and I attempted to find a way to deal with it. I was talking with an elderly gentleman here, and I mentioned it to him, and he said, "Well, you can't say nothing, because they may shoot you in the back, but, next time, why don't you tell a joke." And I said, "Okay, well I need a joke to tell." And he directed me to another gentleman who was a great storyteller. And there's a guy on the corner, and most people would probably not even consider that the man had any value or what have you. But you know, a real nice man, and he gave me a joke.

He continues with an account of how he fought back against this recurring racist behavior:

> And I wrote it down, and I rehearsed it and practiced it and got before the mirror, and actually I did it, and it took me several weeks. But once I got the joke down, then I had to deal with my nerve to do it. You have to realize that at our roll call at the time, there could have been 200–300 guys in there at any given time at our roll call, and of that, less than 1/2 of 1 percent was black. You understand what I'm saying. So, you know, when you tell your joke, you have to come up front and tell it. Well, I had been pondering it for several days, you know, and this one particular night my hand just shot up, and, of course, the lieutenant who was the watch commander, "Oh we have a rookie with a joke. Let's bring him on up here." And I told the joke the guy had given me about a white female

and a black male. And after I told the joke, I laughed and the other black guys almost fell to the floor, but nobody else did. No one said anything. It was just as quiet, like leaving a funeral. And I never heard another joke.

All the jokes told by whites in a particular period were racial jokes, yet another sign of how certain forms of overt racism are still central to society. This example is contextually rich in that it demonstrates many themes about their racialized experiences that are developed by these perspicacious respondents. We see reference to the limited number of black officers in many departments, as well as the importance of sharing of knowledge and support among black officers and civilians. We also see clearly the ideological hegemony that whites have in defining black people and in creating a sense of white networking and solidarity through such activities as regular joke telling. Perhaps most interesting here is the way in which a young black officer worked out a thoughtful response to the racism that he faced.

Despite the curtailing of jokes in this particular department, racial joking is still reported by many African Americans inside and outside police institutions. One respondent seeks to illustrate the seriousness with which he regarded a racist cartoon found on the departmental beat sheet by reading from a letter he had written to the chief:

"On [gives recent date] this department used a cartoon depicting a slave ship with the caption, 'The better-equipped slave ships, of course, always carried a spare,' on the beat sheet. This department also used stereotyped comments about 'Rednecks.' I find both comments and cartoon in poor taste and offensive. Many of the minorities in this department also agree with my sentiments in voicing concerns. However, many of the minorities are afraid to verbalize their comments for fear of repercussions. Although we are diverse in our environment, it still seems like we are still promoting racism and negative stereotypes."

Although the whites in the department may have included a "redneck" joke in order to make the slave cartoon less offensive, this officer rightly criticizes both as unnecessarily promoting negative stereotypes of people whom officers interact with more or less daily. It is important to note too that many black officers are both offended and intimidated by such joking and cartoons, and that some fear for their job if they were to let those feelings be known.

Name-Calling and Verbal Threats from White Officers

Clearly, police workplaces are still riddled with instances of overt racism, even though they may be in decline in many departments. Describing black people with epithets and other names is a way that many whites can express ideological conceptions of African Americans. The goals are to denigrate those targeted and to maintain patterns of subordination. One respondent describes his experiences on his first day of work in the 1970s:

> You know, it was a real strange experience. The very first day that I reported to the police academy on September 17, the sergeant that was out there in charge walked up to me and said, "You fat-ass nigger, get your ass on that damn scale."

Numerous respondents spontaneously recount experiences in which they have been called derogatory terms by fellow white officers or members of the public. Well into the 1980s, these racist practices were so widespread that in some departments superior officers would counsel new African-American officers on what to expect:

> I remember having a conversation with a captain, and he sat me down and he gave me the spiel about, "I want you to know one of the criteria is that you have to have a thick skin. If you can't stand being called a 'nigger' and still do your job, you don't need to be here because you're gonna get called all kinds of names."

Interestingly, this superior officer understood what African-American officers would be subjected to and wanted to make sure that new black officers would accept such behavior without retaliating. Certainly, African Americans do not need to be counseled by white superiors because they encounter name-calling so frequently that they have long ago developed protective mechanisms against it. One respondent illustrates this point:

> I've heard that word, must have been well over 10,000 times in my life. But I can't let it affect me. I know who I am; I know what I can do. I know what I have; I know what I've accomplished and no one can take that away from me.

Key here is the frequency of racist names and incidents for African Americans. Racist comments and behavior are far more commonplace than even sensitive whites are likely to know and understand.

The majority of these black women and men indicate that they refuse to accept name-calling within the occupational setting and have, at least a few times, forcefully challenged name callers to cease or face the consequences. One officer discusses her reaction to name-calling at a law enforcement agency party:

> I had a white supervisor, and she made a statement. She had a swimming pool and she said, "I just got my pool cleaned, [and now] I let you niggers get in my pool." . . . And at that time, my immediate reactions told me to hit her.

She was restrained in her response in the immediate situation but later filed a complaint with a superior officer, which was dismissed. The only action taken was that the black officer was transferred to another supervisor.

Racialized mistreatment inside and outside the workplace by fellow employees is bad enough for black police officers; when supervisors and other officials participate in, or wink at, such racist actions, their impact is usually more painful and long-lasting. We have noted examples of this participation in discrimination by senior officers and officials throughout this and previous chapters. Racial discrimination supported or ignored by supervisors and senior officers often has very negative effects because the targets of discrimination cannot see a way out. There is no one who can provide help and redress. Most regular white officers tend to orient their discriminatory actions to signals that they receive from more senior white officers. Discriminatory behavior that is winked at or rewarded by these senior officers and officials thus tends to be repeated.[9]

Name-calling was also reported as sometimes being gender oriented. Another female officer comments, "I've had suspects say, 'Bitch, you should be home having babies.'" This form of name-calling seems to be as common in many law enforcement agencies as racist name-calling. Yet these agencies seem to be very slow in protecting women from such harassment and intimidation, and women officers usually lack the political clout in such departments to combat the omnipresent sexist practices. A respondent originally from a northern state discusses her understanding of how men generally talk with her in ways that diminish her status relative to theirs:

> One young man sat right here, and said, "Hey girl, how's it going?" And I said, "How old are you?" He said, "Twenty-something." I said, "I'm

forty-one. I don't think you're old enough to call me girl. How old do I have to be before I'm no longer 'girl' and become 'woman?'" . . . Everybody calls you "girl." One white guy called me a "colored gal." Now I laughed; I thought that was so cute. I had never heard that before.

Her reaction to the last example of gendered racial name-calling was to dismiss it as cute because the white man was elderly and not perceived by her to be a threat. However, other gendered comments, although not containing epithets, imply threats that she and other women respondents feel must be taken seriously. These comments seek to enforce the status quo by letting women know their secondary place.

Name-calling and verbal threats are important symbolic weapons used to intimidate black Americans while reinforcing their structural and ideological oppression. Racialized language is very important in the perpetuation of systemic racism in the United States, and it is generally rooted in the social networks and in-groups of white Americans. Thus, the prominent legal scholar Richard Delgado has suggested that a racial insult is not a minor matter, for it "injures the dignity and self-regard of the person to whom it is addressed, communicating the message that distinctions of race are distinctions of merit, dignity, status, and personhood."[10]

Treating Black Officers with Insensitivity and Disrespect

Many respondents report experiences in which whites have sought to enforce their superior position by treating them or other black people with substantial contempt or disrespect. One officer discusses an early experience with the insensitivity of a white officer and its long-term effect on his family:

> As a child, I remember a confrontation that my father had with the county highway patrol. At the time, I think he was attempting to teach my mother how to drive, and the [white] deputy pulled behind him and stopped him, and it was right in front of our house at the time. And . . . it was not a pleasant experience, shall I say, to the point of actually threatening to put my father in jail and carrying us off to shelters, etc. [Just] teaching her, trying to teach her how to drive, and I don't know whether that had an impact on her, but she still doesn't drive.

A day of family unity turned into an unforgettable traumatic experience in which a white officer threatened the parents with jail time and the loss of their children. Our respondents often use such personal experiences not only to understand the operation of everyday racism better but also to guide their job performance. For example, several respondents offer examples of how past white insensitivity has encouraged them to treat people with greater respect and dignity.

Another officer discusses how he and his white partner almost came to blows over the treatment of a poor family:

> [White officers often] don't care about people, and how things affect people. Okay. Well, I've never been like that. As an example, we stopped a guy who had an old Chevrolet, and I do mean old. He had four or five little kids in it over in the projects, and we stopped him because the car smoked and [the city] has an antismoke ordinance on car smoking at that particular time. So, we stopped him, and in just looking at the guy I say, "Man, I'm not going to give this guy a $50 ticket when he's got four or five little kids, and you can tell they don't have a whole lot. And he's driving this old ragged car that's smoking like a house on fire." He's probably doing the best he can do. You know what I mean? And we got into a real argument about that. To the point that he [the partner] said, "I'm not riding with you anymore; let's call the sergeant." I said, "You do whatever you want to do," because I was the senior officer in the car anyway. And I said, "No," you know, "I'm not writing him no ticket, and you're not."

Past experience with poverty and insensitivity of white officers shapes the discretionary behavior of this concerned officer. Having experienced such encounters as a young person, he uses empathy with poor people to place himself in the position of the man driving the car and imagines the effect of a ticket.

In fact, these black officers repeatedly argue that their past experiences frequently give them greater insight into human behavior and allow them to be more human than many of the white officers they observe daily. One respondent puts it this way:

> We handle the black community completely different than [white officers]. Because most of us older cops understood abuse, we understood we have been victimized so we made up our mind we were not [going to] go out and abuse. No, we did our jobs. We didn't make these petty arrests especially with black youth. We sent them home to their mama. A lot of times white cops would arrest the fathers in front of their kids, and

was always roughing them [up] and always handcuffing them. And the kids would start crying. I saw that too many times in my life. We've got enough problems without taking those fathers. . . . A lot of those young white guys, they didn't care because they didn't look at them as humans.

Past experiences with white insensitivity help officers like this respondent to understand its effects on other people. Treating black people with *humanity* is emphasized in many of these interviews.

A detective discusses how her past experience has helped her to treat a sexual-battery victim with greater respect:

I'm always talking to girls about teenage pregnancy because I was a victim of teenage pregnancy. I'm always trying to use myself as a role model. . . . I took a girl home day before yesterday that sat in this office. She reported an attempt of sexual battery. And when you talk about victims being treated differently, well they interviewed her. . . . She's sitting and she's holding her head, and I knew she had been there over an hour. And they were through with her, and I said, "Well, honey, what you waiting on?" And she said, "Well, I'm waiting on somebody to take me home." And I got real offended by that, because she's a victim; she's been through enough. Why are you making her sit here? It was early in the morning. She probably had had nothing to eat. She was walking on the back of her shoes. She was not dressed properly. . . . The way that she looked, the way that she presented herself, she was a very introverted person, you know; she wouldn't speak out. She wouldn't speak up and nobody cared. They just looked over her—which was wrong.

Once again past experience provides not only knowledge but also a foundation for empathy, and thus betters policing. This respondent implies that white or affluent victims of sexual assault may receive better treatment than black or poor victims. Numerous respondents discuss the discriminatory treatment of black suspects, offenders, and victims of crimes, as compared with treatment of comparable whites. They note the differential treatment given to black and white citizens whose property has been stolen or who have lost family members to violent crimes. The effect of discrimination is experienced in part as a dismissal of the importance of black experiences relative to those of whites *and* a denial of the dignity that black Americans should be afforded.

Previous research shows that white insensitivity in these cases often results from ideological constructions of black inferiority and the physical segregation that prevents whites from knowing black people well.[11] Our respondents often discuss attempts by whites, including fellow officers, to deny their dignity. Humiliation is a form of racist practice that serves to define black Americans as inferior. For example, one black officer describes an extended case of racial harassment in which he was threatened and ignored, and in which his credibility was publicly attacked. White officers accused him of siding with the black community against white officers, although he was just trying to defuse a volatile situation. Subsequently, he received hate mail, and a racist note was left on his patrol car. He was publicly accused of writing and placing the racist note on his own car, and then he was asked to take a polygraph test:

> I never felt like a victim. I felt like I had to defend myself the whole time, even after that. And if I get emotional, excuse me. You remember [the city commissioner when] the derogatory note passed around [town]. That could have been politically motivated. The state attorney never asked him to take a polygraph to make sure that he had nothing to do with that. What makes him more credible than me? I was asked by the state attorney's office to take a polygraph to prove that I did not put the note on my car. Yes sir. Now, can you imagine how insulted I was? . . . I was insulted when I found the note. I was insulted when the chief treated the investigation the way he did. I was insulted when the state attorney asked me to take a polygraph. I have never been vindicated for this.

In his experience, whites are deemed more credible than blacks, and the latter's experiences are often deemed to be unimportant. In the face of overt and extremely humiliating harassment, this officer received no sympathy and was challenged by various white administrators to prove that he was, in fact, victimized. The effects of racial humiliation and other forms of discrimination are seldom measured or studied, but they are often serious and long-lasting.[12] Given the important occupational role that these women and men play in society, such discriminatory experiences are detrimental to personal self-image, as well as to the image of black people in general.

Whites often denigrate and humiliate black Americans outside the workplace as well. One officer discusses belittling experiences with whites that occur frequently during shopping:

> I can go into a department store—now here I am a lieutenant on the police department; I work in Internal Affairs—I go in a department store

on a Saturday and I got to stand in line for fifteen minutes while they are trying to verify my identification and my check. And I know why that is. Now, they can't say that it's their procedure because I watch them. And then somebody else who is of a different race goes up there, and they are cleared just like that. So how do you forget when you are reminded; you know? It would be nice to forget, but you can't because you're confronted with it all the time.

This type of experience is very common for African Americans as they venture into predominantly white shopping areas. These well-educated, high-achieving women and men often report that they are treated in a manner that shows the inability of many whites to think of them as intelligent, responsible human beings.

Another respondent notes how, despite being normally calm, she became furious when a white officer from another agency treated her as if she were a criminal breaking into her own home in a predominantly white neighborhood:

I was dressed in a robe, and the officer thought I was breaking into my house. He approached my garage and saw my car and backed off. But as a citizen, I'm not treated as I should be. He saw my color and assumed that I could not live in that subdivision.

After an initially tense situation, the officer noted a police car parked in her garage and thought better of continuing his investigation. In her interview, she adds that she complained to his supervisor, but with no success. She felt belittled by the initial ridiculous interaction and the response she received after complaining. She concludes that despite the humiliation she still feels when reflecting on the encounter, it could have been much worse for her if she had not been recognized as a police officer.

Keeping Black Officers under Close Control

Even while they argue that they are not being racist, many white administrators and supervisors maintain strict supervision over their black employees. Such surveillance has the effect of taking the moral high ground while implementing policies that limit the ability of black employees to question such policies. Thus, during the 1960s and 1970s, most African-American police officers faced incessant attempts by whites to monitor them, control their actions, make them feel uncomfortable and unwanted, and force them out of policing. One officer recounts the tense atmosphere that he once worked in:

> Very harsh. Very harsh. Everything was trial and error. . . . You were not instructed on things or told how to do things. You were basically just put there and left alone, and when something went wrong they were really on your ass. You know, trying to build pressure on you, and run you off. . . . He'd just write you up. And see, when you start doing stuff like that, what you're doing is generating a paper trail. And you really want to try to hurt somebody and start a bad personnel jacket on them, and that's basically what you're doing there.

In his first years, this officer was not properly trained or instructed by whites in charge, and this practice was deliberate. Apparently, the white officers hoped that the forces pressing on the department would wane, and there would be no need to spend time preparing black officers for the requirements of policing. When questions or issues arose, black officers had no one in the agency to turn to for guidance.

Close control and monitoring are explicitly noted as commonplace by more than a third of the respondents. These respondents often link the notion of having to be twice as good as white officers to practices of close supervision. Certainly, superior officers have to supervise the officers under them. However, numerous respondents argue that the differential monitoring of black officers results in a paper trail in their personnel file that can be used against them later on. One officer discusses her recent experiences with supervision:

> I had one supervisor that I just didn't feel real comfortable with him. He talked to everybody, but he didn't say much to me at all. Everything I handed him, it was double and triple checked. And every call I went on, he was making sure that I was there and, you know. It was a real uncomfortable thing to have to deal with. If you look at it from the administrative standpoint, he was just doing his job. But then if you're out there and you look at the fact that he's not doing this to anybody else but you, it kind of makes you wonder. But he never said anything to make me think that he was against me because of my race or my gender. . . . No one else was getting the treatment that I was getting. In fact, other people were doing things that they probably should have been disciplined for, and I was pretty much doing everything right, but yet I was the person that was under the magnifying glass.

This insightful reflection illustrates how these African-American officers learn that in the performance of their administrative functions superior white officers often allow subjective interpretations of racial or gender matters to influence performance of their duties as well as interpersonal relationships. By comparing her supervisor's actions and interactions with her and with others, this respondent is very open-minded and careful but has gradually determined that something is amiss. Such encounters lower the comfort level of officers and, perhaps more important, produce personnel files that interfere with their advancement.

To this point, these respondents have discussed some of the ideological and attitudinal constructions of whites that define black officers as less competent and that often serve to justify discriminatory practices. Both these constructions and the consequent discriminatory practices are persistent, although their forms may shift.

Authoritarian Actions of Whites: Black Officers and Civilians

That many whites understand the superiority vested in their skin color is further evident in their tendency to act in an authoritarian or demanding manner when dealing with officers and civilians. For example, one officer points out the seriousness of this tendency by developing a hypothetical encounter with a white officer during a training session:

[When a white officer would ask stereotypically,] "Why are black people so loud when you're dealing with them?" I might give them a separate clarification. "Why do black officers also feel intimidated by white officers to the respect that they are going to feel that every white officer is going to overexert their power or something?"

Numerous respondents discuss situations in which white officers overexert their authority to intimidate members of the black public, sometimes in the process simultaneously reinforcing their superiority to black officers:

A white police officer comes on the scene and says, "If you all don't shut up, everybody's going to jail." A black police officer's been there like ten minutes. He didn't have no problems. Soon as a white police officer says, "You all don't shut up, everybody going to jail," pandemonium broke lose. He took a bunch of folks to jail. . . . And you got the black police officer saying, "I was there; I'm handling it; there was nothing going on." Sure, they were loud, but he's dealing with it. A white police officer comes because they don't shut up instantly; he takes them to jail.

This type of white action is commonplace. Another respondent notes, "They would love to let you know that [they're] your superior." Acting on a belief system that maintains that African Americans are loud and uncivilized and notions that black officers are not competent to perform their job, numerous white officers treat black citizens as lesser human beings.

One officer notes how powerful whites who seek to maintain their influence in local communities also manifest this behavior:

It was my home, where I'm from, and this son of a bitch didn't want me [there]. Some big-time farmer over there, some important person. I stopped his ass when he was drunk, and I put him in jail. About a month later, I get a letter from that son of a bitch telling me, "You've got to move out." And I said, "Shit, you've got to be joking?"

Many of our respondents indicate that their policing tasks are most delicate when they are dealing with influential whites, especially those who have had little contact with black Americans in positions of police authority.

Some of the female respondents also note the authoritarian behavior exhibited by male officers, who often "will jump in ahead because they want to take control of a situation." Likely acting on learned messages of the secondary importance of women in society, as well as the traditional notion that only men can be effective officers, male officers periodically dismiss the ability of women to police:

There are certain male officers who will cancel a female officer from their call. We have codes and signals that we use over the radio and . . . at my place of employment they always dispatch two officers to a scene. . . . That male officer, if he gets sent with a female officer, he will cancel her. Because a lot of times they feel, if I got to have a female with me I'll just do it myself.

These white male officers assume an authoritarian position in relation to women, which allows them to decide whether or not women officers can perform required law enforcement tasks. Authoritarian behavior by whites, or white men, serves to reinforce existing stratification hierarchies and reproduce conventional ideological notions of white male superiority.

Open Hostility and Harassment from White Officers

One veteran officer captured the intensity of hostility facing many black officers when they started the job:

> It was pretty intense. And I remember that period well, and it was such an eye opener because I didn't think at that time that you were black or white; I just, I really believed that you were "blue." I really believed that we were all out here to accomplish the same thing and we would be dependent upon each other to do the same job, which is a very critical job. I never imagined that there would be such hostility and disdain. . . . I had to just endure a lot of the situations whether they were subtle situations or whether that they were very overt, negative, hostile situations.

These comments set the tone for this section. Most of our respondents seem to have initially shared the idea that by becoming police officers they were moving ahead and leaving behind an overtly racist past in law enforcement. Most had heard of the fraternal unity of police officers and felt that they would be more or less accepted. They soon learned this was not the case.

Those who became officers prior to the 1980s report that white officers early on, seemingly intoxicated by their authority and supported by agency leaders, pelted African-American officers with nonstop insults and did everything possible to force them out of policing. As the first black women officer in her city, the following respondent suffered incessant harassment:

> I stopped wearing my hair in an Afro. I stopped wearing Jontue. Then I was called "Watermelon Wanda," because you very well know all blacks eat watermelon. So, there was nothing I could do to basically get rid of the prejudices that were there in the department. When I started out, we had a department procedure in which you get on the police radio. You give your call number, whatever you're riding that particular day . . . then you tell them what you have. But in that proper respect, I could not do that, because as soon as they heard my voice on the radio, they would start clicking, and I could not get back on. I could have been getting my butt kicked or anything could have happened, but they didn't care; they just resented the fact that I was there.

She was crying as she recounted the trauma of going to work in this period. She faced the humiliation of never-ending attacks on her appearance and the fear of being unsure she would receive backup. In her interview, she expressed her gratitude to the black male officers who supported her, backed her up, and helped her survive during this very trying time. Her discussion again underscores the often distinctive position of black women in law enforcement agencies. They report facing racialized harassment from white people because of their race and sexual harassment from (usually white) men who wish to keep women in a subordinate position relative to men.

WHITE RESPONSES TO CHANGE AND CHALLENGE
Reluctance to Desegregate Agencies

Our respondents periodically share with the interviewer their awareness that a majority of whites, including a majority of white officers, still operate from a mind-set that black people should be satisfied with a socially subordinate position. For this reason, many white officers seem reluctant to view discrimination as a problem and to support policies that rectify racist practices. Thus, one savvy officer discusses how white officers are likely to accept changes only to keep their job:

> Can you imagine the mind-set of the [white] administrators that were around here and how they may have felt about African Americans coming into this department? But, accepting them solely because they had to, because the law required it. Can you imagine the mind-set that they may have had about the level of willingness to do the right thing and assist them in assimilating upwards, sideways, whatever way into this department? It wasn't there. It came from a continual pounding at the door. We got to do this, we got to do that, we got to do this, we got to do that: you know, perpetual.

Recognizing the inability or reluctance of most whites to work for changes in the nature of individual or institutional racism, numerous respondents argue that blacks must continually work for changes in discriminatory conditions. Without sustained effort, past gains can be lost, and the future of black law enforcement officers is jeopardized.

Several respondents discuss the idea that they see entrenched in the mind of many whites that discrimination is no longer a problem. This officer summarizes conversations she has had with white officers over the necessity of diversity training in various police agencies:

[They say,] "Well, why do we have to go through that?" You know, "We get along just fine; we don't have a problem. Why are they shoving this down our throats?" And I said, "Well, consider this." I said, "When you go out to lunch with your white friend and somebody at the table used the word 'nigger,'" I said, "When you get to the point where you are offended by that and make that known with that group, you know, until you get to that point, maybe you could benefit from cultural diversity training." When I get to the point, if I'm not at the point yet where when I go out with my black friends or somebody brings up the word "cracker," and I'm not offended by that, maybe I can benefit from cultural diversity training.

Note the evenhanded approach of this respondent in pointing out that all people, white and black, can benefit from insightful diversity training programs.

Expecting Support and Gratitude from Black Officers

When members of the dominant group seek to demonstrate that they are concerned for the plight of black people, sometimes they demand at the same time that blacks express some gratitude. One respondent discusses a memorable encounter that forever changed his relationship with a senior white officer:

When I was a sergeant, my lieutenant called me in and asked me to move a desk for him. I was like well, "I can call some of the maintenance guys; that's part of their job description. I don't think it's something we normally expect our sergeants to do." He said, "Well, ask some of your guys." I refused because I didn't want to lose credibility with the men. It was like he wanted me to do something subservient to justify why I'd gotten ahead. He said, "After all I've done for your black ass, you won't do this for me?"

This officer asserts his positive image of himself in a difficult situation. Many of these women and men report experiences with certain white officers who expect demonstrations of gratitude, apparently to reinforce their dominant position or image of themselves. These officers also report that white officers often do not feel that black people should be police officers or believe that they cannot do a credible job and therefore should be grateful that they have a job at all. One officer discusses how he arrived at this conclusion by listening to the comments of white officers during training sessions:

> Some of the guys at the agency there are used to the good-old-boy-type network. You know, we are supposed to be happy with just being given whatever we get. We shouldn't want to be supervisors; we shouldn't want to go to impact positions.

White expectations of gratitude seem to reflect ideological constructions of black inferiority, and these whites further seek to contain the advancement of black officers. Once again, we see the critical importance of established old-boy networks.

White Backlash: Self-Pity and "Reverse Discrimination"

Similarly, several of the African-American officers note that white officers and administrators periodically respond to black understandings of discrimination and attempts to rectify discrimination with self-pity, as whites define themselves as the real victims. Several respondents report that certain white officers reinforce their dominance by lashing out against efforts of black officers to promote change. Thus, fourteen of the respondents specifically discuss various manifestations of this lashing out, as in this pointed comment by one officer:

> I don't think that you can ever get to a fair department to work at. I don't care if you put a black man in charge, a black woman, a white woman; I think then whites are going to complain, "It's going to be the reverse discrimination."

Demonstrating an understanding of the structuring factors in contemporary racism, numerous respondents explain conditions under which they encounter white backlash. One notes that backlash is less likely in times of economic prosperity because there is enough to go around and everyone is able to achieve her or his goals. However, during economic uncertainty, as this officer explains,

> you're talking about struggling people, middle-income, you know, trying to get your kids in college. You're trying to do more for your family than the opportunities were there for you. So when you're caught up in that struggle, you're caught up into typecasting. . . . It's referred to as

displaced aggression, displaced venting. . . . "Well why is that blankity, blankity 'nigger' here?"

Economic and occupational competition, therefore, remains intimately tied to racial constructions and behavior.

When many people compete, they implicitly or explicitly invoke the value of past practices that protected them against competition from employees of color. Black attacks on segregation policies and development of strategies that ensure that they are able to compete can weaken the economic security that whites have historically been afforded because of their racial characteristics. Several respondents conclude from their many experiences that white insecurity periodically manifests itself in a backlash that questions the competency of black employees or calls for a reversal of equal opportunity policies:

> I think that we're [black officers] very competitive in this agency as well, as far as promotion and advancement and things of that nature. And I think a lot of [white] people will blame their shortcomings as far as if they compete against an African American. And even though the test scores are right there—it's posted—they still may resent that person getting promoted and feel that they're getting promoted and such because they're black.

Numerous respondents discuss encounters in which whites have argued that the only reason black employees get certain positions is their race. In this manner, whites reinforce notions of black intellectual inferiority, support policies to limit black participation, and challenge attempts to redress injustice. One officer discusses a particularly hurtful experience in which white coworkers reacted negatively to his promotion in a small law enforcement agency by quitting:

> We have two people that quit. Two supervisors that were equal to me. . . . The chief picked me out of them. Now, instead of them saying, well, the chief feels that I'm more qualified for whatever reason, he had the innuendos that the black community pressured him. . . . I can't speak for them; [but] I guess they assumed that they should have been given the position because they were better than me or better qualified. I don't know what they felt that made them more qualified. . . . We had been in law enforcement for about the same period of time. But as far as education, I had them all by far. The female . . . I was very disappointed when

she quit because I knew her and I liked her, and I still do. But she had a reason. . . . She had prepared for the meeting [and] she interrupted the meeting and handed out a letter to everybody in the department; she quit on the spot. . . . It just took all of the fire out of the joy at the time . . . at the time the promotion wasn't fun to get. The male, he left also, and he was very disheartened. Well, I spoke to him right after, and he said, "You know you don't deserve this position, and I got the fucking balls to tell you that"—and this is, I'm quoting him—"I have the fucking balls to tell you that and I'm getting away from this place." And he did quit. . . . I just wished they would have given me a chance to see what I do, and if I didn't do it, then I could see them quitting. But to quit a job . . . without another job just because I got promoted doesn't make sense.

This respondent searches for other reasons that might explain why the two white officers quit but must conclude that his own racial characteristics and their negative perceptions of his ability were determining factors. Indeed, he is one of only two black officers in a community that is nearly half black, and it appears that the white officers are not accustomed to dealing with black officers in command roles. A respondent from another department discusses a similar response that occurred when an African American moved into a leadership position: "I'm sure a lot of it's race. You should have seen the white police officers bail out after he [assumed leadership]. Quit. . . . and they'll tell you, 'I ain't working for a black man.'"

Anger at Black Officers Who Point Out Racism

Strong emotional responses from whites frequently make it difficult for African Americans to address concerns about continuing racial discrimination successfully. Those who question stereotypical attitudes and discriminatory actions, or address them as injustices and offer remedies, are frequently considered by whites to be overly sensitive. Indeed, they may be labeled as a "troublemaker" or "radical." Many respondents discuss how their demands to be treated fairly have been met with this white response:

Some people used to say I was a troublemaker. I said, "Troublemaker, how? What have I done to cause trouble? Because I won't let you say 'nigger' in front of me? That's a troublemaker? Because I won't let you treat people wrong; that's a troublemaker?" I said, "Come on; get with it; who's the troublemaker? Because I won't let you push my face in the mud? And I'm a troublemaker?" Come on; let's be real!

In his interview this veteran law enforcement officer also notes that his more than twenty years of service as a police officer are all the more remarkable given this negative attitude imposed on him by numerous white officers. Long after initial confrontations have passed, African-American officers too often carry the label of "troublemaker" throughout their career. Indeed, older white officers do not forget about, and newer white officers are often socialized to avoid, certain African-American officers who are outspoken.

Another officer makes a comment that elaborates on the character of the threat that whites often perceive:

> I was seen as very unfavorable by a lot of people, and perhaps I still am
> because I sense that a lot of people see me as a threat. The fact that
> you're advocating for change or the need for change [threatens them].
> And it wasn't done in such a way that I was trying to attack any individ-
> ual; I was simply being outspoken about the changes that I felt were nec-
> essary, to change the system from within and make it better.

His understanding of solutions that would make the agency better for officers of color is not shared by many of the white officers. He also describes feeling, a few years back, the tension as he walked by white officers after he had challenged some promotion tests. Today, even though he serves in a command capacity, he finds that whites still perceive him as "radical" and are sometimes reluctant even to interact with him. The legacy of being a member of the racial outgroup lingers for a long time even as organizations change.

Another senior officer describes white officers' reactions to the formation of a black association in her agency. Some white officers regarded the process as unnecessary and threatening:

> A few years ago we started a black police officer association at the
> department. And even though I was not directly experiencing problems, I
> am certainly sensitive to the needs of those who are. And I remember
> that started a lot of controversy at the department, because, you know,
> people felt like, "Why do the blacks need that; it's gonna be a radical
> group; they're discriminating; it's only for black officers." If we started
> an organization just for white officers, there wouldn't be a problem.

Individual officers who challenge racist practices become a threat to many whites in traditionally white agencies. In addition, black officers' organizations are an even more potent threat to established patterns of discrimination and are attacked and resisted by many white officers. Individual officers who file lawsuits can have an impact in addressing specific discriminatory policies, and formation of black organizations can work to change a wide range of departmental policies. This previous respondent notes, interestingly, how exclusive organizations promoting white interests seem normal to whites, yet organizations representing the will and desire of black officers are often forcefully resisted.

Retaliation against Those Who Protest

One respondent commented on the level of tension in his agency after he successfully challenged promotional exams as being racially biased: "The fact that they had to reverse that portion of the test infuriated hundreds of people around here. It was so tense that you had to almost use a machete to walk through the building." The perception existed that a critique of promotional practices was somehow a critique of whites generally. Interestingly, in this case changing the exam procedures even benefited some white officers in this agency, yet they too demonstrated their anger by refusing to interact with him normally.

Other respondents also report suffering from white anger. One man reports how his reaction to a single encounter resulted in his becoming an object of scorn:

> I saw the police officer when he knocked him off the bicycle with the patrol car. The man went down to the ground, the officer put a chokehold on the man, I got there, the officer struck him a couple times in the solar plex[us] with a night stick and was choking him to the point where his eyes, he had lost body control, he had urinated over himself, his mouth was foaming and his eyes was going back which he was losing a lot of, I guess, what you call your involuntary muscle control and the voluntary muscle control, he was losing that, so that gave me an indication that we're about to kill this person.

He proceeds to describe his own wise actions:

> So I got out and I said, "Turn this man loose; he's going to die on us. Take your hands [from] around his neck, and let me have him." So the

officer was really upset but he did what I asked him. Then I went in and talked to his sergeant about it. . . . His sergeant said, "Well if you've got a complaint, you need to forward it to the lieutenant because I didn't see anything." I said, "Okay." [Another officer] which was one of the other officers, after we turned the guy loose, he says, "You motherfucker." . . . The guy sued, and the department settled out of court, but there was implications that we was in this thing together because we was black. I was asked questions such as, "How long you been knowing this man?" I never [had] seen that man before; I just knew he was a man. [Whites asked,] "Did you get a kickback? How much did he pay you?" Things like that . . . I was interrogated by investigators from the insurance company, from risk management, [the] police department. "How did you buy that [names nice car] out there?" [Other officers] stayed away from me . . . and if I didn't dot all my *I*'s or crossed all my *T*'s on some reports, sergeants were ready to write me up.

Various white officers in the department saw this one officer's complaint of excessive force as an affront, and the complaining officer was a target of considerable anger. Agency leaders' did not accept the fact that racial characteristics could have been a factor and address this incident in a forthright way. Acting on the basis of what he considered just, he encountered almost daily harassment and intimidation, and he ultimately retired early.

Calling racist ideologies or behavior to the attention of whites can create anger, resentment, and a redefinition of the complainant as a problem. Many whites seek to punish the complainant and force his or her silence in the future. In interviews numerous respondents discuss how their complaints or other protest actions have challenged existing relations of power to the extent that they encountered the wrath of fellow officers and superior officers.

One respondent discusses the result of his intervention in what was seen as a case of excessive police force:

[An African-American male] was on the ground and the officer kicked him and the guy started hollering and screaming. . . . And he started attracting a crowd. Then he started hollering at my partner: "Man, you guys just gonna let this guy do this to me? I haven't done anything." The [white officer] got him handcuffed and my partner says, "Come on; let's go; we don't want to be caught in this; let's go." So, we start toward our car, we look back and somehow or other this guy's gotten loose and gotten control of the officer. And so we go back over and get him off of him, and put him in the back of the car and say, "Hey, look, take him and get on out of here." Which is what happened.

Yet, this was not the account that was passed along in the white network, as he now makes clear:

A couple of days later they called my partner and I in, and said that we refused to aid him. . . . That little rumor spread that we did not assist him so for a while there, I guess about a year, we couldn't depend on anybody coming to assist us. We had to assist ourselves. So, if and when they separated us—one of us was on one side of town and one was on the other—usually we didn't care what we were doing, if we heard something of a serious nature come up where one of us were involved, we'd just head across town, because we knew that they weren't going to come and assist us, no matter what happened.

Two African-American officers were informally isolated from others and could not count on backup or support. Despite their actual assistance of the white officer in difficulty, his word carried more weight than theirs, and they were subjected to various retaliatory actions. In some departments, the white administration is directly involved in shaping policies of retaliation against black officers. Another officer describes what happened in her agency: "A black police officer complained because a white police officer used excessive force. They wind up investigating the black police officer for making the complaint. And he did nothing wrong. So, and that was the flavor there."

Once they are targeted, the retaliation that black officers face can be lasting and multifaceted. One officer who filed a lawsuit faced reassignment to a basement office and found himself cut off from departmental communication and some policing authority:

As a result of me filing my lawsuit, I had incidents where like I would make an arrest and I'd turn them over to an officer. Like I would be off duty, somewhere working off duty, I'd turn them over to an officer, and next thing I know, they turn him loose, disregarding my authority as a police officer. They were subverting my authority as a police officer.

Subverting a black officer's authority and failing to respond to backup calls are overt forms of retaliation that can threaten the officer's physical safety. However, retaliation most often includes more subtle actions such as constructing a paper trail that places the black officers on notice:

> I was on the board of directors for the National Black Police Association, and I was denied a raise because of that, one of my step raises, because of that. . . . I took the action in court. . . . That [was] the beginning of what we used to call "the training," when they want to get rid of you. They start little things just to put little letters of reprimand and discipline within your personnel file, so if it builds up, then they can do other things to you. . . . It was just a thing of where they were trying to build a case upon you so two or three years down the road, "We're going to ease this in, we're going to ease something else in, and two or three years down the road, we'll have a nice case file built upon you."

As retaliation in the form of "the training" unfolds, several respondents note that their potential for advancement ends, that interpersonal relations are disrupted, and that communication with superior officers is significantly diminished. Issues of job security become constant sources of stress. One officer describes this poignantly: "I have been blackballed. In this department, I have put in for numerous transfers. I have never gotten one. You dissociate yourself from the job. You just do it. You become robotic." The costs of racism are manifold for individuals, families, and communities.

White Fear of Black Officers' Unity and Independence

An optimist without knowledge of U.S. history might expect that police organizations would represent the interests of all officers, including African Americans who face discrimination by their supervisors. Yet, even a brief look at U.S. history reveals that white police officers have often perpetrated the worst forms of oppression targeting African Americans and other Americans of color. From the late nineteenth century to the 1970s many white police officers were active members of white supremacist organizations such as the Ku Klux Klan and participated in many openly violent attacks on African Americans, or winked while other whites carried out this violence. Those participating included not only rank-and-file officers but also police chiefs and sheriffs, especially in the border states, the southern states, and southern areas of some northern states.[13] In more recent decades, white officers in all regions have been implicated in various forms of discrimination against African Americans, and occasionally in organized white supremacist activity.[14]

Thus, as we discuss in chapter 6, organization is a strategy of resistance that black officers often consider necessary to combat continuing racial hostility and discrimination in policing. In the respondents' experiences, whites often respond to such active organization with fear or anger, as if they are threatened by efforts of African Americans to improve their lot. Indeed, whites have frequently attacked black officers' unions as unnecessary. The Fraternal Order of Police (FOP) and the Police Benevolent Association (PBA) have historically served the interests of their white members well. Whether intentionally or not, these organizations have generally allowed entrenched racist ideologies and practices to be perpetuated without working actively to eradicate them.

Numerous respondents discuss how, although they are members of a traditional police union, they have no real voice and feel they are completely ignored. One respondent discusses how these feelings culminated in black officers' taking collective action:

> The union was putting some proposals on the table that would adversely affect blacks and, of course, promotion is always a big one. . . . I think sometimes as black officers, you're taken lightly because there's not that many of you. . . . So, we pretty much launched the campaign that we would pull out of the PBA and go with the FOP, and that's exactly what happened; and the PBA lost our contract, and which the FOP now has. . . . And I mean even now, you know, every four years we go through out contract agreements and we have to make it clear that we are supportive of the union. However, if you pass or support policy that adversely affects African Americans, we're not going to be a part of it.

From this perspective, only careful monitoring and timely pressure can ensure that traditionally white police unions will back the issues of critical importance to black officers. Many have responded by joining black organizations that promote unity, that accent issues of concern to black officers, and that provide assistance to communities. The continuing split in the interests of black and white officers, manifested in the structure and operation of traditional unions, is further indicative of the entrenched nature of the color line.

In addition to noting white fear of black organizations, our respondents report that some white officers feel threatened by black officers' working together in other capacities. Some seem to view any group of black officers as a threat to white hegemony and seek to keep black officers isolated from the dominant networks. For example, one black supervisor discusses the mix of white and black officers on her squad:

> We were about half and half. And it was pointed out to me at that time by my supervisor that we needed to transfer some people off my squad because nobody wanted it to look like all the blacks were being put on my squad—even though there were other squads that were either [with] all white, or either one black. So it's just, see, that thing about race is always there. . . . I mean what was wrong with a squad that just happened to have been all black? What would have been wrong with that if when we put on our uniforms, we were just police officers?

Her question arises in response to an evaluation of the contradiction between white notions that racism is a myth and nonsensical practices that reproduce racial differences. If racism were in fact dead, would it not be acceptable to have an all-black squad or department? However, many respondents maintain that persistent racism forces white officers to regard a substantially black police squad as somehow threatening.

POLICE BRUTALITY: BLACK OFFICERS' PERSPECTIVES

Physical violence by police officers is an important form of overt discriminatory behavior that enforces compliance with the status quo and serves as an important reminder to black Americans of the extent to which whites will allow them to participate in a white-controlled society. White police officers have historically controlled black communities, and for that reason there exists in the general framework of black Americans' knowledge of racism some specific knowledge of the centuries-old history of police violence.

The topic of police malpractice remains one of great concern in black communities across the country. Some researchers have described how forceful administration, better police training, and strict police professionalism can reduce unnecessarily violent behavior of police officers and alleviate racial tensions in most cities.[15] In spite of attempts at reform, police malpractice remains a serious problem across the United States. Human Rights Watch, the largest U.S. human rights group, has recently concluded from a study of police behavior in fourteen cities that police "brutality was one of the most serious, enduring and divisive human rights violations in the United States [and] members of the black and Hispanic minorities were the victims in disproportionate numbers."[16]

Our respondents are generally quite aware of the historical patterns of brutality of white officers and of the impact of that violence in shaping black communities' understandings of policing. Indeed, as we have seen, many have witnessed the use of excessive force by white officers or felt threatened by white officers at some point in their life. Still, when discussing their experiences in policing, many respondents were somewhat reticent about discussing the issues of police violence and brutality in interviews. What may have motivated this reluctance could be that most interviews took place in police stations, often with other officers nearby. In addition, it appears that many officers want to reduce tensions at work and lower their stress level. Some, as we have already seen, may fear retaliation by their white counterparts.

Thus, it is very significant that, in some manner, nearly half the respondents addressed varying manifestations of police violence. Some did so in roundabout ways, yet it became clear in the interviews that this is an important issue with which all of them must deal. For example, one officer describes how a past experience with police violence reminds him of the racial nature of police brutality:

> I remember that vividly, where an officer struck a young female with his weapon across the mouth, knocking out several of her teeth. . . . Officers knew he was wrong also and knew that he was prejudiced and was abusive toward African Americans. . . . That would not occur if it had been a white young lady and in a white hospital in a white community.

This incident occurred in a hospital in the daytime and suggests that police brutality has been common and overt. Certainly, incidents such as this serve to keep the victim in a subordinate position and remind other black citizens who witness it, or are aware of it, of what could happen to them.

Another officer suggests that police violence disproportionately affects black prisoners, who are authorities on this subject:

> There has been more brutality on black people going to jail than white folks going to jail. Well, I haven't done a study, but all I can say is what I know here. Just like the guy who was beaten so bad his eye came out of his socket. And there's a lot. Some time when I take a different route, some of the prisoners I have in the back of my car say, "What you going

to do, take me somewhere and beat me up?" I'll say, "I'm going to take
you to jail." . . . So they're expecting you to do something to them
because it may have been done before.

This comment implies that white-generated brutality is frequent,
although it usually occurs out of the public's view and away from officers not supportive of such violence. Other respondents underscore this
point with explanations of how specialized agency divisions that have
excluded black officers sometimes have a culture of aggression or violence that becomes accepted, promotes group solidarity, and remains
relatively hidden with the agency. For example, one officer discusses the
all-white K-9 division: "Now, I've heard stories about a particular dog
handler. He would release a dog on anybody and wouldn't care anything about it. I haven't seen it yet. . . . I know it's there."

A respondent from another law enforcement agency discusses how
a squad of white officers engaged in severe brutality yet faced little
punishment:

> Just a few years ago, we had an incident where this particular little squad of
> white officers took one black suspect and picked him up from the predomi-
> nant low socioeconomic area of the city, took him to a baseball park, and
> did a "ring of fire" on him. A "ring of fire" is where they take this black
> suspect and put him in the center of a ring of cars and shine their bright
> lights on him. It's a form of terrorism. . . . A lieutenant filed a long hand-
> written complaint on it, but nothing ever happened to any of these officers.
> What the administration did is tore this group apart, took the sergeant that
> was in charge, and put him in charge of internal affairs. There was nothing
> we could do because they kind of kept it hush-hush. Nothing was ever done
> about it. Yep. This is the cruelty I'm telling you about.

Black officers are often reluctant to become involved in such incidents
because of fear of retaliation and ostracism. Administrations that refuse
to become involved give implicit support to such behavior, perhaps
because of close ties shared with the offending officers or a reluctance
to face the wrath of police organizations.

In many respondents' experience, many white officers fear black
officers' unity with black communities and seem to feel that black officers can only be "real" police officers to the extent that they do not
identify with those communities. More experienced black officers
sometimes note that younger black officers are pressured by white offi-

cers to prove that they are, in fact, "real" officers by engaging in abusive behavior against black citizens. Thus, one respondent discusses in poignant detail an incident in which his career was negatively affected by white officers' expectations:

> We had a white officer that allegedly beat a black male with a flashlight . . . and the black male received forty-something staples in his head. . . . And I was the supervisor at the time. I came to the scene. . . . And I sent the officers away from the scene, and I stayed there and handled it. I was the only black officer there at that scene. . . . Now I used my head when I sent them away. I knew what I was doing. Now I'm going to show you how blacks can be scrutinized. These are fellow officers. I'm looking out for their safety and the safety of the citizens, okay. Now, you've got a large black crowd accumulating; you've got a black male that's bleeding. You've got two white officers standing over him. Now you've got about 50 blacks coming up. The smartest thing to do is to get those two white officers out of there before more blacks come and say, "There they are; let's get them!" It could create a riot situation, okay? So I got them out of there.
>
> Now, my white officers assumed that I got them out of there so I could solicit complaints. You get what I'm saying? I got them out of there so they wouldn't get killed or have to kill anyone. And I calmed the people down. It worked. We did not have a riot. I told the people, I said, "Well, if you think they are wrong, we'll look into it. And if they are, we will deal with that." But I had to do anything I could do to calm those people down, and I knew these people, and I knew what I needed to do. . . . Now, these officers wrote complaints on me, which they were unfounded, but this is how you're scrutinized. . . . They didn't look at me as an officer; they didn't look at me as trying to calm the situation down; they looked at me as a black just like these people.

Attempting to perform his job to the best of his ability and dissolve a potentially violent situation, this senior officer was perceived by white subordinates as siding with the black community against his police agency. He was ostracized by fellow white officers, chastised by his chief, and forced to the brink of resignation. In his and numerous other officers' experience, whites feel threatened by any suggestion of unity, however inaccurate, between black officers and members of black communities.

The extent of black officer involvement in brutality against black citizens is not known, as no major studies have been undertaken. No

respondent described an incident of violence in which he or she participated, although some male respondents did discuss feeling the need to
be aggressive at the beginning of their career under pressure from older
officers. Numerous respondents indicate that younger black male officers may be more likely to fall under the influence of the policing ideas
of white "good old boys" in certain networks that accent excessive violence. However, almost unanimously, the respondents suggest that
black officers as a group are less aggressive toward all citizens. The reasons given include a more acute awareness of past police brutality, their
own experiences with police brutality, and the fact that many of them
live in or near the community that they police, unlike most white officers. One officer explains: "You have a little more respect, I think, for
the people you're dealing with. Because if you rode anywhere in the city
you'd see the same people out the window. I didn't want to mistreat a
guy tonight and see him at the grocery store the next day."

Despite a reluctance to discuss incidents of police violence openly,
these black officers are aware of its persistence and its effect of intimidating citizens in black communities. Police violence harms not only
particular victims but also the larger black communities, as the victim's
experience becomes part of general community knowledge. Although
many respondents acknowledge an awareness of excessive violence in
their law enforcement agency, only four respondents discussed some
actions that they have taken to address violence that they have witnessed or have had knowledge of in their agency. In each instance, they
report that they faced retaliation that affected their career. Clearly, the
awareness of the possibility of retaliation is intimidating in itself.

CONCLUSION

> You want to call it progress because there aren't big jokes in the briefing
> room; the word "nigger" is not used in the briefing room. You'd like to
> call it progress and to certain people in certain respects, that's exactly
> what it is. But the hard answer is that those feelings will come out.
> They're starting to come out in certain policies, in certain decisions that
> are being made—that is very, very concealed because what you do is you
> prevent the fact that there is an agenda of making sure this person is kept
> down [from being revealed].

Much contemporary research has shown that everyday racism, as a
manifestation of white authority and power, seeks to suppress the views

of those who are dominated and to contain them in traditionally subordinate positions.[17] As we have seen in this and preceding chapters, the strategies used by whites at all levels to accomplish such goals range from constructing stereotypes and notions of racial superiority to exhibiting open forms of hostility and recurring discrimination. These black officers provide ample evidence that discrimination by whites maintains the status quo, in part by limiting black participation in historically white institutions. Such white efforts involve ideologically reinforcing the idea of black inferiority and creating institutionalized practices that seek to create constant barriers.

These black officers report that most whites in their job sphere deny that racial discrimination is still a serious problem there, or that they participate in such discrimination. This shifts the blame for continuing racial problems to African Americans, while absolving the collective conscience of white people. The respondents note that when black people point out racist attitudes or acts of discrimination, whites often become defensive or angry. As a result, the complainants frequently face backlash or retaliation. Despite white claims that racial discrimination is dead or dying, these women and men discuss how they daily encounter ways in which whites overemphasize the differences between white and black people, or between black and white communities. Examples include the racist talk that reproduces hoary stereotypes of black inferiority and the racialization of tasks that reinforces notions that black employees cannot competently perform certain job tasks. Finally, our respondents' discussions often illustrate the importance of the techniques recurrently employed by whites to pacify or intimidate black officers. Clearly, hostile racial climates in law enforcement workplaces are still a serious problem in U.S. law enforcement agencies as we move into the twenty-first century.

These law enforcement officers discuss important containment strategies that they have encountered at the hands of whites, thereby providing important insights into how they understand whites. Their reported experiences with everyday discrimination are usually interactive events, and these experiences generally indicate that white and black officers operate from different theories as to the place of whites and blacks in the social world. Our respondents report how being police officers instills in them feelings of pride, purpose, and responsibility, as well as a sense of legitimate authority. However, they report that many encounters with whites revolve around efforts by whites to strip away these feelings and to enforce a subordinate position of black officers to white officers, as well as to white people in general. Therefore, these black officers understand that such containment strategies often foster a sense of white superiority and solidarity that is important to the perpetuation of racial differences and maintenance of different status. The many accounts in the interviews indicate how whites, intentionally or unintentionally, activate their racist notions, employ racist language, and engage in discriminatory behavior in order to conform to the expectations of important others. Constantly, we see the importance of white old-boy networks, for whites generally perform these actions to be part of a larger group, to show group solidarity. The respondents report in detail how most white officers have access to greater material rewards, as well as to more interpersonal camaraderie and emotional support, because of their membership in the dominant network in their organization.

Our findings provide much evidence for the cumulative and shared general knowledge of discrimination and other aspects of systemic racism that black officers develop over time. They, too, have important networks and support groups that are essential to their survival in a world of daily racism. They learn an array of countering strategies that are essential in their dealing with racism in their workaday lives, strategies that we will examine in detail in the next chapters. Yet, their interviews also indicate that white strategies of containment and restriction are, in part, dependent on this process of sharing among the black officers. In their interviews, these officers note how their experiences with police violence and with racist talk in their department affect them personally. White intimidation is enhanced when black employees communicate information about negative encounters with whites to other black officers, who in turn take defensive precautions because of this information. Those who do not successfully learn these messages or who reject them may find themselves subjected to prolonged periods of harassment. The resulting stress and insecurity produced by white-generated harassment and other forms of discrimination can make an officer's workaday life a living hell.

6.

Black Officers Transform Policing

There is nothing that I would do over again because that's just life. I'm proud that I was able to get more blacks hired and to get more blacks able to work throughout the police department. You know, when I ride around and I see black females and I see black males who have stars on their collars—they're supervisors; they're administrators. Not just supervisors, they're administrators. And that's what I'm glad of, you know? A lot of them—all of them came under me. But, as I had a number of them tell me, "Hell, you should have been here; you should have been there." I said, "Yeah, but you've got to realize something; the people that fight are the ones who end up not getting the things that they fight for," I said. And I realize that there were people before me who fight, so they didn't get what I got, so I don't have that problem, if you understand what I'm saying.

This insightful senior officer takes credit for the advancement of black officers in his law enforcement agency, at the same time giving credit for his own success to those who preceded him. His comments embody the spirit of commonality of interest, struggle, self-sacrifice, and transformation reflected in discussions with most of the officers we interviewed. In chapter 2 we showed how, and how much, these officers have learned about the operation of everyday racism in policing. They have developed their views as local and national political and economic contexts shape and reshape the struggles over how police agencies should operate in communities. Historically and currently, many white business and political leaders have used their influence to demand stricter social control over communities of color or, less often, to promote more humane policing.

Much scholarly work and media commentary leave the impression that African-American officers are little more than pawns in struggles to reshape historically white police agencies. However, given an opportunity to discuss their views, African-American officers see themselves as far more than mere pawns. Drawing on the detailed accounts and commentaries by respondents, we move beyond these prior analyses to focus on how black officers have fought for and transformed policing within the larger context of social and political movements to change U.S. racial relations.

In response to those who have argued that white racism has ended and that we currently live in a color-blind society, a number of scholars in the experiential-racism tradition have convincingly demonstrated that racism still operates in complex forms and along myriad dimensions in our everyday world. Most important, our evidence derives not from ivory tower ideation or media-driven anecdotes but from in-depth conversations with nearly five hundred African Americans over fifteen years. These interviews demonstrate that white-determined racism contextualizes the lived reality of African Americans today and still causes them great physical and emotional harm. As we have shown in previous research, these interviews also show how the matrix of racial domination produces a recurring dialectic of resistance.[1]

Much of our insight into racism in the United States is derived from those thinkers who have emphasized the active resistance of black Americans. We are impressed by Herbert Aptheker's accounts of the hundreds of slave insurrections and conspiracies to revolt, by W. E. B. Du Bois's analysis of how slaves' "general strike" was the key to the defeat of the Confederacy in the Civil War, by the many thousands of brave black Americans whose nonviolent efforts overthrew legal segregation, and by the continuing organizational efforts of black Americans to dismantle the structure of U.S. racism.[2] Indeed, the constant efforts of African Americans, now over hundreds of years, to achieve freedom and equality have made their struggles and movements a model of action for oppressed peoples across the world.

Those African Americans we have spoken with over the years have shared with us their deep understandings and profound knowledge of how the daily operation of racism can be successfully countered through daily struggle. The development and organization of resistance to white racial domination, as individuals and as part of their community, is a constant and vital theme in the interviews of most African Americans who have talked with us. In this chapter we give voice to their views and perspectives on individual and collective resistance.

In addition to delineating the important aspects of this seldom studied African-American culture of resistance to racism, we trace out how specific racialized encounters—as well as individual characteristics such as gender, class, and age—must be understood in order to gain a more complete comprehension of the character and dimensions of black resistance strategies for dealing with individual and institutionalized racism. Most previous scholarly work on black resistance, including our own, either concentrates on large-scale community movements or probes the array of individual strategies that counter racist challenges. In this chapter we develop a deeper understanding of these two dimensions of resistance by using the accounts of respondents to examine how societal struggle is dialectically linked to individual and small-group resistance within a specific institutional setting such as that of a law enforcement agency. We see that maintaining strong ties with the black community has informed and guided the daily actions of black officers in this often racially hostile organizational setting. Clearly, we can conclude, the efforts of African-American officers have significantly transformed the character of U.S. policing in recent decades.

ACCOUNTS OF RESISTANCE: BREAKING DOWN SEGREGATION

African-American officers have often been pioneers in their community in challenging the old racial hierarchy. One officer discusses at length how a black officer in his area became the first to arrest a white person:

> The first officer to make an arrest on a white person, open in the streets, was Officer [name]. And [he] and I played football at the same university, and . . . he was about 6'7", three hundred and about fifteen pounds. And he actually had a fight with the guy. A white lives in the [white] area that was over here, and he had had some white lady around the Holiday Inn . . . and they were drinking and had partied, and he had beat her up. And some of the guests next door to his room heard the commotion and called the police out. So, as [he] answered the call he drove to the front entrance of the motel, and it just so happened this guy was leaving. . . . He stopped the guy to talk with him, and so [the officer] at that time

told him, "Sir, we're going to have to go back and check on the welfare of this other person in this room that you were in. I want you to accompany me back up." [The white man] says, "I'm not going anywhere with you." I'm witnessing this now because I was [his] backup. . . . [He] said, "Oh yea you're going back now. We got a problem up here in this room or I wouldn't be here and you, you're gonna go back." And [the white man] said, "Buddy, I, I, I'm not going back." He said, "You're fooling with the wrong people. You need to be down there with your people."

After noting that the white man was referring here to the black community, this officer continues:

So, [the officer] went to go into the hotel with him, and he pulled back and said, "I'm not going." [The officer] said, "Listen, let's go on up to this room." So, so at that time [he] had to actually grab the guy and force him to take him back because we can do that . . . in a situation . . . [when] we suspect a crime has happened. . . . So, he put a resistance and actually started fighting. So, [the officer] picked him up . . . and pushed him down through the hood of the car. Just folded double, then grabbed him in the pants as if he was almost unconscious, just drug him up to the room and conducted his business and found out the lady had her teeth, all her teeth knocked out. And she was in dire need of medical attention bad because she had a severe head injury. And her teeth were all out in front. He had just bust them out, you know beat her up. So, [the officer] put his butt in jail where he should have been.

This officer recounts in detail an incident with profound consequences: a black officer seized the authority to arrest white offenders in spite of being assigned to patrol a black area with no authority to arrest white people. In their interviews two other officers recounted in depth, and with pride, how black officers broke segregation barriers and began to arrest white offenders despite "getting their butts chewed out" afterward. Clearly, once these black officers acted to break down the old rules, others followed suit, and there was no going back. Soon, black officers were proving that they were active, competent protectors of the public will rather than powerless tokens.

Michael Olivas has emphasized the critical importance of accounts of resistance from ancestors and predecessors in helping current generations of Americans of color to counter racism.[3] In our interviews these African-American officers accent the necessity of understanding their own and their predecessors' accounts of how they have changed polic-ing. Collective experiences with racist encounters are shared among members of black communities, including these black officers, and they help to form a framework of understanding and support that serves as a basis for resistance. Without their accounts, one might assume that whites had decided, out of the goodness of their heart, to change polic-ing institutions to allow black participation. In fact, African Americans and other Americans of color actively fought racism in law enforcement agencies and thus played a key role in changing the nature of policing in many areas of the United States.

Another officer explains how black officers in his agency fought for integrated patrol cars in the 1970s despite official intransigence:

> We were riding segregated cars. [We] fought for and got integrated cars. . . . I'd say the mid seventies or early eighties. And [we] went up and got a lawyer and [went to] the sheriff and under sheriff. And we said, "Look, we'd like to be, we'd like to be full police officers. We're relegated to black areas. We'd like to ride the entire county and if on these nights when my black partner is not there, my black behind is out there, my black behind rides by itself. If there is a white officer, why not put him with me?" "Well, because we don't do that." "It's about time we started, you know; quit hanging me out there to dry." . . . So, "Well, you're black." "Well, I'll be damned! I wear the same, the same uniform. My body doesn't stop any more bullets than anybody else, you know; I bleed the same. If I get shot I'm going to bleed." So, those kind of things and "We don't have enough blacks." "That's not my fault that you're not hiring enough blacks!" You know? So, "You're going to keep me out here riding the beat forever because we're not hiring enough blacks?"

This discussion shows how white senior officers often had points of view that promoted segregation in policing and were reluctant to move toward professionalism in these matters. Black officers had to speak out and teach white officials that adequate protection of the public could not be achieved if police strategies remained rooted in outdated segre-gationist notions and practices. Resistance to racism in the 1960s and 1970s, therefore, occurred within both the larger societal context and the contexts of specific institutional settings.

Another officer recounts the story of a black officer who did not passively serve the interests of his segregationist employers and worked to change organizational and societal injustice simultaneously:

> I had a partner named [officer's name]. We came on about the same time. He lived across the street. . . . And we were riding together one night, and he said—we came in one afternoon down at the precinct to gas up— he said, "I think I'll"—we had two fountains one white, one was for col-ored—and he said, "I'll see how this white water tastes." And so he drank out the fountain. And the mechanic saw him, and before we could get back to our beat, he had called our lieutenant and told him about it. So he calls us on the radio and tells us to meet him at [a nearby intersec-tion]. And he said, "Which one of you boys drank out of the fountain down there?" Well, we knew he knew who we were because they had told him. . . . [The officer] was suspended for three days, but it looked so bad they decided to let it go. But they had a punishment beat . . . on the midnight shift from eleven to seven.

Not long ago in the United States, drinking water from a whites-only fountain was an act of overt resistance; the incident provides a com-mentary on the contradiction of hiring black officers to enforce laws that still disadvantaged them. White leaders inside and outside law enforcement agencies naively assumed that black officers would follow unjust laws without challenging them. Confronted with the absurdity of this assumption, the white lieutenant was at a loss to decide how to punish the black transgressor. The black officer took responsibility, and punishment was meted out. Importantly, the account lives on well after the death of the officer and serves as a reminder to others that acts of resistance can have powerful consequences long after the moment of action.

KNOWING ONESELF IN RELATION TO WHITE RACISM
The Importance of Officers' Backgrounds

In these accounts of action and agency, we see black officers' willing-ness to use their entry into policing as an opportunity to challenge seg-regationist practices that have been characteristic of racial interaction in many areas of the United States since the 1880s. In chapter 2 we examined the importance of many of these black officers' growing up in a segregated community, an experience that had a significant influ-ence on their understanding of the socioracial world around them. These experiences shaped their goals and strategies of resistance.

According to the accounts of our respondents, certain factors seem to increase the likelihood of a black American participating actively in risky change efforts like those noted. Reflecting on his first decade of police work, this older officer notes the importance of serving in the military:

> [I] didn't take bullshit. If you said something to me, and you were wrong, I spoke up. The blacks in the South, especially black men, was seen as submissive, and not prone to stand up for themselves. Other guys, who'd gone and fought or who'd been in the military and prepared to fight, I think we were different about things in life, period. Because we went over there to fight for what I thought was supposed to be this country's best interest, perhaps it was time to fight back here for what I perceived to be our people's best interest. It was just that I had seen stuff coming up as a small child. I had said, "I'm not going to let this happen to me, you know; I'm not going to take this anymore."

Being raised in a segregationist setting kindled the fire, but serving in the military and fighting overseas struck the match of resistance. This service to country clarifies the contradiction of fighting for freedom abroad while being denied freedom at home and has often culminated in a new perspective for many black women and men who have served in the military, both in the past and in the present.

In addition, the military has accented the idea of betterment through education and has often provided assistance to its members in obtaining education during and after their period of service. This opportunity corresponded with the centuries-old goal of black communities: to gain freedom through increased education. Those black women and men who achieved higher levels of education from military and other programs and later joined police agencies often became a threat to white-centered policing, especially in those agencies composed mostly of poorly educated whites. Another officer explains some of the consequences:

> The racial problem was there. It was always there, but like I said before, it was compounded by the educational differences. . . . And that's what they didn't like about college-trained blacks. We didn't ask what the rules said. . . . We went everywhere. We didn't want their interpretation. We knew lawyers. We knew black lawyers, and so that [racism] became a problem. Well, we got job slots; we forced the sheriff at the time, the white sheriff, to open up job slots for black officers. We showed the need for black officers. We had nothing to do directly with the actual hiring of

who got the job, but we fought for the job slot. We fought for officers to work in the police department. Like now, we have blacks all over the police department.

Black officers emphasize that they have transformed policing. Those who had military experience and those who were college trained were clearly vital to the struggle for desegregation. Accumulated knowledge about racism allowed these officers to form a sophisticated understanding of its manifestations. Their experiences and training allowed them to be proactive and to develop preemptive strategies to counter organizational racism in policing rather than just to react to individual problems.

We should note the continual use of the word *we* in discussions throughout this chapter and previous chapters. This is a group and community struggle. Officers like this man maintain that the struggle against racism must be one that changes institutions, yet he accents a key point about sources of personal strength:

> Because number one, I think the reason for that is because I never forgot where I come from. And not, I mean, not to say that I was showing favoritism; I knew the area that I was living in. It was predominantly black. I'm black, nobody have to tell me that, and I have no intentions of moving out of my community.

Again and again, commentaries like this give us a sense of the collective and ongoing character of the struggle against discrimination inside and outside U.S. police departments. These officers understand that they are part of a long-term and collective struggle. That this officer emphasizes the importance of not leaving his black community provides insight into how self-definition, which is essential to resistance, is rooted in one's background and sense of community.

The Importance of Self-Image and Self-Esteem

Cumulative experience and collective knowledge are keys to formation of a "humanist vision of themselves and others,"[4] which is central for resistance to racism and action to expand social justice. One does not just learn and then act, for actions to combat injustice create a fecund atmosphere for deeper understandings. If clarity of understanding about the nature of racial interaction shapes one's self-image, struggle and the knowledge gained from it further shape one's self-image and self-esteem. This officer discusses how his awareness of the historical mistreatment of the African-American community by white officers is linked to his personal sense of empathy:

> I think I brought patience and understanding, empathy to people's problems, other than looking at the physical and law-abiding solution. [When] I first came on the police force, I made up my mind that I was going to show some feelings and empathy toward people. . . . Anybody can slap somebody in jail, but I made [up] my mind that I was going to put myself in their place and deal with their problems, or deal with their breaking of the law from that perspective. And I think I have accomplished that because [of] the respect and the cooperation that I have received from the community while I was an officer.

Because of the community's positive response to his ability to treat individuals as human beings rather than as depersonalized criminals, he feels a strong sense of accomplishment. The strength of the conventional police culture in creating an "us" versus "them" approach to civilians withers in importance in comparison with the strong self-image and empathy forged from direct experiences with racial oppression in policing. Other officers often see themselves as not fitting the traditional mold of the "aggressive crime-fighting officer." Instead, they typically have a more holistic view of themselves as officers, which seems rooted in collective bonds with members of their family and community. As this officer indicates, they protect the public while serving a multifunctional role:

> I think that I'm a people-person to a certain degree. I believe in upholding the law. I like doing things to help people; I like, I like, feeling as though I make a difference. Being a police officer requires you to be some of everything, I think. I mean, because I find myself . . . preaching to people, I'm teaching people. . . . You have to use your imagination, and you have to, like I say, be able to function in almost any capacity because . . . you're marriage counselors, you're guidance counselors, you're giving all kind of advice all the time.

This sense of service, and of self, is oriented to community betterment in a way that would be difficult to understand if self-image were just an individual and internal matter. Many respondents indicate that they need to feel that they are making a difference in communities to feel a sense of accomplishment.

Their actions have an impact not only on them and their families but also on their communities and, ultimately, societal patterns of racial oppression. As other committed police officers do, these black officers often attempt to affect others off duty as well as on duty. Who they are is intimately intertwined with those with whom they interact:

> To my kids or my wife, I provide for the family. I'm a role model. That's one of the reasons that I'm back in school to show them that my life has—I want them to see that you can achieve higher level of education, a degree after high school. I encourage them to do that. For citizens out here, you can see me as a respectable person trying to serve the community. Whenever they see me, I'm polite . . . no one's ever seen me wandering around cheating on my wife or hanging out with drug dealers, taking money from them, buying or selling. Actually, I guess I'm just trying to set a good example for other people to see that you don't have to be one, what people say you are. You can achieve what anybody else can achieve. You don't have to be what people say you are—you have to be this; you have to be that. I've overcome that. I am someone; I am somebody.

Repeatedly, we see the importance to these women and men of being respected as officers *and* as members of their communities. This self-image emerges in part from a common experience of oppression in which individuals are denied basic humanity and are treated with disrespect.

Another officer shares the importance of treating people with humanity and of defining one's role as a problem solver rather than an aggressive crime fighter. Her perspective is further rooted in her experience with sexism as well as racism:

> I know that I'm certainly not as strong, as tall, as big, as physically, you know, together as male officers. But you'll find now that society is at a point where it takes much more than muscle, that you get a lot more done by talking things through and showing your human side. And I think that's why women are so good in police work because . . . we're good listeners. And we know that it'd be much easier and better for everybody if we could talk it out, because we can't duke it out like the guys. And so I think the days of the big macho, strong police officer are

over, and it takes someone who's willing to get out there and work through issues and problems and really try to deal with problems as opposed to symptoms of problems.

The similarities of her comments to those of the male officers is clear, but she further promotes a positive definition of herself, and of other women officers, as sensitive and capable interpersonally, perhaps in response to the pervasive discourse that women cannot be good officers because they are physically weaker than men. Her account, like that of many other officers, is continually shaped as a response to the hegemonic white and male discourse about policing and is thus another strategy of resistance. Her self-definition is based on not only positive reinforcement from members of her community but also her reaction to the dominant discourse that she is somehow less capable than men.

Another respondent laments what he and other African Americans could be if they did not have to operate within a racialized reality and its stereotyped images of African Americans. The harsh context means that African Americans are more or less forced to reflect on

racial issues. They're talking about something that really affects, you know, racial issues, about criminals: We've got too many blacks robbing and we have blacks getting discriminated against here, blacks da-da-da. . . . I mean, there's more to life than that. I mean, my brain is more, is concerned with art, music, philosophy, economics; not me specifically, but as a community, we have people that can, that are concerned about those things. But the only thing that comes to the forefront is our concern with racism, and we wear it as a badge of nobility. And I think the only reason we wear it is that because we're the, we're the recipient of it. . . . And plus, it just, it confines us so much from enjoying life, that every time you sit around, people want to talk about racism. Well, I know racism is out there, but I'm not going to just let my whole life just revolve around blacks and whites. There's more to life. There's Asians out there too; I mean there's Mexicans out there. I mean, they've got cultures that I'd like to experience; they've got ideas. I don't want to just spend my whole life just worrying about what white folks are doing and how white folks treating blacks.

If black women and men were not confronted daily by racism, including gendered racism, they would have much more freedom to define themselves and to live life to its fullest. No matter how much they would like to believe that conditions are better, or that who they are is not affected by those with whom they interact, at any moment they can be confronted by whites who thrust discrimination upon them. Accordingly, the officers we spoke with generally see themselves as being shaped by racist acts to some degree and see their self-knowing as constantly invaded by the acts and the discourse that must result from those acts.

Tailoring Responses to Situations

Rooted in a strong sense of self, most of these officers discuss a range of countering strategies they have used when confronted with racism. As we discussed in chapter 2, these strategies are often predicated on a reasoned evaluation of an encounter guided by a cumulative knowledge of racism. An officer's response generally fits the encounter, and each response in some way serves as a mechanism to counter racism.

These fighting-back strategies range from personal perseverance to collective and organized struggles. Each strategy attempts to move beyond racial limitations and to create a freer self, and a more humane world. One respondent discusses how each racialized and genderized situation must be thoroughly considered before an appropriate response can be decided:

> Pray a whole lot. I usually try to confront and say this is what I think is going on, but you usually, there has to be some time-spell to think about it. And you have to weigh your options: Is it worth it? Was it so? I don't know; after being in it so long, you think, is it worth a fight? "You can win the battle and lose the war" is a good saying among cops, and so each situation you weigh your options on whether or not it's worth it. And that's a shame. To say, I wish I could confront every issue, but I don't confront every issue. It's okay if I can get around it without actually saying it out loud, and they get the idea that I don't like it, and they change it, we're okay. And then there are just certain things that I draw the line at. I mean, total outright racism, I draw the line; as far as verbalizing it or anything, that's where I draw the line, I draw the line if it affects, I guess, my pay or my reputation. I'm very proud of the fact that I'm honest or whatever.

From this carefully considered, experience-honed perspective, some battles must be fought immediately, particularly if they involve overt racism or if one's reputation or livelihood is in question. Other more subtle acts and processes must be thought through and discussed with others first, because an immediate counter may be detrimental to long-range outcomes and careers. In our interviews, the desire for change is omnipresent, and these women and men are prepared to counter current injustice. Note too, once again, the role of religious values in responses to racism.

Frequently, these women and men discuss how they have developed a horizon that envisions future struggles for which they consciously prepare with the help of others, as one officer underscores:

> You have to realize that it takes time to change attitudes and maybe some attitudes won't ever change, so you have to keep it in check and go on with your life. And my father-in-law says that you can't fight every battle, but you have to pick the battle. And if ever a time comes that I have to pick one, I'll have to pick one to fight.

This younger officer has yet to encounter overt racism in his agency, yet feels that he possesses the requisite tools of evaluation to understand when and whether he encounters a significantly racialized situation. By discussing past and potential situations with an important family member, he feels ready to respond appropriately. As many other officers do, he links his future responses to past responses developed and honed collectively over many generations. It appears that each time blatant, subtle, or covert racism is countered by an individual officer, or group of officers, the transformation of U.S. policing in the antiracist direction is furthered.

INDIVIDUAL RESISTANCE ON THE JOB
Managing and Enduring Everyday Racism

When black law enforcement officers respond to racialized mistreatment, their strategies of resistance are not static; they depend on location, situation, and point in time. Importantly, therefore, most officers have a repertoire of diverse strategies that they use over the course of their career, which depend on the context of encounters with whites, as well as on their own personal characteristics and styles of interaction.

In chapter 3 we examined the many ways that whites intentionally or unintentionally insult black people's culture, characteristics, and personalities in order to justify their exclusion or marginalization in U.S.

institutions. In the face of overt hostility, black officers frequently report having no choice but to endure quietly and patiently the outright denigration of their self-identity, their family, or other members of their community. One older officer describes what it was like in the 1970s:

> Inside the station house, all the way around you, you just, I tell you it was just almost like meteor showers coming down on you, bombarding you; that's the way you felt. There was no place to hide, no place to run.

Listening to this officer's comments, it becomes clear that white officers then felt that the frequency of attacks might be sufficient to drive black officers away. Yet black officers, such as this respondent, dug in and refused to be driven off by incessant attacks by whites.

Prior research by the authors has shown that the physical and emotional costs of racial hostility and discrimination for African Americans are serious and varied.[5] We see the same reports in these interviews. Frequently, these women and men note or allude to the great range of impacts that racial hostility and discrimination have on them, their family, and their community. These costs of discrimination include many health costs, both physical and psychological. When we went to a city to meet with the very last officer we interviewed for this study, his family told us that it would be too hard for him in his present health condition and initially would not let us visit. Even some white officers advised us to be easy with him. Yet, he insisted and was determined to say all he wanted to say even when he started tiring. This man made what was one of the most emotional comments about the long-term effects of the stress of racism:

> I had heart surgery twice, so I'm on light duty here. I developed heart problems. Well, I'm quite sure stress had a lot to do with it, yes. Some stress. [pause] That's correct. I just lost one of my friends, [name]. . . . I took his place. They shipped me in from the [name] station out here. He died last August. He had a heart transplant. He lived about three years after his transplant. [pause] Then we have Sergeant [name], who had double aneurysms and a stroke and so he is, he's basically a vegetable today . . . he doesn't know himself. . . . His mind goes and comes.

Although this respondent, as other black officers do, realizes that the strains and tensions of everyday life include many factors, he is clear that the stress of dealing with racial hostility and discrimination in his workplace is a major factor in his and other black officers' health problems. Indeed, another veteran officer downplays the impact of the usual stress of the policing role in relation to the greater impact of racism, thereby succinctly summing up the sentiments of many respondents: "It is more stressful dealing internally with the racism that we have. If I didn't have that problem, this job, for me, it would almost be stress-free."

Another officer points at yet other costs of racism, which must be constantly countered:

> Once you experience those situations long enough, you get calloused to them; you get hardened to those situations. You learn how to put them away, and go out and perform, even though it's very stressful. You go out and perform the way you know you're supposed to perform by the rules and by the procedures and by the laws. Because you know now that there's somebody out to bite you in the butt, or to get you placed in prison, or to have you terminated knowing that you've got a home, children, furniture to pay for, debts, bills. So you learn how to put it away.

He continues with a description of some other impacts of dealing with everyday racism:

> I've seen officers [who] drank themselves crazy on the weekend. I've seen officers [long pause], just go away, just shut up in their room for the whole time. Don't bother them. Officers' divorce rates are high, black officers, white too. But I guess to sum it up is that you learn to be hard to that situation. You know it's there until there's some people or until there's some support mechanism that's going to help you do away [with] it or get rid of it, expose it. You should learn to try and live with it and realize that you have a job to perform. And you deal with it at the time, and it's time to deal with it. I didn't carry it around with me. When I got in my patrol car, I left out. I went out and just go out and do my job. I come back in the station, that's when I deal with it. I think that's the way most officers handle it . . . from what I've seen.

This officer's emotions rise to the surface as he recounts the recurring humiliation and pain that are experienced by him and fellow black officers. Many internalize their pain and deal with it in isolation, or with alcohol, because they have no alternative. He points to a partial solution that occurs when other black officers are hired, because their numbers can produce organization and support mechanisms. He and other officers just have to endure until relief arrives. This siege mentality is especially common in the accounts of early black officers, women officers, and those isolated in small or rural law enforcement agencies. They generally discuss facing more overt forms of racism, more white hostility, and a greater lack of support.

How do they endure this? Why do they persevere in such painful settings? Reflecting on the years when he was the only black officer, one respondent provides some answers to these difficult questions:

> You're basically the only black. You come in to work. You clock in. No one talks to you. Not only not talk to you, they kind of frown away from you. Then, you have to deal with that. And I mean that's from the chief on down. Then I have to deal with that. Go to work; no one likes you at the time. And then you have to go out there to the community, and you've got to deal with criminals who don't like you. And you've got nowhere to go. Your camaraderie is gone. . . . Now, you may get on the phone and call a friend, but for ten hours you are just you. And I had to deal with that for a while. I'll work out, that helps; work out vigorously. And I look for better moments, and they are here, like now.

Then he reflects on the situations today, as a senior officer:

> Some of the people are still there, work under me. . . . That was then; this is now. The best way to look at people, instead of getting hate, you look at it as misguided, uninformed. That's the way to deal with it to keep me from holding a grudge, so to speak. I really don't hold grudges, but that hurt me more than that person. . . . So that's just more stress. So I look at it and I looked at it like it was going to get better. But it did get overwhelming at times. It really did. And you just, and I just hate getting in the car. It's almost like you get a sick feeling; I'm going to put on my uniform and go to work for a while. But I had to work; I had to make a living. But I didn't want to—and I had offers; I had a job offered to me in the sheriff's department, but what if I would have left? What path would I have been setting for somebody else, or for the future? I needed to stick it out. So I did. . . . And I feel strong about this community, and I feel attached to the community, and that's why I stick it out.

As with many other accounts in this book, we see in this thoughtful analysis how endurance of racism is not cowardice, or just an individualistic attempt to prove to oneself that racial hatred can be survived. It is a reasoned response to racism that is judged to be the best fit in a particular situation, indeed a situation in a process of slow change. As this man does, many of these officers explain the importance of being strong for the good of the black community and for those black officers who follow. If they were to give up and quit, or explode from frustration, then they might not have a positive effect on the policing institution over time. Again we observe that the strategy of patiently enduring racism is not an all-or-nothing form of internalized resistance. Instead, it is often a useful strategy for a particular context in which one must wait for a better day, in the expectation of achieving long-term collective goals for racial change.

Active Confrontation: Combatting Everyday Racism

Bombarded regularly with racial hatred and discrimination, these and thousands of other black officers have persevered, succeeded, even sometimes thrived in some of the harshest employment conditions of modern society. At times, when they cannot endure the blatancy of the racism any more, they openly confront their white tormentors. The personal frustration and anguish over racial hostility and discrimination are often overwhelming. One respondent assesses the anger many black officers feel because of the continual attempts by whites to humiliate and dehumanize them. He mentions an incident involving white discriminators:

> Yeah, he was white. "Ignore that shit." I say, "Okay." I'd call [a local black leader] of the Urban League; he'd say, "Ignore it." He said, "You've got to hang in there tough." So, I made probation, we got a new captain, and I walked in one morning, and one officer said, "Well, there goes the resident nigger." And I said, "Let me tell you one mother-fucking thing. Ain't going to be no more goddamn 'nigger.' The 'nigger' shit is over with." And, so then, the lieutenant walked in and said, "What's all this damn cussing in here? What's wrong with the nigger?" And I said, "Let me tell you one more fucking thing; that 'nigger' shit is over with." So then, the new captain walks in and says: "Fine. I wasn't going to say nothing until you said something. And you finally decided that you would put a stop to it; it's done. I don't want to hear it again, and if I do, I'm going to bust some ass."

He then recounts that the new captain called him into his office and said:

> "Now, I want to know what took you so long to put a stop to it." And I
> said, "Well, I had to make probation." He said, "Wise damn move," he
> said, "because they would have run your ass off." And we talked for a
> long time. And he . . . said, "You know, I never saw a black person until
> I turned twenty-one years old and went in the navy." He grew up in [the
> Midwest]. He said, "All I was used to seeing was Indians." He said, "But
> I'm finally glad." He said, "All I want you to do is do your job and
> you'll never have a problem with me." I said, "Well, captain, I'm going
> to do that."

This account of confrontation with white officers resulted from very
overt racial hostility and discrimination. He was labeled the "resident
nigger" as if he were a pet with no emotions or aspirations. He further
shares how he told himself just to endure it until he reached a point of
job security. When he turned to black leaders, they would tell him to be
strong or ignore it. Once probation ended, however, his strategy turned
to confrontation fueled by incalculable pain. The result was a redefinition of himself in his agency with the support of a white officer unwill-
ing to risk challenging other whites about their behavior until it
threatened his command.

In other social locations, confrontation with white discriminators
takes various forms. In this next comment, the mutual isolation and
reliance of two black trainees at a police academy were a source of
strength in determining appropriate responses to certain racial encounters:

> We were two [black] officers. We made our grades, kept to ourselves in
> the sense that we didn't associate a lot. We felt like if people didn't want
> to associate with us, then the heck with them. We're not going to try to
> force ourselves on them, but we're going to be respected. So we pretty
> much stayed to ourselves. One of the guys was talking one day, and the
> guy says, "Shut up!" And my friend looked around, and he said, "Why
> should I?" And the guy says, "Who [do] you think you're talking to?"
> He says, "I'm talking to you." And he says, "You can't tell me what to
> say." And my friend says, "Why can't I?" And he says "You're a," and
> [my friend] says, "I'm a what?" And he went ahead on, and he bowed
> himself and he said, "You're a nigger." And about that time he got
> slapped. I think the fact that this one [white] guy kind of typified all of
> this. We were seen in the light of being militants. And we were just there.

I can't care how you feel about me personally. I don't care what you say
as long as you don't say it around me. That's fine if you want to go
home, and you can yell it to the housetop; that's your business. But when
you're around me, you respect me as a person. . . . The book says it's not
proper here, and we're gonna use the book if that what it takes to
straighten you out about this, your behavior.

These black officers were trying to make it through the academy with
heads held high despite actions indicating the white recruits did not
want them. They jointly determined that lack of acceptance would be
endured so long as no one was publicly disrespectful to them. Once a
white recruit crossed that line, he was slapped. Such physical confrontations are a means of last resort for these officers, who indicate
that they prefer to solve racial situations through other means.

Black female officers have, as we have noted, a distinctive position,
in which they often encounter both racism and sexism. In their interviews they discuss confronting whites about overt mistreatment. One
officer recounts an important story of how she found a place in the
department and earned the respect of fellow officers by publicly confronting a fellow black male officer:

I command respect; I wouldn't have it any other way. . . . And when I
got to work one morning at about 6:30 I guess, I walked in the roll-call
room, and I didn't know a whole lot of people because normally, roll-call
back then, we would have about maybe . . . 150 in roll call. You know,
officers that are riding on that shift, and I walked in and I sat down.
They had chairs . . . and I sat down and I crossed my feet like this, and I
had an officer, a black officer I might add, walked up to me. And he
took his nightstick, and he uncrossed my legs. And he said, "Real police
officers don't sit with their legs crossed." And I mean, I could have taken
that several ways. I could have taken that as though he was saying, I was
being wimpy or, or females sitting like that or whatever. And the way
that I handled that probably jumped my career. . . . I could have sat there
and cried. I could have ran to my superior officer, who would have been
my supervisor . . . and said that I felt that he was being sexist or whatever, but I didn't. What I did, I handled him from that day and that was
very early in my career. I told him, I said, "Let me tell you something.
For as long, you don't even know me; for as long as you know me, you
don't ever walk up to me, and first of all put your nightstick or your
hand on me without asking permission to do so." I mean, I knew that

that was considered a battery, but I mean I would not have taken it to those extremes. And I told him that the way that I sat had nothing to do with anything. . . . If you've got a problem with the way that I'm sitting, that's your problem. The way that I'm sitting has nothing to do with how well, or how well I may or may not be able to do my job. And I mean, I pretty much took a stand and it was done around other people, and I think from that point, people knew that they couldn't just walk up to me and bully me or say something to me that I did not like or did not agree with because they knew that I was going to voice my opinion, and I started that from day one. I handle people on the streets the same way. I will not allow people to talk to me any kind of way, you know, even when I work.

This officer delineates her process of evaluation, the other actions she could have chosen, as well as some potential outcomes of her choices. Her confrontational response was measured and specifically addressed the gendered affront in that situation. More important, she implies that her action demonstrated to the many other officers that she was not someone who would take gendered or racialized abuse without confronting it. Numerous officers like this woman discuss how resistance has allowed them to remain in or advance in policing and indicate that this ultimately benefits African Americans as a group.

Improving One's Readiness: Education and Training

In previous chapters, we have shown that these officers believe they have to be twice as good as white officers. Consequently, they frequently discuss improving themselves and working within the boundaries of the system for change. They believe that by becoming the best officer they can be, they can protect themselves from the attacks of whites. Discussing his agency, one officer demonstrates his understanding of a fundamental contradiction in policing:

Well, I'm vocal; I'm a mouth opener. There's a way—remember me saying, too, it's not what you say as how you say it. There are ways to do things too and not be on the radical end. I can be the silent motivator, so to speak, and get things done silently . . . that's my approach. I'm not a radical by no means, and I'm a conformer. I work within the system and learn the system, and always have made a point of learning the system, work within the system, and make the system work like it should.

When black officers speak out and confront racism, they may be labeled radical. Many take pains to point out that they are not radical. This officer sees himself as more or less conforming, yet he has an understanding that the goals of police professionalism are skewed to the extent that police agencies operate in a racist manner. Therefore, he aspires to learn policing, advance in his agency, achieve command rank, and require his subordinates to police the community according to the stated goals of policing rather than the dictates of racism. To do this, he must endure many things, and he does speak out when appropriate, yet his master strategy is to work behind the scenes.

These African-American officers report that they must continually strive to be better. By choice or not, they are held up as examples. They realize that their success or failure can reflect positively or negatively on other black Americans. They often feel compelled to participate in professional training to further individual and collective goals:

> I've had to change course, and really, through advancements, see things
> in a different light. And I think one of the most important things with me
> was realizing that sometimes . . . you admit that you don't know; you
> can learn faster. But if you go into a thing and you know everything,
> then you can bring about a whole lot of division, and I just admitted that
> I didn't know. But I got busy in the books and while here, I've gone back
> to college and just tried to improve me all around, you know? Not just
> through advancement, but . . . then you know, say hey, I need some more
> schooling; I need some more this. I'm an instructor, and I push for excel-
> lence, you know, because it just won't happen automatically.

This officer was careful not to create division and catalyze white reaction by overtly demonstrating his significant knowledge. He is reflective about his own shortcomings and stresses personal improvement, individual success, and agency leadership. Many respondents also link individual success to collective success in ways that whites do not.

Other officers may have other long-range goals yet similarly recognize the necessity of learning more about good policing if they are to be successful. One female officer explains,

> I was very inquisitive, and like when calls and things go out on the radio,
> I would always be real observant and listen. And when things go out
> over the radio, I would say, "Well, what if we had gone to that case and
> this had happened?" In other words, I was always giving him scenarios

and telling him, "Well if this happened, could we have done this?" And
they saw that as me being a person that was willing to learn, wanted to
learn, wanted to learn how to do police work. I was always throwing
questions, asking questions, giving them scenarios. Well, we would go on
calls and I would say, "Well I know we handled this like this, but if this
had happened, couldn't we, if this had happened and couldn't have done
such and such and such?" And they saw that as "You know, this girl is
really trying to learn police work," and I think that played a very, very
great part in how people treated me as a police officer, how my coworkers treated me as a police officer.

Perhaps all new officers should be required to engage in a similar inquisitive process and become the best-prepared officers possible. What sets
this officer and her strategy apart is that she enters policing as a black
woman, and whites may be inclined to reject her presence and dismiss her
as a "girl." Being an inquisitive, active learner can force other officers to
view her as competent and accept her. To the extent that she is successful, she is able to navigate racism and sexism more or less successfully and
thereby demonstrate that black women can be very good police officers.

Personal Goals Are Linked with Collective Goals

These officers often see their entry into policing as reflective of the
desires of black Americans generally. Therefore, most do not just accept
their new job with individual gratitude but rather work to ensure that
black officers will be an integral part of all policing activities. The
repertoire of coping and resistance strategies is often manifested individually but is always collectively oriented.

We have previously discussed the importance of the civil rights
movement and the political struggles of black communities to the entry
into and perseverance in policing institutions of black officers. Of further importance is recognition that the support of others led to their
success; that acknowledgment guides their formation of personal and
professional goals, which often emphasize giving back to their community. One officer explains that by making policing more professional he
works to remove racial markers and presses whites to perceive black
Americans as fully human:

My goal is always strive to do better and to go higher and continue to
try to be an influence, positive influence on everybody so that they'll say,

"Yeah, he was a good man." If they want to know what race I was, you know, they could say, "Yeah, he was a good African American," or whatever the case may be, but either way, they're going to say that I was a good administrator; I was fair and honest. And [for] those who may feel that there is a difference in the color of your skin whenever it comes to ability, this will—my having done a good job—dispel that particular myth. And they can say, "Well, I don't think color has anything to do with it; this guy was black and he did an excellent job." And I want to continue to try to do my best to set that example and be the best, you know, continue to climb as high as I can.

Black officers are in the distinctive position of exposing many racist contradictions in their agencies. To the extent that they prove themselves, they can dispel myths about black people in general. To the extent that they work at being professional and at demanding professionalism, they can positively impact the police culture and shape the future administration of agencies.

These black officers can also be important examples for younger black people and signal that there are hope and opportunity in spite of the historical reality of racism, as this female officer notes:

That role model thing; I'm not like [Dennis] Rodman, and I'm not like those other guys who don't want to be a role model. I'm saying, Hey, look at me, okay. I'm not perfect; I've got plenty of flaws. But you know what, I'm trying. And I'm not going to do something to you out of mean-spiritedness. I'm going to do what I need to do because this is the law, not because of your color. I could hate you all day, okay. There's some blacks that drive me bananas. And I say my people, my people— and then some days I dissociate myself from the black race. There's some females that drive me up the wall, and I dissociate myself from the female gender. But you know what; I come back and I think about it. They got a better chance with me than with a lot of folks. Because at least I'm open for change.

This officer's common heritage with other African Americans is clear, even while she emphasizes she is a unique individual. She implores us to see her as human while she maintains the realistic understanding that her success can and should serve as inspiration to other black women and men that it is possible to persevere and make a difference. It is clear in most of the interviews that these officers have frequently made certain personal sacrifices to get where they are now in their career. Their sacrifices and trials are a critical source of both knowledge and motivation for the present and future.

In the interviews these women and men often suggest that their personal sacrifices promote a collective good. This officer discusses how he uses reflections on racism as motivation to persevere and improve conditions for others:

> I used it as motivation and energy. . . . I don't know if I'd be where I am today, had I not experienced a lot of the racism that I did. Because some of the things, you know, actually cause me to go home and sit and meditate on them. And, you know, dog-gone it, I'm going to do something about this. . . . I felt that it was my responsibility to go through the ranks and diversify the command staff and to present an African-American perspective to the changes that we're going to be facing in the future and that was my sole purpose for promotion. . . . It's my obligation to take it and to go and to fight racism and harassment, and to make sure that the things that I've experienced do not occur anymore to anybody. And that's pretty much my life mission as long as I'm a trooper.

Women officers report that the pain and humiliation they have endured, the accumulation of confrontations they have had, and their efforts to better themselves and policing have a purpose well beyond the individual level. This female pioneer at a large law enforcement agency shares this understanding:

> The first female, who should have been the first to graduate, she ended up having a nervous breakdown, and to this day I understand she still has not fully recovered. Because I was a stronger person, I took the blows and I did not crack up. I thought I was, and they tried to make me, but I didn't. And I think by someone being able to take it and withstand it . . . the more people you have on the department of a minority, the more you accept them and learn to exist and cohabit.

Although racial discrimination is energy sapping, it often generates a strong determination to resist and to ensure, if one gets the necessary authority, that other black Americans, and women, do not have face similar problems. Through speaking out and making other personal sacrifices, numerous officers have placed their own advancement at risk and have faced retaliation. Despite these dangers, many find their responsibility to challenge racism must take precedence over worries about personal advancement and security. Indeed, these officers' emphasis on recognizing their role in shaping the current and future nature of discrimination in policing through their own actions is a significant finding that is distinctive among analyses in the literature on policing in the United States.

Numerous officers stress that proving themselves, and continually learning and fighting back, are ways that they can generally improve the conditions for other African Americans as well. One officer notes the improvements in protest capabilities:

> I think the older guys, most of them were out, they were the pioneers so they had to take the [brunt] of all the ignorance that was available. Luckily now we have a few processes where you can remedy that situation. Back then they didn't have . . . a discrimination suit, or anything like that. Now you have that capability.

Early officers endured and confronted racism on the job to transform police agencies and permit the entry of greater numbers of black officers. To the extent that more recently hired black officers do not encounter discrimination and overt racist behavior by white officers, the efforts of their predecessors were successful.

COLLECTIVE RESISTANCE
The Importance of Mutual Support

Early black officers proved that they could withstand withering racial hostility and create institutional space for increased numbers of black and, later, women officers. They endured, challenged overt practices, and sometimes moved up in law enforcement agencies. In such a capacity, they have served as guides and as support for later entrants into policing, who are often unprepared for what they encounter. Women officers, and particularly black women officers, have experienced intense animosity and coordinated efforts to force them out of this traditionally male-dominated profession. Our respondents frequently tell stories about mistreatment of women in policing and discuss how black officers draw on their negative experiences to help them, as in this example:

> I remember the first white female that came to the street. They hated her guts. These were white officers, but the blacks were the ones who helped her. You know, so what I'm saying is that black folks have always been,

black police officers have always been the ones who really hold up the
police department in terms of morals and things of that nature.

Again, in numerous agencies black officers suggest that they are the
ones who often uphold the proclaimed standards of professional and
nondiscriminatory behavior. It is not only male officers who discuss this
assistance; black women officers also acknowledge the support they
received from many black male officers.

One female officer discusses in detail the pain and humiliation she
suffered in her agency and credits other black officers for their support
in tough times:

> [Other black officers] would come by and check on you, and see what's
> wrong. I mean, "You need some help? Can I get something for you?"
> And I've had officers to do that for me, and we do it for other officers,
> especially on the squad. You do have that common bond with somebody
> to come by, and check on your fellow officers.

Even today, the camaraderie necessary in this dangerous policing profession tends to be segregated. Despite the claim that "blue is blue," the
most critical support and care generally are provided by members of
one's own racial group.

This is an enduring consequence of white old-boy networks, which
are still often racially exclusionary in regard to important policing matters. To counter these networks, black officers have had to create their
own support networks and police organizations. For example, the
respondents discuss radioing officers whom they feel comfortable with,
meeting them, helping them through tough times, and backing them up
in time of need. One officer discusses the importance of this type of
relationship and the pride he has in his role:

> We almost have a support group between black officers. It's a lot of us
> there, and we can all communicate. They make a call that makes them
> upset, and I back them up on that call. I know what they're going
> through. So I kind of step in and take care of it. You know, because
> they're from [the same community], and we can have that relationship;
> we have a relationship where . . . maybe I'm going to finish this call for
> you. "Why don't you just sit down and take a break?" Whatever, like
> that. So we have that. When you walk through the hallway, and one of
> us is upset, we can stop and say, "Hey, man, are you all right?" And

with a bad attitude, "Well, why don't you meet me outside?" And we can talk about it that way. And now that I'm in a senior role now, I'm like a senior officer even though I've only been there two years, but that two years is more than a lot of people.

This support is frequently discussed as essential to individual perseverance, as well as a crucial base on which to develop more formal organizations. These informal support groups serve as precursors to black officers' associations. Yet, most agencies do not yet have such formal organizations. White administrators often thwart attempts to organize in many agencies, and in some agencies the numbers of black officers are too low for successful organization.

Still, many officers in agencies without these formal associations maintain informal groups that also work to increase or maintain the number of black officers in these agencies. This officer discusses the ongoing efforts of black officers in her department to prepare younger people for careers in policing:

> We have a cadet program, an explorer program, as a way to develop African-American police officers. And recently we have hired two that came through the cadet program. We have some in training, and some in the academy. So that program has helped attract African-American men. In the past, you would have to pay to go to the academy to be certified and that was another way that white males got hired. But the process now, we will hire noncertified officers and send them on to the academy. And both of these programs have helped bring on a number of primarily African-American males.

In every type and size of agency, these officers report the importance of mutual support, yet it seems particularly vital in smaller police agencies, in rural agencies, and in those with fewer black officers and no formal organization to represent their interests.

Formal Organizations and Associations

These African-American officers endure, confront specific instances of discrimination, and work for change within the system because they understand that their role is of vital importance to their communities. But what is the impact of their efforts on policing in the United States? As one officer notes, "If you have a complaint, what are you going to do to solve it? What is your contribution to the change?" Another officer pointedly provides the answer; first he notes, "Nobody voluntarily gives up power; rules change but power remains the same." Then he argues that formal organization with collective action is the key to forcing change in the face of extensive discrimination and intransigence.

Many officers underscore the necessity of forming unions and associations to promote black officer solidarity, which can serve as powerful tools to alter policing through the recruitment and training of new black officers. One officer discusses the continuing need for black solidarity in relation to white opposition to inclusion of black officers:

> [New black officers] didn't want to have anything to do with us. It's so obvious. Now [they're] in trouble; now the system is showing that [it doesn't] care who you are. The bottom line you know you're still black. And, you know, it became a revolving door with them. They were good kids, but you know they needed, as a matter of fact, we were forced to form a black association, a black brotherhood of police officers. We tried to bring those cops in and tell them this is how you survive the system. Because the blacks down there with rank or status, they were black, they were never nothing else; they were black. You know, they did their jobs, they were confident, they didn't try to be anything else. There was one that tried to be something different, but as soon as he got in trouble, as soon as he forgot who he was, as soon as he forgot what color he was, as soon as he got too comfortable, [he] made mistakes in the system. The system, the system did it again. That still goes on down there. Every once in a while you see that in white guys, you know, every once in a while. . . . You may be the man, but, brother, you are still black. Michael Jackson, you may be the man, but, brother, you are still black. You say that to a lot of people of influence today who think that they are untouchable, [but] . . . the system has a way they love to bring them back to reality. You may be all of that, you may have all the money in the world; the bottom line is you're still [black]. Colin Powell knows how far to go.

Black officers who endured and survived racism at the inception of their job learned quickly how racial hostility and discrimination operated in their institutional setting. As their numbers have grown, black officers have usually shared their experiences and knowledge with new recruits and showed them how to survive in difficult circumstances.

This was and is accomplished informally in many law enforcement agencies, but in those with a large number of black officers, it has sometimes been formalized in black police associations. These associations have necessarily developed and codified a range of strategies to deal with the forms of racism in specific settings. Several officers like the following note that the continual recruitment of black officers ensures that positive changes in departmental racial patterns continue:

> We decided we'd take our organization on a different mission, and that mission was that we were going to go out and actively recruit black police officers. And tell the story of what was going on in the police department. . . . It wasn't until '83 that we reached a hundred black police officers; and that was due to raising total hell with the sheriff. . . . That wasn't done because they wanted to do it. . . . If you truly want to hire African-American police officers, it's a constant struggle, and you have to keep pushing.

This organizing is an appropriate strategy for the long-term, protracted struggle against racial hostility and discrimination. Members of black police organizations understand that the future of blacks in policing depends on organized struggle.

Yet, recruiting is not enough. Efforts are necessary to guarantee the retention of black officers who are recruited and to move them into positions of authority. Support, training, and mentoring are important responsibilities taken on by organizations of black officers, as this officer makes clear:

> Our black police organization? One of the main reasons that it was formulated was to serve as a mentor program for new recruits coming in the department to let them know that "Look, when you need help, you don't only turn to your field training officer, but there is another resource out here, another avenue that can help you with your difficulty before it's too late. You know, don't wait till the day before you're dismissed before you ask for help." We introduce ourselves to the new recruits long before they get into any difficulty. And I think it just helps them feel more welcome here, too. You know, the police culture, I mean, it's a strange culture; it's so fraternal that when you're coming inside from the outside, it's difficult I think, particularly as an African-American officer. We've tried to beef up our FTO program and get more black training officers.

These black police organizations fill important gaps in officer support that are not addressed by traditional police unions such as the

Police Benevolent Association (PBA) and the Fraternal Order of Police (FOP). These latter organizations traditionally deal with labor issues and are likely to reflect the particular interests of white officers. Black associations are much more likely to deal with civil and human rights violations and to work to ensure that they are rectified.

However, in many areas the black police association and the traditional white police associations are dependent on each other to accomplish common goals of betterment for their members. Therefore, black associations influence policing by actively, collectively shaping these traditional labor unions. As one officer explains from the experience in her agency:

> Before we had FOP, we had the Police Benevolent Association, who was our union group. And, you know, every four years we vote on a contract, and we were approaching time to vote again. And I knew that the union was putting some proposals on the table that would adversely affect blacks and, of course, promotion is always a big one. And, you know, I felt like there was no way that blacks should support an organization that supports procedures that adversely affect African Americans. And so, at the time, I was the president of our black police officer's association, and we had launched a campaign to completely pull out of the union. And I think sometimes as black officers, you're taken lightly because there's not that many of you. But we figured if we pulled out of the union, there was going to be over $300,000 lost to the union per year. So if, you know, if they thought we were not that significant, we proved to them that we were. And it was also coming up on a time where there were a lot of people who were, blacks and whites, who were dissatisfied with the union. So, we pretty much launched the campaign that we would pull out of the PBA and go with the FOP, and that's exactly what happened. And the PBA lost our contract, and which the FOP now has . . . that was like '92. And I mean even now, you know, every four years we go through out contract agreements and we have to make it clear that we are supportive of the union. However, if you pass or support policy that adversely affects African Americans, we're not gonna be a part of it.

Clearly conceived goals, such as promotion of talented black officers, and strong organization can pressure otherwise less than supportive police unions to negotiate with and support the aims of black officers. Those unions that continue to support discriminatory policies, intentionally or by oversight, will learn the error of their decisions by the extent of the financial and political losses they incur as black officers leave the unions.

Moreover, if white leaders still do not get the message that black officers want real change, political demonstrations can be used to push the agenda of black officers in the face of white resistance:

> Well, it all depends. Because, see now, if there is an issue that's a real concern to us, we are going to speak out about that issue. And I'll give you one, of the previous sergeant's exam. There were a lot of problems with that written test, you know, and we made a few white officers join. We stood right there on the steps of the police station, fifty-five of us, and said that this test was the wrong test.

Collective organization and action usually improve the workplace conditions for black officers, and these improvements sometimes extend to all officers, as in the preceding example. Numerous African-American officers point out that among their goals are greater professionalization of policing and better working conditions for all officers.

LEGAL PROTECTION AND LAWSUITS

Civil rights movements and other political struggles by African Americans have increased legal protections against discrimination for African Americans, as well as for all other Americans. The civil rights laws have provided African Americans with an institutionally sanctioned means of redress for their concerns. In addition, these movements forced the creation of the Equal Employment Opportunity Commission (EEOC) and of many affirmative action programs, both of which have been important weapons in the arsenal of black resistance to racism.

Numerous respondents accent the role of equal opportunity and affirmative action policies that support hiring and advancement within historically white departments. One senior officer discusses why such equal opportunity programs are important:

> I'm always in favor of it because without that, there wouldn't be any incentive for whites to even consider blacks for [a] position. . . . I'm a minority and I have nothing unique to bring to you that you can't get from anybody else in your own racial group; what would make you

consider me? Unless you've got something to force them to look at other issues—nothing. I mean there has to be something there to make you consider me in order for me, as an average guy, you know, to stand a chance of getting a job. Because, just simple mathematics, always I'm going to be outnumbered as far as number of people that are participating, even though our skills may be identical, you know. . . . I also understand too that people have a tendency to look out for their own.

Once again, we see that these officers recognize the social cloning that goes on in most historically white institutions. This officer notes that "like seeks like" in traditionally white police agencies. Whites are most comfortable with their own kind and, as we discussed in chapter 3, frequently rely on racial stereotypes to justify their social distance from black people. Programs to end racial hostility and discrimination must therefore press those in control for change, for otherwise there would be little or no incentive to step outside the racial comfort zone.

These respondents also note the necessity of having legal recourse, as well as willingness to turn to it, in responding to discrimination by white officers and administrators in historically white agencies. Soon after their entry into policing, black officers sometimes had to turn to legal remedies, as in this man's situation:

The basis for the lawsuit was, there were no lateral training. See we couldn't, black officers couldn't, work traffic at that time. All the other officers were fully educated or trained to work the criminal shift and traffic. We were only given the criminal part of the training. We could only work [in black communities]. Those were the black sections. And it was about '74 when we got our first traffic training and started working traffic in our own districts, I mean the black districts. But see, what we had to do was we had to call white officers in to work traffic calls in the districts that we patrolled.

Racial change is often reported to have been very gradual, and these officers often took action to achieve small but important gains. This officer notes that the lawsuit was intended to force white agencies to train black officers for traffic duty because of white agencies' resistance. Yet, after they filed the suit and received the right to be trained, they still could only work in black communities. Despite their win in this specific battle they were still officers in a segregated agency.

Officers in other agencies also fought and forced white leadership to accept agreements that allowed black officers entry into more specialized areas:

> Right, that's when we filed a conciliatory agreement where we felt that we're being excluded from certain classifications and positions and so forth within the department. And we had no training officers, no corporals, no motorcycle riders and these sort of things and from that point, from '76 on, it changed.

In the mid-1970s one agency was forced to train black officers for traffic duty, while yet another agreed not to block black officers' movement into other positions in the agency. Collectively, and across agencies, black officers have analyzed the problems they have faced, formed solutions, and taken appropriate action in order to persuade white officials to agree to necessary changes. Mutual support and organization have been key, and legal remediation is one instrument of resistance and transformation.

In another agency there was a collective effort that culminated in filing an equal opportunity complaint against the city, which resulted in a favorable judgment that facilitated the promotion of black officers:

> The city then agreed to enter into an agreement with the EOC that said from 1980 through 1985, a five-year period of time, that any black who had taken the test, passed it and qualified—I emphasize qualified—qualified for promotion. The third promotion to sergeant, every third promotion to sergeant for that five-year period, would be a black person, and what that equated to was, for that five-year period, five sergeants were promoted to the rank. Five blacks were promoted to the rank of sergeant from a formal standpoint.

This officer emphasizes that those promoted were qualified, a response to much racist discourse by whites that suggests that black employees are not qualified. Yet it takes more than good qualifications. It often takes legal actions such as this to produce an increase in black officers in law enforcement agencies. Five black sergeants translate into five supportive, rather than racially hostile, supervisors for younger black officers. Most important, perhaps, they may become leaders in the agency down the line.

These respondents stress the importance of black leadership in the transformation of contemporary policing institutions, but black

Americans have had to organize and fight to force law enforcement agencies to allow the growth of this black leadership. One officer in another agency describes what happened there:

> What happened was eventually about six of the officers, myself included, got together and decided that enough is enough. We were subjected to more or less what I looked upon being unfair disciplinary process, where for the same offense that a Caucasian officer would do, then they would give them lesser punishment than for what we would do. And we get a more severe punishment so eventually, about six of us got together and filed . . . contacted the EEOC and Justice Department, and filed a discrimination suit against the department. And at the same time, we pretty well contact the Justice Department, and . . . it was in the process of having all of the funding for the department cut off till such time that the discrimination lawsuit was resolved.

He continues, describing a petition that was circulated to black officers in the department:

> They petitioned that all Afro-Americans—at that time, had probably about twenty-one officers on the force and everything—and asked them if each one of them felt they had been discriminated against, or for a promotion or for a reassignment . . . or even, you know, as far as being unfairly disciplined or whatever, felt that they had been a victim of either one or the other, they go ahead, and they had them to sign this petition. What happened, after they got about thirteen names on the petition, one of the Afro-American officers got a copy of their names and took it up to the chief at that time, and the thirteen people who was on that list pretty well was identified. And then from that point on . . . we were probably [unfairly] disciplined, more or less, not something you put your hand on, but you could pretty well tell what took place. Well anyway, as a result of this, we finally met with the city manager, as well as the city commission. . . . And met with some of the community leaders and let them know . . . of our concerns. . . . We were given some choices to either go ahead on and be given to a black captain—I think there were two lieutenants and a sergeant—or else they would go ahead on . . . and put a black chief down there. And that's when [names black officer] became the black chief.

A number of black officers in this medium-sized department sought redress for multiple instances of discrimination. Though betrayed by one officer, and burdened with punitive agency reactions, these officers persevered. The result was that the majority of the participants never significantly advanced in their agency, but by their sacrifices they were successful in getting the first black chief in the agency's history.

BUILDING AND SECURING BLACK LEADERSHIP

As we have seen, many of these black law enforcement officers describe and emphasize the importance of having black officers more up into higher-level positions in agencies. The strategies to increase the number of African-American officers, as well as to change patterns of racial hostility and discrimination in policing generally, often rely on the presence of some black command officers.

Our respondents often argue that sustainable changes in policing can only occur if black officers are in most divisions and levels of law enforcement agencies. One officer notes that black supervisors are essential to reduce the occupational and social distance between command staff and patrol officers:

> We need more people in command positions. We have some. . . . But in midmanagement, the lieutenant positions and sergeant positions, there needs to be more black supervision in that. . . . That will be one of my goals that I will deal with. . . . We've got to get more of these guys to come in and take the sergeant test.

The goal of creating a black middle management in larger agencies is important to the day-to-day support of black officers and to the enforcement of departmental regulations aimed at promoting internal equality and the elimination of abuse of members of black communities. Also of importance is the promotion of black officers to leadership positions in which they can place issues of importance to black Americans on the agency leadership's agenda. As the following officer describes, otherwise the concerns of black officers and black communities are too easily ignored:

> The police department, police profession, is a very status quo–oriented profession. And because people don't get confronted—when I say people, I'm talking about chiefs primarily and deputy chiefs—do not get confronted with some of these issues that are involving the lesser percentage of people in the workforce, they never get dealt with. I think my efforts,

and the efforts of others in this police department like me who are bringing forward issues to the chiefs—bringing forward issues to the deputy
chiefs—has resulted in our hiring policy being more inclusive, has helped
to increase that number of, the number of blacks and Hispanics in this
police department, and females too, if you look at the percentages. It certainly has helped to, to open up opportunities in transfers where detectives and other people—our criminal investigation division, at one point,
never had any more than two blacks assigned there as detectives. And
I'm talking about in a group of eighty-plus detectives. But we now have a
situation where there are a few more in there, and they're in there based
on their abilities and the fact that they have shown that they can do the
job. I personally have called special meetings . . . with the deputy chiefs
and with the chief to talk about the issue of race and to talk about the
issue of fairness.

Once promoted to a sufficiently high level, these officers have the ability to set agendas, attend meetings, and communicate black concerns to
community and agency leaders. They have a rare ability to work for
major changes in the internal operation of policing in historically white
institutions. Thus, another command officer stresses his role and his
dedication to removing barriers in the treatment and hiring of black
officers:

The interview process—Then we have a process where we implement it
now that I'm on that committee . . . I've taken an active role in this
process, having been there, and am very vocal about it. Where we have
the applicant review committee where now we have appointed marshals,
two appointed marshals and a training personnel on this committee, we
have the final say whether that person's hired or not. . . . I look at some
of this garbage, and I can say, well, no, this is not fair, whatever, or this
person should not have gotten here for whatever reason. And we can
eliminate him at that process; now I do have an input into that.

Black command and supervisory staff can be effective role models
for younger black officers, increase black participation in all areas of an
agency, reshape internal political processes, and work to transform the
nature of departmental racism. For example, one department head,
arguing that structural changes in the department were not enough,
described how part of his mission is to promote diversity training to
effect changes in the attitudes of white officers:

Force-feed it, that's the only way we've got to the point that we are now. The system or the legislature or our overseers had to literally open the mouth of police agencies and dump diversity into their esophagus. . . . We're going to need more force-feeding of diversity training; I think it's probably going to take more than once every four years. It should be something that's an annual training, to where they're so sick of hearing from it, they'd either get on the bandwagon, you know, and really sincerely realize that people are people regardless of what color they are . . . or they'll get out, because we don't need law enforcement officers carrying guns that harbor, you know, such biased views. . . . The people that don't have a problem with diversity, they're not going to have a problem with more training and more force feeding. In fact, they'll accept it. . . . That's what's got us to the point that we are now, and that seems to be the only thing that works—to attach their career to their ability to treat everyone fairly and with equal justice.

This administrator recognizes that much change must be initiated and pressured for from the top. With that pressure, as the rapid desegregation of the U.S. military by President Harry Truman demonstrated in the late 1940s, even severe patterns of racial hostility and discrimination can be substantially overcome. This is particularly true for the military and for paramilitary organizations such as police departments.

In many agencies, our respondents note, this diversity training is merely perfunctory and often used as a means of achieving accreditation rather than real change. However, as black officers move into leadership positions, including as academy teachers and as facilitators of diversity training, they can use diversity training as a way of pressing for change in racial attitudes. One officer explains what can happen:

I'm a human diversity instructor for the [agency]. And in my courses, I teach them, I studied on how Asians act or how Caucasians may act, how African Americans act, and I think with this course, officers have to take sixteen hours of human diversity. And in my classes, I've gotten a lot of positive feedback. I got them to where my classes start off—it's real quiet—I would say probably an hour into my class I have police officers in there about to actually kill each other. I mean they're screaming and they're hollering and they're arguing. But at the end of my class, I calm them down so much until they say, "Well, we never realized that; we never understood that." So, and even after my classes, I've gotten some letters that were unsigned and said that I opened their eyes to a lot of different things. I'm not here to change anybody, and you, majority of times, can't change a grown person, but just want to them to open their eyes to a lot of different things and in my courses, I felt that I have made a difference.

This point or similar points are repeatedly emphasized in the discussions by many of these black officers. African-American leaders in historically white law enforcement agencies serve by example and lead by emphasizing equality of treatment as well as understanding of diversity. They often strive to make policing more professional and to live up to the credos painted on the sides of patrol cars.

Discussing the impact of the black chief on his agency, another officer stresses this point:

> But [he] has made it so. If I come, if I come and put in for a transfer to internal [affairs], because that's where I want to go next, I'll have just as much opportunity as the next man—white, black, yellow, red, anybody, everybody. He does everything [by the book]. It's all based on bam, bam, bam, bam. There is no "Okay, you're one of the good ole boys so I'll get you in there." There's nothing like that, and I was glad to see the good ole boy system go out the door when [he] did become [the head of the agency]. . . . [He's] an education man. . . . He thinks that every, everybody in the police department ought to have a degree. And he's hoping everybody will at least have two years by the year 2000. And I don't think the junior college or [the local university] has seen as many police officers enrolled since he's been [in charge].

Clearly, this black chief's goal is a multiracial, gender-friendly force that is well educated and suited to handling any problem that may arise in the community. Black officers have greater opportunity than ever before, and some have been promoted to positions of leadership despite agencywide white disgruntlement.

As these officers see it, truly professional policing is possible only when old systems of racial and gender discrimination have been dismantled in law enforcement agencies. It is clear from these accounts that black leaders are essential to this process. Their positive actions allow an agency to stand out as a model of equity and fairness for the town or city, to control crime better, and to promote positive agency–community relations, perhaps for the first time in its history. A positive agency–community relationship and new role models are necessary to foster the flow of young black people into institutionally important positions and to continue dismantling racism, as this very insightful respondent makes clear:

> It's kind of difficult to teach children that they can—little African-American children—that they can be anything other than basketball players if they don't see us in positions doing anything other than playing basketball—i.e., being doctors and lawyers, and, and politicians, and other professions. Same thing in a police department; it's hard for that new black officer coming on out of the academy to believe that he could ever be deputy chief if he never sees anybody, any blacks, who are deputy chief. And I think that it's a great mentoring program at the department to see black managers, see black supervisors, see black chiefs who are qualified to do the job that they're doing. See blacks used in areas throughout the department; see blacks in internal affairs as opposed to just working the west side of [the city] in the black community; to see blacks in recruiting, recruiting other blacks; see blacks in planning and evaluations where traditionally blacks have not been employed. I think, yes, it's important to see that because, you know what, we bring a different perspective.

From this perspective, black leadership has an important role to play but must also be understood as a specific outcome of a continuing struggle by black Americans. The transformation of the internal organization of policing is just one part of the equation. Another part that officers stress is continually working to better police–community relations and thus to better citizens' everyday lives.

IMPROVING LIFE IN BLACK COMMUNITIES
The Provision of Social and Educational Services

The strength of the connection black officers share with black communities is emphasized over and over again in their very nuanced and considered discussions. Solidarity is essential among black officers, and solidarity is also important between black officers and local communities. These officers generally understand that racism and its impact cannot be addressed just by transforming policing but also must be addressed in other important institutions and societal settings more or less simultaneously.

A substantial majority of these women and men discuss the necessity of working with their community in order to combat everyday

racism and improve the quality of life in many arenas. One older officer delineates how he and others have worked to improve life in their local community:

> This PAL [Police Athletic League] they have now, an officer and I started that . . . and we would do that with the youngsters, and it's a big thing out there now. But he and I took some old balls and bats, and whatever, and played football and baseball with the kids and it grew from that. . . . One of the officers that got killed, he started a savings and loan club he turned into an organization . . . and from that we were able to do a lot of things for the people who were needy that we knew about. We would provide food for them or clothes or whatever the case might be. Every Thanksgiving and Christmas we would give food baskets, and it was real beneficial.

In their interviews these officers generally realize that solutions to complex problems require more than individual success and perseverance in careers. Officers from segregated black communities often develop a sense of responsibility for these communities beyond that which many white officers may have. Providing aid for the needy and recreation for young people strengthens community ties in the face of continuing racial animosity and discrimination. More important perhaps, the police department becomes a more community-centered organization, rather than just an outside and often oppressive force.

Another officer discusses the range of needs that young people have and how his organization attempts to meet them:

> This is a program that has a little bit of everything that you can think of: educational programs, computer education, uh, all kinds of sports. You know, you name it, we do, and it's not just locally; we participate in the state and national level also. So these kids get a lot of exposure to things. I think that's important. . . . I started pestering the board of directors about let's let the kids travel some. Let's let them see something other than the ghetto because most of our kids at that time were low income, you know poor kids. . . . And I said, "These kids needs an experience; they need to see something outside of their normal environment. They need to stay in a hotel. They need out, eat in a restaurant. They need to see other Afro-Americans who do well, okay? And that will help them to decide what they want to do with themselves."

He continues with an explanation that he took a couple of years to persuade the board of directors to do it:

> We started watching the behavior. We noticed that if you took a group on an airplane to play in a national tournament somewhere they were never the same, okay. Yea, they were never the same. And even those directors who came around, and they started to know that. They say, "You know, when you first started this season, these kids acted one way. They were all loud and hollering and screaming and doing this. Now they come in, it's all business; they're doing what they're supposed to be doing." . . . We built that building next door. We only had that now; let's see, we opened that building in October; it's all education, and everybody said, "What do you want to do that for? They got schools, they got." I said, "Yeah, but they can't have that hands-on control that we can have." You know we take some kids that have some discipline problems, and we start from scratch. And what we work on is teaching them, first of all we want them to understand self-esteem. And then another thing that I learned as a young kid that teachers at my school said, "Remember, son, you control your own destiny, okay?" And that's our message for these kids. You control your own. Nobody else can do that for me, you know; you have to decide what's best for you and if it means that, you know that you got to go to school. And if you don't like the teacher, you got to sit there and listen to what she says and behave yourself so you can get an education; that's what's best for you.

Such strong community orientation among police officers requires a deep understanding of local community problems. Numerous officers make comments that suggest that if racism had really been eliminated, it would not be necessary to adopt strategies such as building schools for disadvantaged children, sponsoring food drives for communities, or raising money to send youth to college. The range of strategies that they consider and get involved in strongly reflects their understandings of the long-term and institutionalized nature of contemporary racism.

Although the characteristics of these officers vary, most describe or suggest the importance of their community to who they have become, to their sense of self and responsibility. Thus, one officer describes the magnitude of the commitment she has to other members of her racial group, as opposed to her gender:

I may have a week of training and . . . can't do any public speaking and fund-raising. The next week, you know, I may have just time off. I can do some stuff. But people forget that you're human. They expect so much, and I tried to tell one supervisor one time, a white female supervisor, that the stress I had from the black community was totally different than she would experience as a white female. Because people are dependent upon me; I am now put up there like the gift horse, and I've got to make things happen because the community is so small. And I am one of the reasons, whether I want to be or not. I hold a job; I hold . . . a leadership position.

As many officers do, she feels that there is little time to accomplish all that needs to be done. The community can be very demanding on those who are successful in education or their occupation. Being in a position of visible authority often forces these officers to take responsibility for and in their community. They work individually and collectively in a capacity beyond the usual role of a police officer.

Despite their often-heroic efforts, these women and men do realize the size and scope of the community needs, as well as their limited ability to address all that needs to be done, as is clear in this comment:

I feel like I'm a member of the African-American community first. Second, I'm a police officer, and I . . . don't have a problem putting the two together. I have a concerned interest in this community, being born and raised here. . . . We're breaking down barriers, like I said; it's getting a lot better. . . . Naturally we can't save every kid because some of them are just too far gone. What we do here at the agency is we try, as far as the black officers, we have a organization here. And, you know, the white officers they seem to think it's like we have some sort of Ku Klux Klan or something, but it's not. It is just we put black officers together, we do fund-raisers, and we give out scholarships every year to minority inner-city students who want to go to college. And the only prerequisite is that they have to write a paper on how crime or violence impacts their neighborhood. So, you know that is some of the ways we as officers try to go back in and try to make a difference. But, no, we're just a fly on the wall; it's going to gonna take so much.

Clearly, these officers understand the enormity of the problems that black communities face.

Black officers have some ability to work for specific changes in policing and in communities, yet institutional racism persists in policing much as it does in other societal institutions. Another officer concurs that discrimination and inequities can, therefore, only be solved by a tremendous effort involving coalitions of agencies and concerned individuals:

> I'd be quite suspicious of someone who said that they're going to come in and do it all by themself. You can't. It's just an array of issues there that you just can't deal with it in one single issue. We have a . . . house after school program, and the population—it's an after school program for disadvantaged youth—the population right now is predominantly high-risk African-American males. When you come to that house—I make it my point to go there twice a week—when you set down and listen to the array of concerns that these young individuals have, there is no way in hell that one single entity is going to address that. You've got to form a coalition with other groups that are experts and the various entities, and then you pull them together, and then you can address some of the problem.

Respondents like this man call into question some ideas about the impacts of racism that suggest they can be remedied in just one area or setting. Numerous officers suggest that a multifaceted, broad-reaching approach to racism and its consequences is necessary to create fundamental changes in neighborhoods, cities, and the larger society. Although most display a strong desire to improve the life of people in their community, they feel limited by the scope of the problems, their lack of funding and resources, and the work-related requirements of policing.

COMMUNITY-ORIENTED POLICING STRATEGIES (COPS)

Beyond their commitment to the social welfare of black communities and their educational efforts, numerous respondents also promote community-oriented policing strategies. These strategies seek to empower black communities to provide their own security, promote better police–citizen relations, and increase community control and supervision over local policing. Older officers sometimes take credit for initiating these strategies in their community with little or no agency support:

I got out of the police car before it was popular to get out of the police car. Meaning, I got out and talked with folks before it was popular. And not only in the black community but also the white community. I had no problems. I just got out, I talked with folks, and folks talked with me. I mean I was in one of the worst white areas in [the] county. I had people calling me and giving me vegetables that they grew, and all kinds of stuff. Wanting me to have dinner because I went out as a police officer. And of course, there were whites who didn't want me out there. They didn't want this "nigger" in their neighborhood, but that didn't bother me. Because I knew for everyone that didn't want me, there was one who did. And what I did, I resolved the crime problems. I wasn't there to make friends; I was there, you know, I was hired to do a job. And I was being paid with their tax money. . . . And the thing about it, you find out what black police officers in a white neighborhood [mean]. They change, overnight. They change overnight because people are people. And once they see that you are genuinely concerned about them, and you're going to do whatever the job is that you are hired to do, that's all they want. And then the niceness comes out. I mean the regular people come out then. And they were that way all the time. But they just didn't know you. They just didn't know you. So, they have no background information on you in which to make an assessment of you.

Not only did he initiate community policing in his patrol area but also he feels that the effort benefited residents in both the black and the white community. Black communities generally experience most white officers as treating them more or less as objects to be controlled. Being policed by black officers is thus a new experience, and despite some hesitation, many develop trust in black officers who get out of the patrol car, talk with them, and treat them as human beings. Of further importance is his discussion of how his policing strategy also appealed to many members of the white community. Stereotypes that governed their understanding were challenged, and continuing face-to-face interaction apparently helped to set the stage for some changes in local racial group relations.

COPS programs have spread to many law enforcement agencies in an array of communities. These officers feel that the benefit of such programs is clear:

I've seen my, the community that I grew up in go from a beautiful community where everybody loved everybody to a run-down little dope community, and they're selling dope right in front of my parents' home. I've seen them do it, before I became an officer. And, you know, I've seen it go back to you know a quiet community again because of police action.

As a policing strategy, COPS programs often have some success in fostering better police–community ties, which in turn help to reduce street crime and improve local living conditions. This officer discusses obvious changes in her community since the implementation of community-oriented policing. However, some researchers have argued that COPS has become a halfhearted undertaking, which in many areas is a way to attract federal dollars for traditional crime fighting strategies and the militarization of policing.[6] One influential officer feels so strongly that he argues, "COPS should be a philosophy, not a tactic. Some do it, but the whole agency is not involved. A lot of officers believe that we should tell them how to be policed and not listen to how they feel they should be policed."

Statements like this recur in the interviews, for numerous black officers feel that COPS is more important to them and the black communities they police than it is to most white leaders and officers, who prefer to promote traditional notions of crime fighting. It must be understood that there is a historical-collective imperative that often drives black officers to support COPS programs. As strategies to transform racist policing practices are developed, community-oriented policing allows black officers to redefine how agencies should police local black communities, a point this officer underscores:

> Things have improved from that standpoint. And because the nature of how police officers are deployed now through community-oriented policing is such that a lot of these black officers are put in situations in these lower socioeconomic communities where they are counseling kids, counseling parents. . . . Now there is more balance to what a black police officer does out there.

These black officers generally maintain that their collective efforts in programs like COPS can operate in the best interest of policing and in the interest of controlling street crime, as well as in strengthening of black communities by helping to overcome some of the harsh consequences that ultimately stem from racial oppression.

CONCLUSION

Across the United States, African Americans have historically been targeted and harmed by economic exploitation, political disenfranchisement, marginalization in or exclusion from many organizations, and a racist ideology that legitimates racially oppressive structures and processes. In the face of hostility and discrimination, the residents of black communities have continually resisted this mistreatment and have fought to determine for themselves just who they are and what they can be.

These black officers discuss and dissect the great hatred and intense discrimination they have encountered from whites since their entry into historically white policing institutions. In previous chapters, we have documented the complexity of their discriminatory experiences in detail. We see it throughout the interviews. Thus, this older officer reflects on his experience to leave us with a summarizing impression of how he sees himself:

> In 1973 I had experienced everything you could possibly experience, or either a variation of it one way or another. . . . I mean you look back on it, and . . . I wouldn't take a million dollars for it. And I wouldn't take ten [million] to go back through it again.

In spite of obvious pain he has experienced over the years, he makes it clear in his interview that he sees his entry into, and longevity in, policing as valuable to the larger community.

Constantly, these officers' accounts and discussions force us to see the *agency* of black Americans, in this case of black officers. We see the extent to which their *actions* have transformed historically white police institutions, designed to contain them through legitimated violence. This makes policing a better place to work. The comments of this female officer, hired in the 1990s, are an example:

> Being a police officer is the most wonderful thing I think I could experience. I think it's somewhat completed my life. You have excitement; you have the ability and capability of being able to help people. It's a great job. You meet thousands of people. It's just great. . . . It's not a profession that you're going to receive many riches. A lot of times you're not going to receive [your] due graciously for the things that you have done, but if you're looking for something that's going to be fulfilling to you, then this is the ideal way to go.

How do we account for the differences between the experiences and impressions of the officer hired in 1973 and the one hired in the mid-1990s? Although institutional forces shape people's lives, institutions are not static. They can be transformed, usually through human activity. Some change in policing is a result of larger economic, political, and cultural processes outside the law enforcement agencies, yet much change has stemmed from the actions of African-American law enforcement officers. As we see in this chapter, these officers should not be viewed as individuals in isolation but should be seen as active participants in their department and their community. These black officers grew up understanding racial hostility and discrimination through shared knowledge and accumulated experiences evaluated collectively in their communities. They have developed the analytical tools to evaluate the general manifestations of racism in their life, and they share that knowledge and their goals of what can and should be in the present and future of U.S. institutions, including law enforcement institutions, in their interviews.

Numerous officers entered policing at the behest of community leaders and endured the hostile reception they had with the support of these leaders and communities, in order to produce eventual change in local policing practices and thus to have a positive impact on the local community. They were rarely alone, and many goals were not merely generated individually. With this collective support, they endured, confronted whites, and worked from within, even as many whites hoped that they would quit or that, at least, their numbers would remain low.

As these officers established a beachhead of sorts and more black officers were hired, older officers often provided collective support and shared knowledge and survival strategies with new officers. Where possible, they organized black police associations to fight for greater recruitment and hiring and advancement in policing. As black political movements have fought for legal protections across the society, black officers have periodically used legal strategies to uncover and fight discrimination. Their efforts ultimately have reshaped the nature of social interaction within police agencies and often created greater space for members of nontraditional racial and ethnic groups.

Clearly, the concerns of these and other black officers are rarely far removed from their community. They have entered and survived police agencies with the help of the black community, and they understand that their ultimate success is measured in part by diminishing the hostility that has historically existed between police agencies and black communities. Many officers recount with pride that they see themselves as providers of needed social services to black communities, as role models and teachers for young people, and as promoters of community-oriented policing. These African-American officers strongly suggest that their efforts have made policing more professional and more humane despite the resistance of the traditional culture that still permeates policing in the United States. To the extent that police agencies have incorporated black officers and have been transformed by their efforts, new black officers will encounter less overt hostility and thus can spend more energy doing their job and feeling positive about opportunities for career advancement. When problems arise, they can now turn to black organizations, black leaders, and legal remedies.

Still, this process of change is by no means universal or complete, nor does it have a transformative logic outside continuing human action. These officers generally are aware that even in the most transformed law enforcement agencies, racial hostility and discrimination still operate in various, if more subtle and covert, forms to disadvantage black officers and citizens. Racism must be constantly documented, analyzed, and fought. Furthermore, there are many historically white law enforcement agencies, particularly those that are small or rural, in which there are still very limited numbers of black officers, who are especially likely still to encounter blatant racial hostility and humiliation with little hope of remedy. In addition, black women officers face distinctive and continuing forms of sexism and racialized sexism that have operated to keep their entry into and advancement within policing institutions very limited. Many important changes remain to be accomplished.

A Better Future for All Americans

It is something that kind of lights a fire that smolders and burns, and you just sort of think. You don't forget that in a lifetime. Those kind of memories always stick with you. I guess it's our way. Good things seems to kind of flame and then die. But the bad it, it flames up and embers. Just burns and churns, and stays a lifetime with you. Yeah, you know it's kind of like a bad meal you consume, and then regurgitate it and taste it all over again.

In this book African-American police officers provide much evidence of everyday racism in the routine operation of policing within major law enforcement agencies in Sunbelt areas of United States. The racial hostility and discrimination documented in our respondents' accounts are commonplace, recurring, variable in terms of overtness, and damaging to many people, both officers and civilians. Notably, we see in these interviews the development of a cumulative, shared body of knowledge on which black officers rely to understand this everyday racism and to counter particular racist practices in their workaday lives.

In this analysis we have explored how black officers use this knowledge to identify patterns and forms of racism in policing. Research studies that examine the complexity of human interaction and attempt to understand the difficult contexts of experience and knowledge in real life are not common. Studies that allow African Americans to be the central respondents and to develop detailed accounts of their experiences, interactions, and reactions to everyday racism are even more rare. Today, thus, black Americans' understandings of how policing and the criminal justice system impact their daily lives are largely missing from the research literature. There is a growing body of scholarly work, the experiential-racism tradition, which stresses interviewing respondents of color in the field to examine better their experiences with regard to the importance of critical issues, such as racial hostility and discrimination, in their everyday lives. We would urge more researchers, including criminologists, to go out into the field and do research to study the everyday experiences of Americans of color in general, and criminal justice agents of color in particular. This would help to overcome huge gaps in the social science knowledge of the everyday world of Americans.

In much social science research and in much public commentary on law enforcement issues, "black" is now more or less a demographic variable that is analyzed quantitatively in relation to other demographic variables or in regard to certain street crime data. As we discussed earlier, many research studies in this area have downplayed the importance of racism in understanding law enforcement practices and the criminal justice system.

To explore the understanding of racism shared by African-American officers and how their experiences shape and are shaped by this understanding, we have developed a thematic analysis of fifty open-ended interviews. These African-American officers are a diverse group of women and men of different ages and from different law enforcement agencies in a variety of rural and urban areas. Particularly significant is that most are veteran officers, and just more than half are in supervisory or command positions. The indictments of racial hostility and discrimination in policing by these experienced black officers are particularly significant since much scholarly and media commentary suggests that the class status of middle-class African Americans insulates them from racial hostility and discrimination. This view is naive and clearly refuted by our research data. These successful and well-educated officers constantly describe how racial hostility and discrimination remain very important factors that sabotage, trouble, and shape their daily life over the course of a career.

Virtually all of these experienced and articulate respondents demonstrate through their detailed discussions the dynamic and fluid nature of racial hostility and discrimination, which are detrimental forces in their workday lives and not some abstract phenomena of the past, as many whites assume. These African-American law enforcement officers discuss with clarity and substantial detail the persistent ideological, structural, interpersonal, and attitudinal processes that produce, or reproduce, patterns of discrimination in their career and life. This recurring racism tries to define them as second-class citizens and legitimizes a great array of racial barriers that block their ability to be successful and fully equal to typical white citizens.

KNOWLEDGE ABOUT EVERYDAY RACISM

Our data clearly show that these generally experienced African-American officers have a cumulative knowledge of the operation of racism that guides and assists their understandings of daily encounters with white Americans, both white officers and white civilians. Interestingly, these officers outline a somewhat more complex and collective process of learning about racial hostility and discrimination than that discussed in the one other major study of this knowledge, that of the pioneering scholar Philomena Essed.[1] Our interviews show a very dynamic learning process in which black women and men not only acquire knowledge about the operation of racism but constantly add to and redefine it in interaction with important others. A theoretical implication of our study is that ongoing experiences are central to African Americans' interactively developing ever more cumulative understandings of everyday racism.

These African-American officers explain clearly how the structural conditions of discrimination and interpersonal interactions within discriminatory settings shape the general knowledge of racism that they acquire, as well as their skills to interpret the meaning of encounters with whites who discriminate. Learning about racism results from differential exposure to a range of discriminatory settings and supportive black settings that guide life decisions and shape self- and collective identities. Although African Americans' ubiquitous experience with racial hostility and discrimination provides them with a substantial basis for group solidarity and mutual understandings, we do see that differences among them in terms of gender, class, age, and occupational position sometimes shape the nature of their understandings about particular issues.

We see from the black officers' multifaceted accounts that everyday racism has a hoary ideological base that has long been built on white notions of black personal, social, and cultural inferiority. An important aspect of everyday racism is that it is experienced and understood somewhat differently by African Americans to the extent that the structural and institutional processes they encounter are different. As children, African Americans encounter whites with some knowledge that they have garnered from family and friends, and this knowledge accumulates as they get older. The African-American officers we interviewed frequently focus on the importance of family, religion, education, and community organizations as early and continuing sources of important knowledge about the role that racism plays in society, and about ways to counter it. These officers have learned an interpretative methodology that allows them to understand discriminatory encounters with whites as they occur.

As they have moved into occupational settings previously denied to them, including policing, African Americans have had to develop specialized interpretive tools to deal with the distinctive types of discrimination that appear in the diversity of occupational settings finally available to them after centuries of exclusion. Our respondents repeatedly report on how the extent of knowledge of racism needed by African Americans changes as the institutional settings change, or as the nature of racial discrimination mutates in the larger society. Although a comprehensive knowledge of racism is essential to their ability to survive and adapt in a relatively new occupational setting, such as policing, African Americans also draw on their interpretive skills to develop a specialized knowledge of the operation of racism within the particular institutional setting. An understanding of subtle and covert racism in an institutional setting like that of law enforcement agencies requires an interpretive ability gained through everyday experience therein. To this end, most African Americans use interesting methods of comparison and experimentation to determine whether unpleasant encounters they have with whites are indeed racial discrimination. Their care and caution in making judgments about racial hostility and discrimination are often impressive.

In their interviews, these African-American officers note and discuss three forms of experience with everyday racism at the hands of an array of white Americans. The first is vicarious experience. Discriminatory encounters that impact particular individuals are shared with other black officers, and these accounts thereby affect other members of the black community. The second is passive-receptive experience in which black officers, in the routine activities of their occupation and daily life, are acted upon by some form of racial discrimination. The third is active, goal-oriented experience in which these black officers consciously attempt to better understand racism through personal or group investigation and experimentation in an attempt to address or change some form of discrimination that they have identified as affecting their life. This latter case also includes their responding actively to patterns of racism in their department. Our respondents regularly report gaining more knowledge about the reality, operations, and complexity of everyday racism and about their sense of self during ongoing struggles against particular forms of discrimination.

These officers report that information about negative encounters with whites is often shared with other black Americans, thereby adding to the general base of knowledge about discrimination within black communities. After a particularly serious encounter with racism, one officer ordinarily processes the experience carefully and may as a result share her or his account with other officers or with relatives and friends, all of whom can help in collectively determining its meaning. A particular encounter thereby forms part of the community's shared memory of the operation of racism and can have a cumulative impact on understandings and strategies of those who become aware of it.

Demonstrating the extent and sophistication of black officers' knowledge of racial hostility and discrimination is a first step in delineating the meaning of this racism in policing across the United States. As we will argue, one can learn much from attending to our respondents' accounts of the complex interrelationships of the many structuring social, economic, and political factors that shape the contours of the racial hostility and discrimination that they face on a routine basis. These shaping factors affect the character and location of the discriminatory and other negative encounters with whites, as well as the extent to which black Americans understand these experiences and encounters as racialized. Experiences with discrimination generally have a cumulative effect on these black officers, as on other black Americans, in regard to personal health, self-image, their family, and many important life decisions.

DENIGRATION OF CULTURE AND PERSONALITY

Our respondents recount in detail how white officers and civilians legitimize black exclusion from occupational and societal benefits by means of a panoply of ideological constructions about black inferiority. Such racist constructions are used to repress black attempts to address and change the nature of continuing injustices inside and outside the work-place. In the process of growing up, these respondents were frequently made to feel inferior whenever they encountered white individuals or white-dominated institutions. They report often being treated as back-ward or as less than civilized. Through frequent interactions they have become aware that many whites have attitudinal notions of racial or cultural purity that deny that white and black people share views and values as equivalent human beings.

Entering law enforcement agencies as well-educated officers, these women and men have found that these racist constructions, sometimes subtle and sometimes blatant, still permeate the workplace. Accounts in their interviews reveal how many white administrators and officers continue to view black Americans, including black officers, as some-how inferior to white people. Many respondents lament how white offi-cers continually underestimate their abilities and treat them as less intelligent or less able to perform their policing duties. Such white notions also promote disproportionately negative treatment of black citizens, including negative treatment of off-duty black officers by white officers. Many respondents not only discuss firsthand experiences with outrageous police mistreatment but also report witnessing incidents in which white officers have unfairly denigrated or attacked members of black communities.

An example given repeatedly in the interviews relates to the way African Americans are unjustly criminalized in white attempts to limit black advancement and reinforce a subordinate status. Many of these black officers have themselves experienced racial discrimination as they drive the roadways of their town or city, where they too are repeatedly stopped and questioned by white officers for no good reason. Some report that shopping in local stores or walking the streets means being under distinctive white surveillance. Daily activities that whites take for granted are made much more difficult for most African Americans, including police officers, as their racial characteristics mark them to whites as "racial outsiders" with values and perspectives different from those of whites—thus as a potential threat.

Problematization as a form of racism is contingent on ideological conditions that stimulate and legitimate other forms of racism. It allows whites to rationalize patterns of discrimination and legitimize strategies of racial containment and other discrimination. Many of these black officers suggest that the attribution of biological, personality, and cul-tural problems to explain black people's secondary status gives whites a way of arguing that racism is no longer a causative factor in creating negative living and working conditions for African Americans.

MARGINALIZATION, EXCLUSION, AND RETALIATION

These African-American officers give many detailed accounts showing how, when, where, and why racial oppression still shapes their experience inside and outside the law enforcement agency workplace. Together with data from other research studies, these accounts reveal how continuing patterns of imposed segregation in neighborhoods and workplaces result in the recurring marginalization and exclusion of African Americans from many opportunities, positions, privileges, and rewards available to whites. As we have noted in previous chapters, many studies have documented the high level of segregation of racial groups in the United States, and the ways in which white Americans have created and maintained segregation and discrimination in most institutions. Residential segregation and homogeneity remain very important buttresses of racial hostility and discrimination in other areas, such as the workplace. For centuries, white Americans determined that whites and blacks should not live together, socialize, or intermarry, and in contemporary society in many ways these earlier patterns of racial segregation and oppression continue. African Americans have paid a heavy price, in the past and present, for this omnipresent oppression. Thus, compared with white Americans, whose families' average time in North America is less than that of average black families, black Americans remain disproportionately poor, undereducated, consigned to substandard housing, and at greater risk of violence from police and other sources. Absent four centuries of racism, this would not be the case.

Our respondents see segregated structural conditions as shaping two distinct life experiences, one white and one black. Because everyday segregation occurs, and because whiteness is the cultural norm, whites are generally able to distance themselves from black Americans and, if they desire, to more or less ignore them in the course of their life. Because of this segregation, people do not socialize much across the color line, at least on a sustained equal-status basis, and thus whites and blacks have few shared understandings of numerous racial matters.

Recall that much social science research on organizational workplaces shows that informal social networks are very important in shaping workplace norms and much everyday behavior within a typical organization. As we have seen repeatedly, informal networks of white law enforcement officers shape much of the way that their workplace organizes and operates. Assessing what happens in law enforcement settings, our respondents frequently note the importance and impact of informal, old-boy networks of white officers. It is within these informal groups that antiblack stereotyping is supported and that discriminatory actions are often conceived or reinforced. In historically white law enforcement settings, many white officers discriminate as prejudiced individuals, but much of their power to harm results from their membership in influential, white-dominated networks.

White networking patterns are important in creating the workplace frameworks that catalyze knowledge acquisition about racism for black officers. This networking typically means social isolation from black officers, which in turn feeds the antiblack stereotyping. With negative stereotypes circulating among many white officers, African-American officers face a difficult task in trying to become fully integrated employees in historically white agencies. Not surprisingly, our respondents report that many white police officials and officers see them as intruders into white comfort zones within their agency.

Racial barriers in law enforcement agencies limit advancement opportunities and thereby have a significant impact on the law enforcement career, as well as on the family and community, of black officers. Racial barriers vary in form, ranging from subtle to covert to overt, yet together they are part of continuing, systemic racism in the society. The interviews outline how discrimination shapes how black officers are evaluated and disciplined, where they are assigned, and whether they are transferred to desirable positions or promoted. Such racial barriers limit not only how far officers can advance but the length of their career as well. Because of continuing discrimination, numerous black officers opt for early retirement.

Furthermore, the interviews indicate that although racial barriers have an impact on all black officers, certain groups are afforded even less protection against racial hostility and discrimination, especially rural and female black officers. Although existing research on discrimination in policing focuses on urban agencies, our interviews suggest that discrimination is even more overt in rural areas and smaller agencies. In these interviews, discrimination is also more overt where there is no active organization of black officers and little legal or political protection.

It is also significant that all the female officers in our sample report experiencing gendered racism, that is, racism that has strong elements of sexism. Evaluating the actions of white male officers, numerous black female officers often note significant differences in the treatment of white women and of them. These female respondents also discuss how institutional barriers increase competition among them for available positions.

Whereas some literature on policing suggests the declining significance of racism in the law enforcement system, these black officers demonstrate the what, how, and where of the many continuing racial barriers in law enforcement. These barriers continually exclude them from entry to policing, or from advancement once hired. Such barriers vary from overt to covert, can be societal or occupational, and are generally buttressed by attitudinal and ideological racism.

As we have seen, numerous officers discuss how white individuals and white-dominated institutions legitimize their containment and restriction within subordinate societal and institutional positions, despite their efforts to advance professionally. These respondents encounter racial oppression as white people suppress black people's definitions of reality and deny that racism exists, while still engaging in discriminatory behavior that often humiliates black people and reduces them to stereotypical caricatures. Indeed, many officers discuss the pain they feel when exposed to racist jokes, cartoons, and derogatory language, including a range of racist insults. They have pride in their abilities and see the importance of being in these positions of authority for black communities. Still, when they discuss encounters with whites, they frequently describe the pain, humiliation, and stress created by treatment as second-class employees or citizens.

Some respondents also discuss the physical threat that whites continue to pose to them, their family, or other members of the black community. They report being intimidated by white officers acting in an authoritarian manner or by threats of retaliation if they engage in behavior deemed unacceptable by white officers. Such threats act to prevent some black officers from advancing and help to maintain their subordinate position. Many respondents further discuss their awareness of physical violence against members of black communities and personal experience of reprisals from whites for making malpractice incidents public knowledge.

Fear of retaliation from whites extends to organization by black officers. To resist retaliation, they may organize to implement changes in the discriminatory operation of their agency. In addition, black officers often promote milder "color-blind" remedial strategies for problems within their agency, not because they are in their best interest or will pre-vent racial injustice but because in doing so they can prevent white back-lash. Such backlash often occurs if black officers are perceived as going too fast in seeking institutional changes, thereby threatening the interests of white officers and supervisors. This type of antiblack action not only reinforces the racist notion that black people belong in subordinate posi-tions relative to whites but also fosters a sense of white solidarity that is important to the perpetuation of differences. White people who share racist notions, employ racist language, and engage in racist behavior to conform to expectations of other whites are seen by many respondents as able to share in the material rewards guaranteed whites while main-taining blacks as subordinates.

Our respondents discuss in some detail the impact of the continual stress and anxiety that everyday discrimination in law enforcement agencies produces. Continually facing monitoring, experiencing daily pressure to conform to white expectations, facing fear of retaliatory actions when they do not meet expectations—these life experiences emphasize the detrimental and cumulative impact of everyday racism on the physical and emotional well-being of these black law enforce-ment officers. These negative encounters with whites are stressful not just for individuals but often for their family and community as well.

BLACK AGENCY AND RESISTANCE

Out of this individual and group experience with everyday racism African Americans have created a strong set of strategies for resistance. There is indeed a type of oppositional culture that underlies individual and group strategies to resist everyday oppression. In chapter 6 we saw clearly that these black officers are not just targets of everyday racism, for they collectively develop strategies to fight back against the negative treatment that they receive at the hands of whites. In their interviews, we observe accounts of many different countering strategies designed to allow them to thrive and to survive in spite of constant marginalization and exclusion efforts.

From the early 1600s and their early enslavement in North America, black Americans have been individual and collective theorists of their experiences. Indeed, some of the greatest American theorists of liberty have been African Americans: From David Walker in the early 1800s, to Frederick Douglass and Anna Julia Cooper in the late 1800s, to W. E. B. Du Bois in the early and middle twentieth century, to Fannie

Lou Hamer, Dr. Martin Luther King Jr., and Malcolm X in recent decades, African Americans have forcefully articulated the great ideals of liberty, justice, and equality. Millions have joined with their leaders in centuries of antidiscrimination efforts, protests, and movements. Our respondents are very much in this long interpretive and protest tradition, and they too strongly assert these ideals of liberty and justice as they strive to made sense of their own experiences with systemic racism.

Throughout the interviews we get honest, if often pessimistic, accounts of the current levels of racial hostility and discrimination in law enforcement agencies. Yet, at the same time, most officers see signs of change, some of which are the result of pressures by black organizations and individuals inside and outside these agencies. In their interviews they assert that their protest and reform efforts have made their law enforcement agency more professional and less discriminatory, even in the face of much white opposition. To the extent that these law enforcement agencies have incorporated their suggestions and demands for change, younger black (and sometimes white) officers encounter fewer problems and spend more time and energy just doing their job.

It is indeed the activism and agency of the veteran officers that have made policing institutions better for African-American officers and civilians. Note this eloquent comment by a successful senior officer:

> A lot of these community members know the black officers, so that helps, whereas before . . . the African-American community saw the police as the enemy. Because they didn't come into their community unless they were called to make an arrest, so that was the only encounter they got from them. Now, we have black troopers that are serving as recruiters, we have black troopers that are serving as public information officers, DARE officers. You know, they go into the schools, and they put on programs and talk to the kids. And the kids see this diversity in every agency that they've come in contact with. So they feel that "Hey, if I want to be a policeman, I can be a policeman. If I want to be a deputy, I can be a deputy." And it opens up more opportunity for more diversity because it sends a positive message. I think the same is true for females. It's given us a lot of resources where before, we didn't have them.

IMPLICATIONS FOR PUBLIC POLICY

Our interviews with these officers reveal that racial hostility and discrimination still occur and still are systemic, not only in law enforcement agencies but in other institutions of the society. Clearly, much work needs to be done if the United States is ever to achieve its ancient and revered ideals of "liberty and justice for all." Indeed, there are great many lessons to be learned from listening to the experiences and ideas of these African-American officers, most of whom are seasoned veterans of law enforcement.

One critical lesson that needs to be learned well by most white Americans, including most policy makers, is that a focus on individual bias and discrimination is not sufficient for dealing with, or even understanding, the continuing production and reproduction of racial inequalities across major institutions. The experiential accounts of these African-American officers demonstrate unequivocally that modern racism is a complex of cumulative practices of individuals who are firmly set within supportive social networks and institutional settings. The accounts of discrimination by these perceptive officers do not describe individual incidents only; usually they delineate a pattern of incidents that have tremendous psychological, physical, family, and community impacts for black officers and communities.

Listening to Experienced Black Voices

Traditionally, most analysts and scholars of the U.S. justice system have assessed policing more or less in a vacuum and neglected the impact of larger societal setting and processes on the operation of policing institutions. In contrast, our respondents discuss societal patterns of discrimination and segregation in order to emphasize the importance of looking beyond particular police settings to the contexts that routinely shape policing. In one important example, they note that continuing patterns of residential segregation across most U.S. towns and cities have a serious impact on the ability of particular agencies to recruit adequate numbers of African-American officers.

Much previous research on U.S. law enforcement agencies suggests that "blue is blue," thereby implying or asserting that officers of color are part of the culture and generally pattern their policing views on those of the white majority. However, this is not the case. Although they agree on many routine-policing matters with the white majority, at some point most of these respondents focus on the differences between white officers and officials and them. Thus, instead of being authoritarian or abusive to citizens of color as many white officers are, these black officers generally suggest that they consciously consider their own negative experiences with police in order to be fairer and less abusive to all citizens, including citizens of color. These officers also show a keen awareness of the limited protection that they themselves are afforded by their occupational status from persisting acts of discrimination, retaliation, or even violence from whites, including white police officers.

Clearly, it is important to get out of the academic's ivory tower, or the mass media or other organization's office, if one is to begin to understand the deadly reality of contemporary racism for African Americans and other Americans of color. In this book we report on long conversations with women and men who collectively have about *eight hundred years* of law enforcement experience, a considerable fund on which to draw for conclusions about the current state of law enforcement agencies. Examining their everyday experiences furthers an understanding of racism in the entire social system and can lead to ways of transforming that system. Consequently, an understanding of the U.S. justice system can be dramatically improved by looking to the experiences, accounts, and viewpoints of those who work in that system and must experience the destructive realities of white-imposed racism as part of their workaday life.

Given the time and space to define their experiences, these women and men explain the complexity of the relationship between racial characteristics and policing beyond the simplistic analyses too often found in the mass media and mainstream social science literature. They offer evidence for a collective, shared knowledge of racial hostility and discrimination among people in black communities, as well as of the cumulative impact of this racism on individuals, which extends well beyond a particular racist encounter. Vicarious experiences with racism of black individuals, including black officers, frequently have an impact on many other members of black communities.

Given the sordid and painful reality of contemporary racism, what can be done? First, all those involved in the criminal justice system and the legislative and executive branches linked to that system must carefully listen to their accounts. The legal scholar Richard Delgado, among others, has suggested that the prevailing mind-set of dominant group members is a principal instrument by which the racial hierarchy is maintained.[2] This mind-set often seems to be set in concrete, and it is too rarely challenged either in the schools or in the media. A majority of white Americans, including a majority of the police officers, judges, district attorneys, and others in the criminal justice system, likely harbor at least some negative stereotypes of African Americans and other

Americans of color. These views very likely have a regular impact on their decisions.

Delgado sees one solution for this situation as lying in publicizing the experiential accounts of African Americans and other people of color, accounts that must be more widely circulated in order to challenge this prevailing mind-set and the racial status quo that it justifies. As we have noted, the ability of African Americans to produce and share their life narratives is structurally and institutionally limited, often severely. They have little access to the white-controlled mass media, and they are also limited in the extent to which they can protest racism to their superiors or to local political officials, the majority of whom are usually white. Limitations are also faced by social science researchers who wish to tell the larger story of racism in policing, or of racism in the country as a whole. Not only do these researchers have less access to the mainstream media and to most legislators and policy makers than more conservative analysts but also the currently dominant research methodologies in social science limit the type of research that is considered legitimate and that is well funded. In addition, traditional social science researchers' uncritical relationships with funding agencies and the dominance of mainstream journals limit the research that can be done on the oppressive realities of systemic racism and sexism in U.S. society.

When space is created in which African Americans can construct detailed accounts and narratives of their workaday lives, as it is here, their responses are often viewed by many white commentators and traditional researchers as just "perceptions" of racism. This common white perspective indicates how the prevailing mind-set frequently dismisses the views of subordinated groups, especially when they are critical of existing social relations and systems. Therefore, the dismissal of the experiential accounts of African Americans as perceptions grants dominant-group members the opportunity to fully discard, reinterpret, or redefine these accounts. It is significant, too, that most whites rarely see white views on racial matters as mere perceptions. The consequences of the white dismissal of black experiences are serious, for understanding these experiences is essential to breaking down the hegemony of the dominant racist ideology in the United States.

If, in contrast, we take these accounts from black law enforcement officers as based on real experiences with racial hostility and discrimination over long days, weeks, months, years, and lifetimes, then their significance for reforming policing institutions becomes great. A report of a critical experience with discrimination by one officer typically represents much more than a single event or impression at a distinct point in time and space. It typically involves a series of past events, happenings, and incidents that are stored in memory and thereby included in the reactions to, and coping with, a present discriminatory situation or encounter. One experience thereby transcends a single moment and a single individual's interpretation of that particular moment. This experience is usually cumulative and includes shared understandings that make it collective as well. Individual experiences are shared and thus form the basis of a group's general knowledge of a subject; in this instance, antiblack hostility or discrimination. Over generations, and across current time and space, the citizens of black communities add to and refine the general knowledge of the subject of racism on the basis of their negative and positive encounters with white Americans. Experience and knowledge are dynamically interrelated and guide a group's beliefs, values, and actions through a complex, ever-transforming social world. In this way, they become veteran analysts and theorists of their own experience, and of racism in the society as a whole. They must do so to survive in a racially hostile world.

African Americans should be facilitated in providing accounts and understandings of the racialized events and incidents that shape their everyday life, instead of being generally ignored by influential figures in policing, the media, and the academy. Change and reform must begin from a realistic understanding of the nature of everyday racism as those who are targeted concretely experience and counter it.

Expanding Learning about Racism

Racialized encounters are interactive moments that involve a meeting of two divergent sets of understandings and experiences about "race" in the United States. When encounters between different people or groups involve distinct views of racial matters in the social world, the contradictions and dilemmas that arise can create a fecund atmosphere for learning about other groups. Elsewhere, we have shown how social factors and forces shape the doing and interpreting of racialized events, including how whites' racial beliefs and actions impact the everyday lives of those who are not white.[3]

In this book, African-American law enforcement officers discuss the separate worlds of white and black Americans as they experience and understand them. Clearly, we see in these accounts that both groups develop different beliefs and values about discrimination and other racial matters. As individuals with different ideas meet, the resulting conflict between competing ideas can provide an opportunity for each to understand what the other believes. However, it seems very clear that it is black Americans who do most of the learning and changing, as they often must to survive or thrive in their career and life. It seems that only a minority of white officers and officials in law enforcement agencies have as yet entered the learning mode about how workplace racism harms not only officers of color and their agencies but also the larger society. Indeed, some of these black officers indicate that those whites in their agency who have begun to understand the realities of contemporary racism and have actually taken important antiracist actions in the agency often themselves become targets for retaliation and marginalization by other whites.

These officers also discuss situations in which the discrimination they face seems to be more or less unconsciously delivered—that is, it is not clearly linked to a white discriminator's avowed intent to harm a particular black victim. The discriminatory actions by whites seem to be unreflective and customary. Thus, some of the discrimination that these officers encounter seems to them to be less than consciously intentional; yet it is still reflective of the socialization of whites that determines their positive views of whites and their negative views of African Americans. This finding of less than fully conscious discrimination has substantial significance for contemporary legal and judicial thinking, which usually requires a demonstration of intent to discriminate in order to prove that discrimination is a factor in a process that damages African Americans and other Americans of color. Listening to the nuanced accounts of these African-American officers makes it clear that there is much for those in the legal and judicial system to learn about the routine, half-conscious or unconscious, implementation of everyday racism by white Americans.

Taking Action at the Top: Specific Strategies against Everyday Racism

Our respondents provide specific insights about government policies that can break down patterns of racial hostility and discrimination in policing institutions. In spite of the transformations in the nature of the racism reported by many of the respondents over several decades of policing, much of which has resulted from their actions, there is still much discrimination of all types to be faced in historically white police institutions. Important for public policy is that overt forms of racism are encountered less frequently in police agencies when respondents have significant legal recourse or are watched over by a few highly placed black officers or by influential organizations of black officers. Most respondents indicate that the greater the subjectivity permitted in organizational decisions in police agencies, the greater the possibility that racial prejudices and stereotypes can impact the organizational decisions and the informal or formal organizational policies they are based on. The problematic character of this subjectivity is compounded by exclusion of black officers from command positions in most agencies, as well as their scarcity in many specialized and supervisory positions in the same agencies. Thus, one policy conclusion to be drawn is that racially linked subjectivity in decision making by those whites in higher-level positions should be reduced as much as possible by workable procedures and reviews.

One remedy, too, is to ensure that more black officers are hired through aggressive outreach programs in black communities and through cadet programs. Most law enforcement agencies still do not have representative numbers of black officers, or in fact, of other officers of color. This situation needs to be immediately remedied, so as to create the likelihood of the creation of a critical mass of African-American officers who can support one another against various forms of departmental discrimination. Such a mass also has the potential to change the traditional, white-centered police subculture, as the increased employment of black and Latino officers in Los Angeles area police departments reportedly demonstrates.[4]

Successful black officers should be able to be promoted and to move into higher-level positions, and thereby be permitted to have an impact on the daily operation of agencies. Such promotions and appointments can change the tone and operation of law enforcement agencies. Not surprisingly, perhaps, racial discrimination in the workplace is especially serious when white police chiefs and supervisors allow it to be perpetrated by officers in lower ranks, a common problem reported by these respondents. Discrimination is more difficult for individual black officers to counter when there are no senior police officials pushing for change or when there is an inability to rely on senior officials or legal remedies in one's agency for protection. One clear policy implication of these findings is that much pressure should be placed on whites at the helm of law enforcement agencies and related criminal justice system organizations to make sure that the relevant civil rights laws are respected in operation as well as in rhetoric. Not only should administrators at the top actively abide by antidiscrimination laws, they should also make sure that their subordinates do so as well.

Our interviews also indicate that black officers in smaller and rural agencies, which are a large proportion of police agencies, typically face more difficulties with racial hostility and discrimination, much of it overt. In such agencies, legal remedies are an essential form of protection that must not be dismantled. In an era of attacks on affirmative action programs and legal protections against racial and gender bias, these black officers suggest that dismantling these programs will likely mean increased discrimination in its various forms. Considering their extensive experience, these officers are almost unanimous in their view that discriminatory attitudes and behavior of white officers and supervisors are reduced only when the costs of those attitudes and that behavior are high for the perpetrators.

The top administrators and lower-level managers in law enforcement agencies can take specific actions immediately to foster better relationships between black and white officers, or between officers and civilians, in day-to-day policing operations. Depending on the location of their agency and the number of black officers in it, our respondents report varying levels of respect and acceptance from fellow officers. Some in more progressive law enforcement agencies report strategies such as "salt and pepper" teams (partnerships of black and white officers), which promote more trust among officers of different groups. Such arrangements increase familiarity and provide officers from different groups an opportunity to talk with, and learn to rely on, each other.

In addition, these black officers note how conflict between law enforcement agencies and black communities often has a negative impact on the daily operation of policing. For that reason, they usually support COPS programs. If well constructed, such programs move officers and community residents closer together in dealing with local problems and in working to make communities less crime ridden and more livable. Typically, COPS programs operate to break down barriers to communication between communities and law enforcement agencies, and they promote opportunities for increased understandings between white officers and community residents, thereby reducing tension and potentially violent incidents. Several of these respondents note that local COPS programs are currently successful, whereas others remain perfunctory and are more oriented to attracting funds and publicity than to fostering local change.

The administrators of law enforcement agencies can also take actions to counter the racist attitudes and ideology that are common among white officers. Those officers we interviewed are quite aware that whites' racial attitudes are difficult to change. Yet, numerous respondents note or suggest that multicultural sensitivity programs can be effective in breaking down some racial and gender stereotyping and distrust. The problem is that many existing programs—and not all departments even have programs—are often perfunctory and thus ineffective. As currently operated, they may even promote animosity and opposition to racial change among many white officers.

Another critical area in which action by various officials at the top of law enforcement agencies and political bodies can be important is in facilitating the organization of officers of color within historically white law enforcement agencies. The first step, as we have noted, is to hire enough black officers to create a critical mass, which will in turn allow for the possibility of organization against patterns of discrimination. As we have seen in previous chapters, when black officers organize, they can often protect each other from some discrimination, as well as have an impact on formal and informal equal opportunity policies within their organization. Making it easier for African-American officers and other officers of color to organize will not only give them a greater sense of agency and self-respect but also enhance their input into traditionally white law enforcement agencies. It is important for administrators and policy makers to listen to the views and reports from these organizations. Recently, for example, the National Black Police Association put out a pamphlet, "Police Brutality: A Strategy to Stop the Violence," which calls on all law enforcement officers to report other officers who engage in police brutality and other malpractice. This is an important suggestion for policy makers to consider, as it challenges the traditional "blue line" perspective of many white officers.[5]

Finally, one other policy implication of our data relates to the levels of stress that these African-American officers often report. Most feel that reductions in departmental racism will reduce the stress in their life and thereby improve their physical and psychological health. Moreover, senior administrators should develop new counseling and health monitoring programs for all officers, which should be used not to punish ill health through reassignment but to detect potential problems and help officers handle the high level of stress and anxiety that they must endure. This is true for all officers, but especially accentuated for those officers who in addition to the normal stress of police work must also face the added stresses of racial and gender discrimination. Many of the older respondents report health problems such as high blood pressure or know of fellow officers who have suffered heart attacks or breakdowns, at least in part because of their inability to deal adequately with the stresses of racism or gendered racism in their law enforcement workplace.

CONCLUSION

Macroeconomic and large-scale political processes contextualize the daily lives of people in countries across the world. Each person is born at a particular location and in a distinctive period of time, which is characterized by continually transforming structural, cultural, and institutional processes. However, people create their own history within these institutional constraints. If we desire, our personal efforts allow us to evaluate, understand, and respond to conditions that attempt to enslave us and dictate who or what we should be. Much scholarly work implies that the lives and life chances of African Americans are largely determined by impersonal forces beyond their control, forces that operate in spite of their individual desires and group aims.

Engaging black police officers in conversation, listening to their accounts and reports, disrupt and challenge this fallacious understanding of the world. As we saw in the last chapter, their life accounts force us to see their *agency* in dealing with everyday racism. This agency can be seen in the actions of individuals and in the work of black officers in their own organization within agencies. Although much remains to be done, their brave *actions* against racial hostility and discrimination have transformed most historically white police institutions far beyond what one might have imagined just two or three decades ago. Indeed, historically, African Americans seem to have been those Americans most committed as a group to the American creed of freedom, justice, equality, and equal opportunity. They were key activists in the abolitionist movement against slavery in the nineteenth century. They organized on a large scale, with supportive whites, in the movement against legal segregation in the middle of the twentieth century, a movement that forever changed U.S. society for the better. Individual and collective actions to expand civil rights for all Americans have often been pressed or led by African Americans. Yet, persisting racial hostility and discrimination still frustrate efforts to achieve social justice and equality.

In the United States policing began, in part, as a means of controlling the enslaved and oppressed African-American population. African

Americans were excluded from policing in the segregationist southern states from the years of Reconstruction to the era of civil rights struggles. Therefore, the movement of significant numbers of African Americans into historically white law enforcement institutions in recent decades has become an indicator of black progress in moving up in U.S. society.[6]

To the extent that racial stigma still has a significant impact on the lives of African Americans, including the dedicated public servants serving in various police settings, we can say that the country still has a long way to go before that progress will be complete. Despite the racial discrimination they still constantly face, and an uncertain racial future, the black women and men whom we interviewed by and large view their actions and activities as playing a multifaceted role in countering societal racism and in helping to create more just agencies and a more just society.

The transformation of historically white policing institutions is not a static linear project but an ongoing socially reconstructive process. Allowing black officers to share their accounts and everyday experiences helps us to understand their resistance and transformative agency in creating important change in this society. This is vital to a fuller understanding of the dynamics of "race" and racism in U.S. society. Let us conclude with this sage and mixed review of current affairs by one veteran officer in a department still riddled with racism:

> I guess by virtue of us getting here, we have opened the door for other African-American police officers to come here. Because I guess prior to African Americans' actually coming in law enforcement, we might have had one on the police department, you might have had one someplace, [but] never twenty that's on the department, that makes sixty or seventy people. So we have opened the door for other African-American police officers to get jobs. I don't know if we've made such a great impact, because we're still fighting the same things we were fighting in the sixties. We haven't really changed that much. We're still fighting—we're not getting promoted, we're not getting, we're not part of the upper-middle management and administration. We're still, most of us, most of us are still line officers. So, you know, it's true that we've got some black chiefs, and we've got some black majors and some black lieutenants and black captains, but not in this part. I think that the North is more progressive when it comes to black police officers, and it always makes a difference with the community, what the community does too.

With some hope in his voice, he adds that change remains conditional on the actions of people in black communities:

> Now if you're in a community like ours that blacks are kind of like very passive, and they don't say, well, "We want this, this, this and that," we don't get it. So I guess we have made an impact. I can't say that we haven't made an impact, but we still have a long, long, long way to go because we're still fighting the same things as years ago.

ENDNOTES

Preface

1. Adrian Angelette, "$1 Million Award Upheld against BR," *State-Times/Morning Advocate* (Baton Rouge, LA), June 28, 2003, p. 1.

2. W. E. B. Du Bois, *Darkwater: Voices from within the Veil* (New York: Humanity Books, [1920] 2003), chapter 6.

Chapter 1

1. Samuel Walker, *A Critical History of Police Reform* (Lexington, MA: D.C. Heath and Company, 1977); Homer Hawkins and Richard Thomas, "White Policing of Black Populations: A History of Race and Social Control in America," in *Out of Order: Policing Black People*, ed. Ellis Cashmore and Eugene McLaughlin (London: Routledge, 1991), pp. 65–86; Robert L. Zangrando, *The NAACP Crusade against Lynching, 1909–1950* (Philadelphia: Temple University Press, 1980).

2. Mary Beth Oliver, "Portrayals of Crime, Race, and Aggression in 'Reality-Based' Police Shows: A Content Analysis," *Journal of Broadcasting and Electronic Media* (Spring 1994): 179–91; see also Michael Keith, "'Policing a Perplexed Society?': No-Go Areas and the Mystification of Police-Black Conflict," in *Out of Order*, pp. 189–214.

3. Robin Magee, "The Myth of the Good Cop and the Inadequacy of Fourth Amendment Remedies for Black Men: Contrasting Presumptions of Innocence and Guilt," *Capital University Law Review* 23 (1994): 151–219.

4. William J. Chambliss, "Policing the Ghetto Underclass: The Politics of Law and Law Enforcement," *Social Problems* 41 (1994): 177–94.

5. Cashmore and McLaughlin, *Out of Order*; Derrick Bell, *Race, Racism and American Law*, 3rd ed. (Boston: Little, Brown, 1992).

6. Homer Hawkins and Richard Thomas, "White Policing of Black Populations: A History of Race and Social Control in America," in *Out of Order*, pp. 65–86.

7. David H. Bayley and Harold Mendelsohn, *Minorities and the Police: Confrontation in America* (New York: The Free Press, 1969); Jerome Skolnick, *The Politics of Protest* (New York: Simon & Schuster, 1969); Jim Sidanius, James H. Liu, John S. Shaw, and Felicia Pratto, "Social Dominance Theory and the Criminal Justice System," *Journal of Applied Social Psychology* 24 (1994): 338–66; Bell, *Race, Racism and American Law*, p. 341.

8. Donald Black and Albert J. Reiss Jr., "Patterns of Behavior in Police and Citizen Transactions," in *Studies of Crime and Law Enforcement in Major Metropolitan Areas*, Vol. 2 (Washington, DC: Government

Printing Office, 1967); R. J. Friedrich, as cited in Lawrence W. Sherman, "Causes of Police Behavior: The Current State of Quantitative Research," *Journal of Research in Crime and Delinquency* (January 1980): 76.

9. C. L. Ruby and John C. Brigham, "A Criminal Schema: The Role of Chronicity, Race, and Socioeconomic Status in Law Enforcement Officials' Perceptions of Others," *Journal of Applied Social Psychology* 26 (1996): 95–112; Jerome Skolnick and James J. Fyfe, *Above the Law: Police and the Excessive Use of Force* (New York: The Free Press, 1993).

10. Lawrence Bobo, "Inequalities That Endure?: Racial Ideology, American Politics, and the Peculiar Role of the Social Sciences," paper presented at conference, The Changing Terrain of Race and Ethnicity, University of Illinois, Chicago, October 26, 2001; see Patricia G. Devine and A. Elliot, "Are Racial Stereotypes Really Fading? The Princeton Trilogy Revisited," *Personality and Social Psychology Bulletin* 21 (1995): 1139–50.

11. Eduardo Bonilla-Silva and Tyrone A. Forman, "'I Am Not a Racist but . . .': Mapping White College Students' Racial Ideology in the U.S.A.," *Discourse and Society* 11 (2000): 51–86.

12. Kristen A. Myers and Passion Williamson, "Race Talk: The Perpetuation of Racism through Private Discourse," *Race and Society* 4 (2001): 3–26.

13. Michael Banton, *The Policeman in the Community* (New York: Basic Books, 1964); Michael K. Brown, *Working the Street: Police Discretion and the Dilemmas of Reform* (New York: Russell Sage Foundation, 1981), p. 56; Bayley and Mendelsohn, *Minorities and the Police: Confrontation in America*.

14. Walker, *A Critical History of Police Reform*; Skolnick, *The Politics of Protest*; Bayley and Mendlesohn, *Minorities and the Police*; Skolnick and Fyfe, *Above the Law*.

15. Dee Cray and Barbara Hudson, eds., *Racism and Criminology* (London: Sage Publications, 1967); Michael Tonry, *Malign Neglect: Race, Crime and Punishment in America* (New York: Oxford Press University, 1995), pp. 71–107.

16. Ian Ayres and Joel Waldfogel, "A Market Test for Race Discrimination in Bail Setting," *Stanford Law Review* 46 (May 1994): 993

17. Richard Morin and Michael H. Cottman, "Discrimination's Lingering Sting," *Washington Post*, June 22, 2001, p. A1; T. A. Forman, D. R. Williams, and J. S. Jackson, "Race, Place and Discrimination," in *Perspectives on Social Problems*, ed. C. Gardner (New York: JAI Press, 1997), pp. 231–61.

18. American Civil Liberties Union, "ACLU Moves to Have Maryland State Police Held in Contempt, Press Release," November 14, 1996, at http://www.aclu.org/news/n111496a.html (Retrieved December 10, 2001).

19. Kim Michelle Lersch and Joe Feagin "Violent Police-Citizen Encounters: An Analysis of Major Newspaper Accounts," *Critical Sociology* 22 (1996): 29–49.

20. William A. Geller and Kevin J. Karales, "Shootings of and by the Chicago Police: Uncommon Crises. Part I: Shootings by Chicago Police," *Journal of Criminal Law and Criminology* 72 (1981): 1813–66; Mark Blumberg, "The Use of Firearms by Police Officers: The Impact of Individuals, Communities and Race," Ph.D. dissertation, School of Criminal Justice, State University of New York at Albany, 1983.

21. James J. Fyfe, "Blind Justice: Police Shootings in Memphis," *The Journal of Criminal Law and Criminology* 73.2 (1982): 707–22.

22. Cited in Skolnick and Fyfe, *Above the Law*, p. 30.

23. National Advisory Commission on Civil Disorders, Report (New York: Bantam Books, 1968); see also James N. Reaves, *Black Cops* (Philadelphia: Quantum Leap Publisher, 1991); James B. Jacobs and Jay Cohen, "The Impact of Racial Integration on the Police," *Journal of Police Science and Administration* 6 (1978): 168–83.

24. Geoffrey Alpert and Roger G. Dunham, *Policing Multi-Ethnic Neighborhoods: The Miami Study and Findings for Law Enforcement in the United States* (New York: Greenwood Press, 1988).

25. Liqun Cao, James Frank, and Francis T. Cullen, "Race, Community Context and Confidence in the Police," *American Journal of Police* 15 (1996): 3–22; Scott Decker and Russell L. Smith, "Police Minority Recruitment: A Note on Its Effectiveness in Improving Black Evaluations of the Police," *Journal of Criminal Justice* 8 (1981): 387–93.

26. Howard Schuman and Bary Gruenberg, "Dissatisfaction with City Services: Is Race an Important Factor?" in *People and Politics in Urban Society*, ed. Harlan Hahn (Beverly Hills: Sage Publications, 1972), 369–92; Samuel Walker, Cassia Spohn, and Miriam DeLone, *The Color of Justice: Race, Ethnicity, and Crime in America* (Belmont, CA: Wadsworth Publishing, 1996).

27. Skolnick, *The Politics of Protest*, pp. 242–43.

28. W. Marvin Dulaney, *Black Police in America* (Bloomington: Indiana University Press, 1996).

29. Samuel Walker, Cassia Spohn, and Miriam DeLone, *The Color of Justice: Race, Ethnicity, and Crime in America*, 2nd ed. (Belmont, CA: Wadsworth Publishing, 2000), p. 110.

30. Dulaney, *Black Police in America*.

31. Skolnick and Fyfe, *Above the Law*, p. 241.

32. Walker, *A Critical History of Police Reform*.

33. Samuel Walker, "Trends in the 50 Largest Cities: Employment of Black and Hispanic Police Officers," *Reveiw of Applied Urban Research* 11.6 (1983): 1–6; Samuel Walker and K. B. Turner, *A Decade of Modest Progress: Employment of Black and Hispanic Police Officers, 1983–1992* (Omaha: University of Nebraska at Omaha Press, 1992).

34. Ellen Hochstedler and John A. Conley, "Explaining Underrepresentation of Black Officers in City Police Agencies," *Journal of Criminal Justice* 14 (1986): 319–28; Larry D. Stokes and James F. Scott, "Affirmative Action Policy Standard and Employment of African Americans in Police Departments," *The Western Journal of Black Studies* 17 (1993): 135–42.

35. Nicholas Alex, *Black in Blue* (New York: Meredith Corporation, 1969); Stephen Leinen, *Black Police, White Society* (New York: New York University Press, 1985); James B. Jacobs and Jay Cohen, "The Impact of Racial Integration on the Police," pp. 168–83.

36. Samuel Walker, *A Critical History of Police Reform*; Derek J. Wendelken and Andres Inn, "Nonperformance Influences on Performance Evaluations: A Laboratory Phenomenon?" *Journal of Applied Psychology* 66 (1981): 149–58.

37. Larry K. Gaines, Norman Van Tubergan, and Michael Paiva, "Police Officer Perceptions of Promotion as a Source of Motivation," *Journal of Criminal Justice* 12 (1984): 265–75; John E. Teahan, "A Longitudinal Study of Attitude Shifts among Black and White Police Officers," *Journal of Social Issues* 31 (1975): 47–56.

38. Eva S. Buzawa, "Determining Patrol Officer Job Satisfaction," *Criminology* 22 (1984): 61–81.

39. James D. Bannon and G. Marie Wilt, "Black Policemen: A Study of Self Images," *Journal of Police Science and Administration* 1 (1973): 21–29.

40. Dulaney, *Black Police in America*.

41. Leinen, *Black Police, White Society*, p. 70; see also Thomas Uhlman, "Black Elite Decision Making: The Case of Trial Judges," *American Journal of Political Science* 22 (1978): 884–95.

42. Reaves, *Black Cops*.

43. Cited in Jerome Skolnick and David H. Bayley, *The New Blue Line: Police Innovation in Six American Cities* (New York: The Free Press, 1986), p. 188.

44. Jerome Skolnick and James J. Fyfe, *Above the Law*; see also Wendy Pelle, "A Plan for New Cops," *Black Enterprise* 22 (1992): 42.

45. James J. Fyfe, "Always Prepared: Police Off-Duty Guns," *The Annals of the American Academy of Political and Social Science* (1980): 452; William A. Geller and Kevin J. Karales, "Shootings of and by the Chicago Police," p. 1813; James J. Fyfe, "Who Shoots? A Look at Officer Race and Police Shooting," *Journal of Police Science and Administration* 9 (1981): 367–82.

46. Lawrence W. Sherman, "Causes of Police Behavior: The Current State of Quantitative Research," *Journal of Research in Crime and Delinquency* (January 1980): 69–100; James N. Reaves, *Black Cops*; Thomas Barker and David L. Carter, *Police Deviance* (Cincinnati, OH: Anderson Publishing, 1986).

47. Sidanius, Liu, Shaw, and Pratto, "Social Dominance Theory and the Criminal Justice System," pp. 338–66.

48. W. Eugene Groves and Peter H. Rossi, "Police Perceptions of a Hostile Ghetto: Realism or Projection," *American Behavioral Scientist* 13 (1970): 727–43; Bannon and Wilt, "Black Policemen," pp. 21–29; Eugene Beard, "The Black Police in Washington, DC," pp. 48–52; Nicholas Alex, *Black in Blue*; Collette C. Jackson and Irving A. Wallach, "Perceptions of the Police in a Black Community," in *The Urban Policeman in Transition: A Psychological and Sociological Review*, ed. John R. and Homa M. Snibbe (Springfield, IL: Thomas, 1973), pp. 354–82.

49. Criminal Justice Institute, "Black Police Officers: Do They Really Make a Difference??? The Empirical Evidence," *Blacks in Criminal Justice* (Spring/Summer 1985): 37–39; Decker and Smith, "Police Minority Recruitment," pp. 387–93.

50. Liqun Cao, James Frank, and Francis T. Cullen, "Race, Community Context and Confidence in the Police," *American Journal of Police* 15 (1996): 3–22.

51. Lydia Saad and Leslie McAneny, "Black Americans See Little Justice for Themselves," *The Gallop Poll Monthly* (March 1995): 32–35.

52. Joseph Balkin, "Why Policemen Don't Like Policewomen," *Journal of Police Science and Administration* 16 (1988): 29–38; Joanne Belknap, "Women in Conflict: An Analysis of Women Correctional Officers," *Women and Criminal Justice* 2 (1991): 89–115; Daniel Bell, "Policewomen: Myths and Reality," *Journal of Police Science and Administration* 10 (1982): 112–20; Nancy C. Jurik, "An Officer and a Lady: Organizational Barriers to Women Working as Correctional Officers in Men's Prisons," *Social Problems* 32 (1985): 375–88; Eric D. Poole and Mark R. Pogrebin, "Factors Affecting the Decision to Remain in Policing: A Study of Women Officers," *Journal of Police Science and Administration* 16 (1988): 49–55; Judi G. Wexler and Deana D. Logan, "Sources of Stress among Women Police Officers," *Journal of Police Science and Administration* 11 (1983): 46–53; Susan E. Martin, "Women on the Move?: A Report on the Status of Women in Policing," *Women & Criminal Justice* 1.1 (1989): 21–40; Ralph A. Weisheit, "Women in the State Police: Concerns of Male and Female Officers," *Journal of Police Science and Administration* 15 (1987): 137–43; Susan E. Martin, "'Outsider within' the Station House: The Impact of Race and Gender on Black Women Police," *Social Problems* 41 (1994): 383–401; Kerry Segrave, *Policewomen: A History* (Jefferson, NC: McFarland & Company, 1995).

53. Joanne Belknap, "Women in Conflict: An Analysis of Women Correctional Officers," pp. 89–115; James J. Fyfe, *Police Practice in the '90s: Key Management Issues* (Washington, DC: International City Management Association, 1989); Joyce Sichel, Lucy Friedman, Janet Quint, and Michael Smith, *Women on Patrol: A Pilot Study of Police Performance in New York City* (Washington, DC: Government Printing Office, 1978).

54. See Joe R. Feagin, *Racist America* (New York: Routledge, 2001); Chigwada, "The Policing of Black Women," in *Out of Order*, pp. 134–50.

55. Roi D. Townsey, "Black Women in American Policing: An Advancement Display," *Journal of Criminal Justice* 10 (1982): 455–68.

56. Martin, "'Outsider within' the Station House," pp. 383–401.

57. Frederick Douglass, "The Color Line," *North American Review* (June 1881), as excerpted in *Jones et ux. v. Alfred H. Mayer Co.* 392 U.S. 409, 446–447 (1968). Italics added.

58. Oliver C. Cox, *Caste, Class, and Race* (Garden City, NY: Doubleday, 1948), p. 344.

59. Stokely Carmichael (Kwame Ture) and Charles V. Hamilton, *Black Power: The Politics of Liberation in America* (New York: Vintage, 1967); see also Robert L. Allen, *Black Awakening in Capitalist America: An Analytic History* (Garden City, NJ: Anchor Books, 1970). We draw here on Joe R. Feagin, *Racist America*, chapters 1–2.

60. Feagin, *Racist America*, chapter 1.

61. *Dred Scott v. Sandford*, 60 U.S. 393, 407 (1857).

62. *Plessy v. Ferguson*, 163 U.S. 537, 551 (1896).

63. Gunnar Myrdal, *An American Dilemma* (New York: McGraw-Hill Paperback, 1964).

64. *Brown et al. v. Board of Education of Topeka et al.*, 347 U.S. 483, 692. A number of other social science studies are also cited in this famous footnote.

65. See Feagin, *Racist America*, chapters 3–5; Philomena Essed, *Understanding Everyday Racism: An Interdisciplinary Approach* (Newbury Park, CA: Sage Publications, 1991), p. 52.

66. Nancy Krieger and Stephen Sidney, "Racial Discrimination and Blood Pressure," *American Journal of Public Health* 86 (1996): 1370–78.

67. Gallup, *Black/White Relations in the United States* (Princeton, NJ: The Gallup Organization, 1997), pp. 29–30, 108–10.

68. Lawrence D. Bobo and Susan A. Suh, "Surveying Racial Discrimination: Analyses from a Multiethnic Labor Market," in *Prismatic Metropolis: Inequality in Los Angeles*, ed. Lawrence D. Bobo, Melvin L. Oliver, James H. Johnson Jr., and Abel Valenzuela Jr. (New York: Russell Sage, 2000), pp. 527–29; Jacquelyn Scarville et al., *Armed Forces Equal Opportunity Survey* (Arlington, VA: Defense Manpower Data Center, 1999), pp. 46–78; Office of the Under Secretary of Defense Personnel and Readiness, *Career Progression of Minority and Women Officers* (Washington, DC: Department of Defense, 1999), pp. 46–85.

69. Richard Morin and Michael H. Cottman, "Discrimination's Lingering Sting," p. A1; Kathy Ciotola, "Black Tourists Report Discrimination in Study," *Gainesville Sun*, October 2, 2001, pp. B1, B3.

70. See Feagin, *Racist America*, pp. 137–74; Fair Housing Council of Fresno County, "Audit Uncovers Blatant Discrimination against Hispanics, African Americans and Families with Children in Fresno County," press release, Fresno, California, October 6, 1997; Central Alabama Fair Housing Center, "Discrimination in the Rental Housing Market: A Study of Montgomery, Alabama, 1995–1996," Montgomery, Alabama, January 13, 1996; Fair Housing Action Center, Inc., "Greater New Orleans Rental Audit," New Orleans, Louisiana, 1996; San Antonio Fair Housing Council, "San Antonio Metropolitan Area Rental Audit 1997," San Antonio, Texas, 1997.

71. See Feagin, *Racist America*, chapter 5.

72. Joe R. Feagin and Melvin P. Sikes, *Living with Racism: The Black Middle Class Experience* (Boston, MA: Beacon Press, 1994), p. 16.

73. Joe R. Feagin, "The Continuing Significance of Race: Antiblack Discrimination in Public Places," *American Sociological Review* 56 (1991): 101–16.

74. Feagin and Sikes, *Living with Racism*, p. 23

75. Essed, *Understanding Everyday Racism*, p. 7.

76. Ibid., p. 8.

77. Yanick St. Jean and Joe R. Feagin, *Double Burden: Black Women and Everyday Racism* (Armonk, NY: M. E. Sharpe, 1998), p. 34.

78. Randy Hodson and Teresa Sullivan, *The Social Organization of Work* (Belmont, CA: Wadsworth Publishing, 1990).

79. Randall Collins, *Theoretical Sociology* (New York: Harcourt, Brace, Jovanovich, 1988).

80. See Hodson and Sullivan, *The Social Organization of Work*, p. 187.

81. Larry J. Siegel and Joseph J. Senna, *Essentials of Criminal Justice*, 4th ed. (Belmont, CA: Wadsworth Publishing, 2004), chapter 6.

82. See Douglas S. Massey and Nancy A. Denton, *American Apartheid: Segregation and the Making of the Underclass* (Cambridge: Harvard University Press, 1993).

83. Isabel Wilkerson, "The Tallest Fence: Feelings on Race in a White Neighborhood," *New York Times*, June 21, 1992, section 1, p. 18.

84. Lois Benjamin, *The Black Elite: Facing the Color Line in the Twilight of the Twentieth Century* (Chicago: Nelson-Hall Publishers, 1991); Feagin and Sikes, *Living with Racism*; St. Jean and Feagin, *Double Burden*.

85. Gordon W. Allport, *The Nature of Prejudice* (Reading, MA: Addison-Wesley, 1954); Essed, *Understanding Everyday Racism*; Feagin and Sikes, *Living with Racism*.

86. Gerald D. Runnels, *Blacks Who Wear Blue*.

87. See Alex, *Black in Blue*; Leinen, *Black Police, White Society*; Reaves, *Black Cops*; Runnels, *Blacks Who Wear Blue*.

88. William I. Thomas and Florian Znaniecki, *The Polish Peasant in Europe and America*, ed. Eli Zaretsky (Chicago: University of Illinois Press, [1927] 1984), p. 2.

89. For example, the officers' views and work experiences parallel those in the few other studies that have been done. See Charles E. Frazier, "The Use of Life-Histories in Testing Theories of Criminal Behavior: Toward Reviving a Method," *Qualitative Sociology* 1 (1978): 122–42.

90. These were forty-eight individual interviews and one two-person group interview with black officers in the southern United States.

91. At the beginning of this project, we had a difficult time getting any black officer to commit himself or herself to sitting down and discussing policing with us. These are very difficult issues for black officers. Finally, two senior officers had very in-depth conversations with us, and soon thereafter the number of interviews increased significantly. Some officers called and asked us to be interviewed. During one conversation, an officer jokingly told us that the only reason he agreed to share his experiences with us was that the first two officers had concluded that we were "all right." This suggests that for these African-American officers telling their life story is a form of participation in an ongoing process of racial struggle, and that they wanted to be sure that we could relate to what they had to say without betraying their understandings and trust. Each willingly participated after giving informed consent.

Despite some initial discomfort, all but two of the officers agreed to their interviews' being audio-taped. The interviews lasted about one to two hours each. We edited the quotes from the interviews lightly to delete stutter words (for example, *uh, ah, you know*) and some false starts. Otherwise, we use ellipses where we have deleted material. In general, we have transcribed these oral interviews into written English.

92. Andrea Fontana and James H. Frey, "Interviewing: The Art of Science," in *Handbook of Qualitative Research*, ed. Norman K. Denzin and Yvonna S. Lincoln (Thousand Oaks, CA: Sage Publications, 1994), p. 371.

93. For example, William Wilbanks, *The Myth of a Racist Criminal Justice System* (Monterey, CA: Brooks/Cole, 1987).

Chapter 2

1. See Nicholas Alex, *Black in Blue* (New York: Meredith Corporation, 1969).

2. James W. Button, *Blacks and Social Change: Impact of the Civil Rights Movement in Southern Communities* (Princeton, NJ: Princeton University Press, 1989).

3. Alex, *Black in Blue*; Stephen Leinen, *Black Police, White Society* (New York: University Press, 1984).

4. Eugene D. Genovese, *Roll, Jordan, Roll: The World the Slaves Made* (New York: Vintage Books, 1976), p. 659.

5. See Joe R. Feagin and Karyn D. McKinney, *The Many Costs of Racism* (Lanham, MD: Rowman & Littlefield, 2003), especially chapters 2–6.

6. See, for example, Philomena Essed, *Understanding Everyday Racism: An Interdisciplinary Approach* (Newbury Park, CA: Sage Publications, 1991); and Joe R. Feagin and Melvin P. Sikes, *Living with Racism: The Black Middle Class Experience* (Boston: Beacon Press, 1994).

7. See Feagin and Sikes, *Living with Racism*, chapter 1 and passim.

8. Feagin and Sikes, *Living with Racism*.

9. Feagin and Sikes, *Living with Racism*.

10. See Feagin and McKinney, *The Many Costs of Racism*.

11. See Joe R. Feagin and Hernan Vera, *White Racism: The Basics* (New York: Routledge, 1995).

12. Samuel Walker, Cassia Spohn, and Miriam DeLone, *The Color of Justice: Race, Ethnicity, and Crime in America* (Belmont, CA: Wadsworth Publishing, 1996).

13. See Feagin and Sikes, *Living with Racism*, chapters 4–5.

14. See Yanick St. Jean and Joe R. Feagin, *Double Burden: Black Women and Everyday Racism* (Armonk, NY: M. E. Sharpe, 1998).

15. See Essed, *Understanding Everyday Racism*; Feagin and Sikes, *Living with Racism*.

Chapter 3

1. We draw the term *problematization* from Philomena Essed, *Understanding Everyday Racism: An Interdisciplinary Approach* (Newbury Park, CA: Sage Publications, 1991), pp. 166–70.

2. Richard J. Lundman and Robert L. Kaufman, "Driving While Black: Effects of Race, Ethnicity, and Gender on Citizen Self-Reports of Traffic Stops and Police Actions," *Criminology* 41 (2003): 195–220.

3. See Joe R. Feagin and Melvin P. Sikes, *Living with Racism: The Black Middle Class Experience* (Boston: Beacon Press, 1994).

4. See Feagin and Sikes, *Living with Racism*, especially chapters 4–5.

5. See Joe Feagin and Hernan Vera, *White Racism: The Basics* (New York: Routledge, 1995).

6. Philomena Essed makes a similar point in *Understanding Everyday Racism*, p. 170.

Chapter 4

1. An earlier version of portions of this chapter was published as Ken Bolton, "Shared Perceptions: Black Police Officers Discuss Continuing Barriers in Policing," *Policing: An International Journal of Police Strategies and Management* 26.3 (2003): 386–99.

2. Samuel Walker, Cassia Spohn, and Miriam DeLone, *The Color of Justice: Race, Ethnicity, and Crime in America*, 2nd ed. (Belmont, CA: Wadsworth Publishing, 2000).

3. Randy Hodson and Teresa Sullivan, *The Social Organization of Work* (Belmont, CA: Wadsworth Publishing, 1990).

4. Eugene Beard, "The Black Police in Washington, DC," *Journal of Police Science and Administration* 5 (1977): 48–52; see also Nicholas Alex, *Black in Blue* (New York: Meredith Corporation, 1969); and Stephen Leinen, *Black Police, White Society* (New York: New York University Press, 1985).

5. Simon Holdaway, "Responding to Racialized Divisions within the Workforce: The Experience of Black and Asian Police Officers in England," *Ethnic and Racial Studies* 20 (1997): 69–89.

6. Nicholas Alex, *Black in Blue* (New York: Meredith Corporation, 1969); Gerald D. Runnels, *Blacks Who Wear Blue* (Dallas: Alexander Publications, 1989).

7. Sarah Glazer, "Police Corruption," *CQ Researcher* 5 (1995): 1041–64; James N. Reaves, *Black Cops* (Philadelphia: Quantum Leap Publisher, 1991).

8. See Samuel Walker and K. B. Turner, *A Decade of Modest Progress: Employment of Black and Hispanic Police Officers, 1983–1992* (Omaha: University of Nebraska at Omaha, 1992).

9. See survey data in Joe Feagin, *Racist America: Roots, Current Realities, and Future Reparations* (New York: Routledge, 2000), especially chapters 4–5.

10. James D. Bannon and G. Marie Wilt, "Black Policemen: A Study of Self Images," *Journal of Police Science and Administration* 1 (1973): 21–29.

11. Philomena Essed, *Understanding Everyday Racism: An Interdisciplinary Approach* (Newbury Park, CA: Sage Publications, 1991), p. 230.

12. Jay Bass, "Rural Policing: Patterns and Problems of 'Micro' Departments," *Justice Professional* 9.1 (1995): 59–74.

Chapter 5

1. Richard Morin, "Misperceptions Cloud Whites' View of Blacks," *Washington Post*, July 11, 2001, p. A01.

2. "Washington Post/Kaiser/Harvard Racial Attitudes Survey," *Washington Post*, July 11, 2001, p. A01.

3. See Joe R. Feagin, Hernan Vera, and Pinar Batur, *White Racism: The Basics*, 2nd ed. (New York: Routledge, 2001), especially chapters 7 and 8.

4. See Joe R. Feagin and Melvin P. Sikes, *Living with Racism: The Black Middle Class Experience* (Boston: Beacon Press, 1994); Yanick St. Jean and Joe R. Feagin, *Double Burden: Black Women and Everyday Racism* (New York: M. E. Sharpe, 1998); and Joe R. Feagin, *Racist America: Roots, Current Realities, and Future Reparations* (New York: Routledge: 2000).

5. *Etter v. Veriflo Corporation*, 67 Cal. App. 4th 457, 79 Cal. Rptr. 2d 33 (1st Dist. Ct. App. 1998). We summarize here the discussion in Joe R. Feagin and Karyn D. McKinney, *The Many Costs of Racism* (Lanham, MD: Rowman & Littlefield, 2003), chapter 1; see also Steven Keeva, "A Bumpy Road to Equality: Panelists Say Courts Are Backpedaling on Minority Issues," *ABA Journal* (1996): 32.

6. See Feagin, *Racist America*, chapters 3–4.

7. See Feagin, Vera, and Batur, *White Racism*, chapter 5.

8. Kristen Myers and Passion Williamson, "Race Talk: The Perpetuation of Racism through Private Discourse," *Race & Society* 4 (2001): 3–26.

9. For the general point in the sociological literature, see Ruth A. Wallace and Alison Worl, *Contemporary Sociological Theory*, 4th ed. (Englewood Cliffs, NJ: Prentice Hall, 1995), pp. 290–92.

10. Richard Delgado, "Words That Wound: A Tort Action for Racial Insults, Epithets, and Name-Calling," in *Critical Race Theory: The Cutting Edge*, ed. Richard Delgado (Philadelphia: Temple University Press, 1995), pp. 159–68.

11. See Feagin, Vera, and Batur, *White Racism*; and Feagin and Sikes, *Living with Racism.*

12. For data on this point, see Feagin and McKinney, *The Many Costs of Racism.*

13. See Wyn Craig Wade, *The Fiery Cross: The Ku Klux Klan in America* (New York: Simon & Schuster, 1987).

14. See Feagin, *Racist America*, pp. 147–49.

15. David L. Carter and Thomas Barker, "Administrative Guidance and Control of Police Officer Behavior: Policies, Procedures, and Rules," in *Police Deviance*, ed. Thomas Barker and David L. Carter (Cincinnati: Anderson, 1991), pp. 13–28.

16. Jonathan Wright, "Rights Group Says Police Brutality Rife in U.S." (Reuters, 1998), 1.

17. See Feagin, Vera, and Batur, *White Racism*; and Feagin and Sikes, *Living with Racism.*

Chapter 6

1. See Joe R. Feagin and Melvin P. Sikes, *Living with Racism: The Black Middle Class Experience* (Boston: Beacon Press, 1994), chapter 7; Yanick St. Jean and Joe R. Feagin, *Double Burden: Black*

Women and Everyday Racism (Armonk, NY: M. E. Sharpe, 1998), chapters 1, 5–7; Joe R. Feagin and Karyn D. McKinney, *The Many Costs of Racism* (Lanham, MD: Rowman & Littlefield, 2003), chapters 5–6. Also see Michelle D. Byng, "Mediating Discrimination: Resisting Oppression among African-American Muslim Women," *Social Problems* 45.4 (1998): 473–87.

2. Herbert Aptheker, *American Negro Slave Revolts* (New York: International Publishers, 1943); W. E. B. Du Bois, *Black Reconstruction in America: 1860–1880* (New York: Atheneum, 1983). On the importance of religion in slave resistance, see Eugene Genovese, *Roll, Jordan, Roll: The World the Slaves Made* (New York: Random House, 1974).

3. Michael A. Olivas, "The Chronicles, My Grandfather's Stories, and Immigration Law: The Slave Traders Chronicle as Racial History," in *Critical Race Theory: The Cutting Edge*, ed. Richard Delgado (Philadelphia: Temple University Press, 1995), pp. 9–20.

4. Byng, "Mediating Discrimination," p. 473.

5. See Feagin and Sikes, *Living with Racism*; Feagin and McKinney, *The Many Costs of Racism*.

6. P. B. Kraska and V. E. Kappeler, "Militarizing American Police: The Rise and Normalization of Paramilitary Units," *Social Problems* 44.1 (1997): 1–17.

Chapter 7

1. Philomena Essed, *Understanding Everyday Racism: An Interdisciplinary Approach* (Newbury Park, CA: Sage Publications, 1991).

2. Richard Delgado, "Legal Storytelling: Storytelling for Oppositionists and Others: A Plea for Narrative," in *Critical Race Theory: The Cutting Edge*, ed. Richard Delgado (Philadelphia: Temple University Press, 1995), pp. 64–74.

3. Joe R. Feagin, Hernan Vera, and Pinar Batur, *White Racism: The Basics*, 2nd ed. (New York: Routledge, 2001).

4. See Samuel Walker, Cassia Spohn, and Miriam DeLone, *The Color of Justice: Race, Ethnicity, and Crime in America*, 2nd ed. (Belmont, CA: Wadsworth Publishing, 2000), p. 115.

5. National Black Police Association, *Police Brutality: A Strategy to Stop the Violence* (Washington, DC: Author, n.d.). We draw here on Walker, Spohn, and DeLone, *The Color of Justice*, p. 116.

6. W. Marvin Dulaney, *Black Police in America* (Bloomington: Indiana University Press, 1996).

INDEX